The End Times in Chronological Unfolded Prophecy

Eze Bahii
ezekybbahii@gmail.com

The End Times in Chronological Order: Unfolded Prophecy

Published in 2024

For permissions or inquiries, contact: ezekybahii@gmail.com

Preface

In every corner of history, across cultures and eras, humanity has sensed a profound unfolding; a narrative that speaks of beginnings and ends, a path that hints at both ruin and redemption. This book explores that journey, tracing the fulfillment of prophecies, not as distant or detached events, but as interconnected moments that reveal an overarching purpose. The prophecies that we once viewed through the lens of ancient texts or oral traditions have, over time, transformed into lived experiences. Now, more than ever, these ancient foretellings appear to be materializing before our eyes, leaving no corner of the world untouched.

In each chapter, you will find an era examined, each one revealing layers of prophecy that have emerged across centuries. From the early days following the ascension of Jesus and the courage of His apostles, through the struggles of empires and plagues, to the rebirth of Israel and modern conflicts, we witness a cycle of conflict and hope, of human endeavour and spiritual revelation. As we explore William Branham's warnings about America, modernity, and moral decay, we see how his insights and the prophecies of others align with what our world is now facing; a world torn between faith and disbelief, between the pursuit of material idols and the yearning for truth.

We delve into the rise and fall of kingdoms, the fearsome wars that reshaped continents, and the emergence of ideologies that sought to displace faith itself. Today, the stakes appear higher than ever, with nuclear threats, climate upheavals, and moral shifts that echo the warnings of ancient seers and contemporary prophets. Our exploration is not simply a recounting of events but an interpretation of their meaning, showing how each layer of history has contributed to an overarching apocalyptic vision.

In writing this book, the aim is not to incite fear but to foster understanding and awareness of where we stand in the larger scheme of prophecy. This book serves as both a mirror and a map, urging readers to reflect on their own place in history. As we contemplate these events and prophecies, we are left with questions about our choices, our values, and what lies beyond the last chapter of our story.

This journey, from prophecy to fulfillment, invites you to look deeper; to see beyond the present and recognize the signs that have always been with us. Let this book serve as a guide, a reminder, and perhaps, a call to prepare for what may lie ahead as we approach the culmination of history's most compelling narrative.

Why Believe in Prophecy?

Why should anyone believe in prophecy? This question isn't new; it's one that has been asked throughout history, both by skeptics and believers alike. Prophecy isn't about seeing the future with perfect clarity or dictating unchangeable outcomes. Instead, it's a bridge connecting the divine and the human, offering glimpses of what lies beyond the visible world. Through prophecy, the veil between what is and what is yet to come grows thin, allowing humanity a chance to align its actions, thoughts, and spirit with a higher understanding of purpose and destiny.

Many ancient prophecies were given not only to predict events but to provide guidance, moral clarity, and even warnings. They were intended as markers along the path of human history, offering insight into the ebb and flow of nations, the moral state of societies, and the ultimate direction of humanity. From the prophets of the Bible to modern-day voices, these messages have persisted, often unfolding in the very events they foresaw.

History shows us a pattern: as prophecy unfolds, it leaves markers that we recognize only in hindsight, urging us to believe that these are not mere coincidences. When we look back, we see how many prophecies were fulfilled, Jerusalem's fall, the scattering of Israel, the rise of nations, global conflicts, and even the return of Israel as a nation. When examined closely, these events don't stand alone; they resonate deeply with what was foretold, each event weaving together to form a cohesive narrative.

Believing in prophecy is also about understanding the moral and spiritual framework that prophecy offers. It compels us to examine our own lives, to question whether we are living in alignment with the truths embedded in these predictions. Prophecies remind us that there is something greater than ourselves and our individual lives; a grand narrative that we are each a part of, one with moral implications and a divine design.

In today's world, where uncertainty looms and challenges seem unending, prophecy provides a compass. It helps us navigate turbulent times by showing that our journey is not random; it has a direction, an endpoint. The events we see unfolding now—natural disasters, moral crises, global conflicts; do not need to be seen as isolated crises. Instead, they can be understood as steps along the path that humanity has been warned about for centuries.

Believing in prophecy isn't about forsaking logic or reason; it's about embracing the possibility that history is not accidental. By understanding prophecy, we gain perspective, insight, and hope. In doing so, we begin to see the world not merely for what it is but for what it is becoming.

Why the Bible is Considered the Most Reliable Holy Book for Prophecy

The Bible has long been regarded as a uniquely reliable source of prophecy, not only for its spiritual teachings but also for its detailed, historically verified prophecies that have unfolded across the centuries. When we examine specific books within the Bible; such as Daniel, Ezekiel, and the Gospels of Matthew and the words of Jesus; patterns emerge that reveal an uncanny accuracy. These prophecies are more than symbolic writings; they serve as a roadmap that connects ancient times to present-day events, and they form a cohesive narrative that believers see as evidence of divine authorship.

In the Book of Daniel, we find a clear example of how prophecy has accurately described major historical events. Daniel's visions predicted the rise and fall of empires long before they came into existence, foretelling the sequence of kingdoms in astonishing detail. For example, in his vision of a great statue with different metals representing different empires, Daniel foresaw the Babylonian, Persian, Greek, and Roman empires. History has shown these empires arose exactly as he described, with each one falling to the next, fulfilling Daniel's predictions.

Furthermore, Daniel's visions include references to the end times, a period he describes as a "time of trouble such as never was since there was a nation." This apocalyptic vision provides details that many interpret as still unfolding, making Daniel's words relevant in both ancient history and our present age.

Ezekiel's prophecies are equally profound, particularly his predictions regarding the future of Israel. Ezekiel spoke of a time when Israel would be scattered across the world, losing its identity and homeland; a prophecy that was fulfilled after the fall of Jerusalem. But he also prophesied that one day Israel would be restored and would return to its land.

This prophecy was seen by many as impossible, especially during centuries when Israel as a nation did not exist. Yet, in 1948, Israel was re-established as a nation, an event viewed by many as the fulfillment of Ezekiel's vision. This return is seen not only as a powerful fulfillment but as part of an ongoing prophecy that remains relevant today. Ezekiel's references to the conflict of "Gog and Magog," which foretells a great battle involving Israel in the end times, are still studied by theologians, who connect it to present-day geopolitics.

In the Gospel of Matthew, particularly in chapters 24 and 25, Jesus provides a detailed account of what to expect in the end times. He speaks of wars, natural disasters, false prophets, and a general decline in moral and spiritual standards. Jesus warns that these events will signal the approach of the end of the age. His teachings emphasize not only specific events but the overall progression of moral decay and spiritual deception, which many believe is observable today.

Jesus also mentions the "abomination of desolation," a prophecy from Daniel that many interpret as a reference to future desecration of holy places, and a period of great tribulation. His words connect to earlier prophecies and provide a clearer picture of the future. Jesus' teachings on the end times resonate strongly with events occurring today, offering believers a sense of urgency and an awareness of the spiritual implications behind global developments.

The Bible's prophetic reliability lies in its interconnectedness. Each book builds upon the others, creating a seamless narrative from ancient prophecies to their fulfillment in historical events and beyond. For instance, Daniel's vision of empires aligns with Jesus' predictions of societal breakdown and moral decline. Ezekiel's visions of Israel's scattering and eventual return connect directly to the New Testament's apocalyptic warnings. In Revelation, which references many Old Testament prophecies, the final battle of Armageddon, the judgments, and the ultimate triumph of good over evil bring these themes together in a final resolution.

This interconnected nature of prophecy; spanning centuries, cultures, and authors—suggests a unity of purpose that believers see as evidence of divine design. Each prophecy does not stand alone; rather, they reinforce one another, presenting a tapestry of events that shape the world's future.

The Bible's prophecies do not stop in the past; they extend into the present and the future, connecting historical events to contemporary issues. From the scattering and return of Israel to the moral decay predicted by Jesus, and the symbolic rise of powers like Gog and Magog, the Bible offers a comprehensive view of humanity's trajectory. Many believers interpret modern events; rising political tensions, environmental crises, moral shifts; as the continuation of a prophetic story told thousands of years ago.

What to Expect While Reading This Book

This book was not developed to promote any specific religious belief but rather to present a thorough, research-based exploration of prophecy, history, and humanity's unfolding story. It connects significant events from thousands of years ago to the present, laying out patterns, parallels, and interpretations that span multiple eras and cultures. Readers will encounter a journey through time, beginning in the distant past, weaving through pivotal moments in human history, and leading up to our modern age. It is designed for anyone; whether religious or not; to follow along and draw their own conclusions about the potential meaning and relevance of these events.

The book is structured in a timely, chronological manner, providing a cohesive narrative that explores how historical prophecies, warnings, and visions may relate to today's global challenges. From ancient empires and wars to today's social changes and geopolitical tensions, it aims to present facts and interpretations objectively, allowing readers to assess the evidence and decide for themselves. Finally, it considers what the future may hold based on the patterns that history seems to reveal, offering a look at possible events yet to come.

Whether you are a sceptic, a curious mind, or a seeker of deeper truths, this book welcomes you to consider the connections it presents and examine the potential relevance of these long-foretold events.

Foundations of Prophecy and the Beginnings of Conflict

The Ascension and the Birth of Prophecy (33 AD)

Jesus' Ascension and the Early Christian Church

The Final Days on Earth

After the resurrection, Jesus spent forty days with His disciples, teaching them and solidifying their understanding of His mission. This period was filled with a sense of awe and reverence as Jesus appeared to His followers, comforting them after the shocking events of His crucifixion and demonstrating the reality of His resurrection. The disciples had questions: what would happen to them, to Israel, and to God's promises now that He was alive again? During this time, He promised them the gift of the Holy Spirit, who would guide, empower, and comfort them after His departure.

The Ascension of Jesus

On the fortieth day after His resurrection, Jesus took His disciples to the Mount of Olives, just outside Jerusalem. There, He gave them final instructions, urging them to remain in Jerusalem and await the Holy Spirit. The disciples were filled with anticipation and asked, "Lord, will you at this time restore the kingdom to Israel?" (Acts 1:6). Jesus replied, "It is not for you to know times or seasons that the Father has fixed by His own authority. But you will receive power when the Holy Spirit has come upon you, and you will be my witnesses in Jerusalem and in all Judea and Samaria, and to the end of the earth" (Acts 1:7-8).

As He spoke these final words, something extraordinary happened. Jesus was lifted up, ascending into the sky, until a cloud took Him out of their sight. The disciples stood in stunned silence, watching their Teacher and Savior disappear into the heavens. Two men in white robes, believed to be angels, appeared beside them and said, "Men of Galilee, why do you stand looking into heaven? This Jesus, who was taken up from you into heaven, will come in the same way as you saw Him go into heaven" (Acts 1:11). This promise of Jesus' return became one of the core beliefs in early Christian teaching, fuelling the disciples' mission and hope.

The Apostles Gather and Await the Holy Spirit

After Jesus' ascension, the disciples returned to Jerusalem with a sense of urgency and purpose. They gathered in an upper room with other followers of Jesus, including Mary, Jesus' mother, and His brothers. Altogether, about 120 believers met there, praying and waiting for the promise Jesus had made to them. This gathering was the first organized assembly of believers, and they spent their days in prayer, unity, and anticipation. During this period, the disciple Peter took leadership and suggested that they replace Judas Iscariot, who had betrayed Jesus and subsequently died. They selected Matthias, restoring the group of apostles to twelve; a symbolic number representing the twelve tribes of Israel.

Pentecost: The Birth of the Church

Ten days after Jesus' ascension, during the Jewish festival of Pentecost, the promise of the Holy Spirit was fulfilled. As the disciples were gathered together, a sound like a mighty rushing wind filled the house, and "divided tongues as of fire appeared to them and rested on each one of them. And they were all filled with the Holy Spirit and began to speak in other tongues as the Spirit gave them utterance" (Acts 2:3-4). This outpouring of the Holy Spirit empowered the apostles in ways they had never experienced before.

Pentecost attracted Jews from all parts of the Roman Empire to Jerusalem, and the apostles' speaking in various languages caused a stir among the crowd. Many thought they were drunk, but Peter boldly stood up and addressed the crowd, explaining that what they were witnessing was a fulfilment of prophecy. He quoted the prophet Joel, saying that God would pour out His Spirit on all flesh, enabling sons and daughters to prophesy and old men to dream dreams. He spoke of Jesus' death, resurrection, and ascension, proclaiming Him as Lord and Messiah. His message was powerful and convicting, and about three thousand people believed in Jesus and were baptized that day. This moment marked the birth of the Christian Church and the beginning of its explosive growth.

The First Christian Community: Unity and Persecution

Following Pentecost, the apostles established the first Christian community in Jerusalem. This early church was marked by deep unity, devotion, and compassion. Believers "devoted themselves to the apostles' teaching and the fellowship, to the breaking of bread and the prayers" (Acts 2:42). They met in each other's homes, sharing meals and possessions. Those who were wealthy sold their goods and gave to those in need, living out a lifestyle of selflessness and love. This community cared for widows, orphans, and the poor, setting a standard of generosity and humility that defined the early Christian experience.

The growth of the Christian Church, however, did not come without challenges. The apostles' teachings about Jesus as the Messiah and their miracles attracted attention and opposition, especially from the religious leaders in Jerusalem. Peter and John were arrested and brought before the Sanhedrin, the Jewish council, after healing a lame man and preaching about Jesus in the temple. The council commanded them to stop speaking in Jesus' name, but Peter and John responded boldly, saying, "We cannot but speak of what we have seen and heard" (Acts 4:20). Their courage and unwavering commitment inspired other believers, who prayed for boldness in the face of persecution.

The Martyrdom of Stephen

One of the most pivotal moments in the early church was the martyrdom of Stephen, a deacon filled with faith and the Holy Spirit. Stephen performed miracles and preached boldly, but his words stirred anger among Jewish leaders who did not accept Jesus as the Messiah. He was brought before the Sanhedrin, where he gave a passionate defense of his faith, recounting the history of Israel and calling out the leaders for resisting God's truth.

Stephen's words incited the council's wrath, and they dragged him outside the city to stone him. As he was being stoned, Stephen looked up and saw a vision of Jesus standing at the right hand of God. He prayed, "Lord Jesus, receive my spirit," and "Lord, do not hold this sin against them" (Acts 7:59-60). With these words, Stephen became the first Christian martyr. His death marked the beginning of a severe persecution against the church, scattering believers throughout Judea and Samaria. Yet, this scattering only fuelled the spread of the gospel, as those who fled continued to preach about Jesus wherever they went.

The Conversion of Saul

One of the most significant transformations in the early church period was the conversion of Saul, a zealous Pharisee who actively persecuted Christians. Saul sought to destroy the church, going from house to house and arresting believers. However, while on his way to Damascus to arrest more Christians, Saul had a life-changing encounter with the risen Jesus. A blinding light struck him to the ground, and he heard Jesus' voice saying, "Saul, Saul, why are you persecuting me?" (Acts 9:4).

This encounter led to Saul's conversion, and he became one of the most fervent and influential apostles, known as Paul. He dedicated his life to spreading the gospel across the Roman Empire, establishing churches, writing letters, and ultimately transforming Christianity into a faith that reached both Jews and Gentiles. Paul's conversion and missionary work were crucial in shaping the early church and broadening its reach beyond the Jewish community.

Impact and Legacy of the Early Church

The early Christian Church grew rapidly, expanding from Jerusalem into Judea, Samaria, and eventually to the far reaches of the Roman Empire. Despite facing persecution, imprisonment, and even death, the apostles and early believers continued to preach the message of Jesus with courage and conviction. Their faith and resilience laid the foundation for the global Christian Church that would endure and spread through the centuries. The early church's legacy of unity, sacrifice, and unwavering faith continues to inspire Christians around the world to this day.

The Apostles' Journey; Spreading the Teachings Across the Roman Empire

The Apostles' Mission Begins

Following the ascension of Jesus and the Pentecost event, the apostles were empowered by the Holy Spirit to go out into the world, preaching the teachings of Jesus. Driven by their faith and an unwavering belief in their mission, the apostles were united by a central goal: to spread Jesus' teachings and establish Christian communities across a vast empire. These early journeys would come to change history as Christianity spread beyond Jerusalem, eventually reaching nearly every corner of the Roman Empire.

Challenges and Triumphs in Jerusalem and Beyond

The apostles faced a range of challenges: persecution, social rejection, imprisonment, and even martyrdom. Yet, in the face of such challenges, their dedication to spreading the message never wavered. Initially, the apostles focused on Jerusalem, where their following grew quickly. The early Christian community became known for its acts of charity, helping the poor, the sick, and the widows, and meeting frequently for communal worship, prayer, and the breaking of bread. Soon, however, the apostles knew they would have to expand outward.

This journey was not a straightforward one. Jerusalem's religious leaders saw the growing Christian movement as a threat to their authority and traditional beliefs. Apostles such as Peter and John were often brought before the Sanhedrin, the Jewish council, to answer for their teachings about Jesus. Yet, each time, they boldly proclaimed their faith and were eventually released, though they faced constant threats.

The Scattering of the Disciples and the Mission to Samaria

One of the early critical turning points was the martyrdom of Stephen, a deacon and the first recorded Christian martyr. His death marked a violent turning point, leading to a severe persecution against the early Christians in Jerusalem. As a result, many believers were forced to flee, and this scattering pushed Christianity beyond Jerusalem and into the surrounding regions.

Philip, one of the seven deacons, travelled to Samaria and began preaching there. His message was well-received, leading many Samaritans to believe in Jesus as the Messiah. Philip's missionary work in Samaria is also notable for his encounter with an Ethiopian official. After explaining the scriptures to him, Philip baptized the Ethiopian, who then took the message back to his homeland, further spreading Christianity into Africa. Philip's journey symbolized how Christianity was reaching unexpected places and peoples, showing the universality of the gospel message.

Peter's Vision and the Inclusion of Gentiles

Peter, one of Jesus' closest disciples and a leading figure in the early church, also took significant steps toward expanding the Christian mission beyond its original Jewish roots. In a momentous event, Peter received a vision in which he was shown animals considered "unclean" by Jewish law. God instructed him to eat, declaring, "What God has made clean, do not call common" (Acts 10:15). Shortly afterward, Peter was invited to the house of Cornelius, a Roman centurion. Cornelius was a Gentile, yet he was eager to learn about the gospel. This marked a critical shift, as Peter realized that the message of Jesus was meant for all people, not just the Jews.

Peter baptized Cornelius and his household, which was a groundbreaking act, symbolizing the inclusion of Gentiles in the Christian faith. This decision faced some resistance from the early church, which had largely been composed of Jewish Christians. But Peter's vision and his experience with Cornelius led the apostles to embrace the idea that the gospel was meant for everyone, opening the doors for more widespread evangelism across diverse cultures and regions within the Roman Empire.

Paul's Conversion and Missionary Journeys

Perhaps the most transformative figure in the spread of Christianity was the apostle Paul. Originally named Saul, he was a devout Pharisee who zealously persecuted Christians, viewing them as heretics who had deviated from Jewish law. However, while traveling to Damascus with the intent of arresting Christians, Paul experienced a blinding light and heard the voice of Jesus. This encounter transformed him, and he converted to Christianity, taking on the name Paul.

Following his conversion, Paul devoted his life to preaching the gospel, particularly to Gentile (non-Jewish) communities. Paul's missionary journeys are legendary and are meticulously documented in the Book of Acts and in his letters, which later became part of the New Testament. Over the course of three major journeys, Paul travelled thousands of miles, often on foot or by ship, establishing churches in Asia Minor (modern-day Turkey), Greece, and eventually Rome itself.

Paul's letters to these early Christian communities provided guidance, encouragement, and theological insights. They addressed moral issues, questions of faith, and the challenges of living as a Christian within a largely pagan society. Many of these letters, such as Romans, Corinthians, and Galatians, would become foundational texts for Christian theology and ethics.

Key Locations in Paul's Missionary Journeys

Antioch: This city in Syria became the launch point for Paul's missionary journeys and was one of the first places where followers of Jesus were called "Christians." Antioch was a diverse, vibrant city and served as a significant centre for early Christianity.

Athens: In Athens, Paul encountered Greek philosophers and spoke at the Areopagus, a forum for public debate. He attempted to bridge Greek philosophical thought with Christian teachings, proclaiming the "unknown god" worshipped by the Greeks as the one true God. Although his message received mixed reactions, Paul's engagement in Athens represents an early attempt to contextualize Christianity within a foreign culture.

Ephesus: Ephesus was another major stop for Paul. He stayed there for an extended period, building a strong Christian community. Ephesus was also known for its temple of Artemis, and Paul's preaching there led to tension with local artisans who profited from making idols, sparking an uproar.

Corinth: Corinth was a cosmopolitan city notorious for its immorality. Paul founded a church there, and his letters to the Corinthians dealt with issues like sexual immorality, disputes among believers, and questions about spiritual gifts.

Rome: Though he arrived in chains as a prisoner, Paul's journey to Rome marked a significant moment in Christian history. Rome was the heart of the Empire, and Paul's presence there symbolized the spread of Christianity to the centre of political power. According to tradition, Paul was eventually martyred in Rome under Emperor Nero, but not before he had established a strong Christian community that would endure.

The Apostles and Early Christian Writings

As the apostles spread Christianity across the Roman Empire, many of them began to write letters and teachings to instruct and encourage the new churches. Paul's letters were especially influential, but other apostles, like Peter and John, also wrote epistles that became part of the New Testament.

John, the youngest of the apostles and often referred to as "the disciple whom Jesus loved," wrote extensively on the themes of love, light, and the nature of Christ. Later in his life, John received a vision while in exile on the island of Patmos, which he recorded as the Book of Revelation. This text, filled with apocalyptic imagery, provided early Christians with a sense of hope and a glimpse of the future victory of Christ, despite the hardships and persecutions they were enduring.

Impact and Legacy of the Apostles' Work

The apostles' mission across the Roman Empire transformed Christianity from a small, persecuted group in Jerusalem into a widespread movement. Despite facing imprisonment, torture, and martyrdom, the apostles' determination helped establish a global faith that would shape history for centuries. Each of the apostles left a unique mark on the early church, from Peter's leadership to Paul's theological insights and missionary zeal.

Their work laid the foundation for a new era in which Christianity spread throughout the known world, reaching places as far as India and Ethiopia. The apostles' unwavering faith, willingness to suffer, and commitment to the gospel set a standard that would inspire generations of Christians, even in the face of future persecutions and challenges.

The Jewish Diaspora, Old Testament Prophecies, and Early Christian Anticipation of an Apocalypse

The Jewish Diaspora: Scattering and Resilience

The Jewish Diaspora, or the dispersion of the Jewish people from their homeland, began long before the time of Jesus. The roots of this scattering trace back to the Babylonian exile in the 6th century BCE when the Babylonians conquered Jerusalem and destroyed the First Temple. Thousands of Jews were taken from their homes and forced to live in Babylon, marking the beginning of a period in which Jewish people found themselves living in foreign lands, yet holding tightly to their faith and traditions.

This period was deeply formative. During the exile, Jewish prophets and scholars began to solidify key elements of Jewish identity and spirituality. The emphasis on the Torah (the first five books of the Bible) became central, as did the focus on worship outside of the Temple, which had been destroyed. The Jewish people started gathering in synagogues for prayer and study, practices that would become essential to Jewish life in the centuries that followed.

After the Babylonian Empire fell, the Persian King Cyrus the Great allowed the Jews to return to their homeland and rebuild Jerusalem's Second Temple in 516 BCE. However, many Jews chose to remain scattered across the Persian Empire, where they had established lives and communities. This pattern continued through successive empires; from the Persians to the Greeks under Alexander the Great, and finally, the Romans.

In the Roman Empire, Jews were present in almost every major city, from Alexandria in Egypt to Rome itself. Though they often faced social and political challenges, the Jewish people maintained a strong connection to their faith, rituals, and identity, creating a unique bond that would endure throughout centuries of adversity.

Old Testament Prophecies and the Promise of a Messiah

Central to Jewish belief during this period was the hope of a Messiah, a divinely appointed leader who would restore Israel, bring justice, and establish an eternal kingdom. Prophets in the Old Testament, such as Isaiah, Jeremiah, and Daniel, had spoken of a future deliverer who would redeem Israel and usher in a new era of peace.

For instance, Isaiah prophesied about a "suffering servant" who would bear the sins of the people (Isaiah 53), a concept that many Christians later interpreted as pointing to Jesus. Meanwhile, the Book of Daniel presented visions of a coming judgment and a kingdom that would replace the empires of men with the rule of God. These passages became central to both Jewish and Christian eschatology, or beliefs about the end times.

In the centuries leading up to the time of Jesus, Jewish literature often focused on apocalyptic themes; revelations about the end of the world, final judgment, and the ultimate victory of God. This era saw the emergence of texts like the Book of Enoch, which detailed cosmic battles and visions of heaven, and the writings of the Essenes, a Jewish sect that lived in isolation near the Dead Sea and produced the Dead Sea Scrolls. These writings reflected a deep yearning for divine intervention and justice, resonating with a population that had endured centuries of oppression under foreign rule.

Roman Conquest and Its Impact on Jewish Apocalyptic Thought

The Jewish people suffered particularly under Roman rule. While the Romans allowed a certain degree of religious freedom, they imposed heavy taxes, restricted political autonomy, and tolerated no dissent. In Judea, the Romans installed puppet rulers like Herod the Great, who, despite his grand building projects (including the expansion of the Second Temple), was widely despised for his loyalty to Rome and his oppressive policies.

The harshness of Roman occupation intensified Jewish expectations for a Messiah. Many Jews believed that God would soon intervene to free them from Roman oppression, just as He had liberated them from slavery in Egypt centuries before. Messianic movements became increasingly common, with leaders rising up, proclaiming liberation, and even gathering followers in anticipation of divine intervention. However, most of these uprisings were quickly crushed by Roman forces.

The anticipation of an apocalyptic intervention reached a peak in the years leading up to the Jewish-Roman War (66-73 AD). During this time, the Zealots, a militant Jewish sect, waged guerrilla warfare against Roman forces, convinced that God was on their side. The tension culminated in a full-scale revolt in 66 AD, which the Romans eventually crushed, leading to the destruction of Jerusalem and the Second Temple in 70 AD. This catastrophic event solidified a sense of exile and longing among the Jewish people, as they once again faced dispersion throughout the Empire. The destruction of the Temple was a profound spiritual blow, one that deeply impacted both Jewish and early Christian thought.

Early Christian Interpretations of Jewish Prophecies

Early Christians saw the fulfilment of many Jewish prophecies in the life, death, and resurrection of Jesus. They believed that Jesus was the long-awaited Messiah who had come not to establish a political kingdom but to usher in a spiritual one. According to early Christian writings, Jesus' resurrection marked the beginning of a new age ; the Kingdom of God ; though it would not be fully realized until his return.

The apostles and early Christian writers often cited Old Testament prophecies to show how they were fulfilled in Jesus. For example, they referenced passages from Isaiah, the Psalms, and Zechariah, interpreting them in a way that highlighted Jesus' role as the promised saviour. In this way, they connected the new Christian faith with its Jewish roots, positioning Christianity as the fulfilment of ancient prophecies and the ultimate answer to humanity's spiritual needs.

The Apocalypse and Early Christian Beliefs

The early Christians, particularly the apostles, expected Jesus to return soon to complete the work of salvation and bring an end to the present world. This belief in an imminent return shaped much of early Christian teaching, as seen in letters from Paul, Peter, and John. They anticipated that Jesus would return in glory, defeat evil, judge humanity, and create a new heaven and earth where God's presence would dwell among the faithful.

This expectation is especially evident in the Book of Revelation, written by the apostle John while he was exiled on the island of Patmos. Revelation, with its vivid imagery and symbolic language, describes a vision of the end times; a final battle between good and evil, the ultimate defeat of Satan, and the establishment of God's eternal kingdom. The text depicts cosmic events, plagues, and divine judgments, blending apocalyptic prophecy with deep theological meaning.

The early Christians also believed that they were living in a period of increased spiritual conflict. They saw themselves as part of a cosmic struggle between God and the forces of darkness. This perspective was fuelled by the persecution they faced under Roman authorities, who saw Christianity as a subversive force. Many Christians were arrested, tortured, and executed, including prominent leaders like Peter and Paul. These persecutions reinforced the belief that the end was near and that they were witnessing the signs of the apocalypse foretold in Scripture.

The Legacy of the Jewish Diaspora and Christian Apocalyptic Thought

As the early Christian Church grew, so did the belief that God had a larger plan, one that transcended earthly kingdoms and empires. The Jewish Diaspora and the Roman Empire's vast network of roads allowed Christianity to spread quickly throughout the known world. Jewish synagogues in cities across the Empire provided the apostles with initial places to preach, and many of the first Christian converts were Jews familiar with the Messianic prophecies.

In these early years, Christianity began to diverge from its Jewish roots, particularly as Gentiles (non-Jews) embraced the faith. The belief in Jesus as the Messiah created a new identity for Christians, who saw themselves as participants in God's redemptive plan for humanity. The early Christians believed they were witnessing the beginning of the end; a period of waiting and preparation for the return of Christ and the final judgment.

The combination of Jewish apocalyptic thought, Roman persecution, and Christian teachings about Jesus' return created a potent blend of hope and urgency within the early Church. This anticipation of an apocalypse, shaped by both Jewish prophecies and Christian expectations, laid the foundation for a faith that would endure even in the face of immense challenges.

The Roman Empire and Rise of Christianity (33-476 AD)

Rise of Christianity within the Roman Empire

Christianity began as a small, seemingly insignificant Jewish sect in a distant province of the Roman Empire. After the crucifixion and resurrection of Jesus Christ, his followers, primarily a small group of Jews, began to spread his teachings throughout Jerusalem and the surrounding areas. As they grew in numbers, the followers of Jesus; soon called "Christians"; quickly attracted attention within the Jewish community and eventually from the Roman authorities themselves.

The apostles, particularly Peter and Paul, played a central role in the growth of Christianity within the Roman Empire. Paul, once a Pharisee and a persecutor of Christians, underwent a profound conversion and became one of the most influential figures in early Christianity. Known for his missionary journeys across the Mediterranean, Paul established Christian communities in major cities such as Ephesus, Corinth, and Rome itself, adapting the message of Jesus to resonate with Gentile (non-Jewish) audiences.

Over time, Christianity began spreading along the Roman Empire's trade routes and bustling cities. Roman roads, originally constructed for the military, became vital channels for early Christians to spread their faith. Ports and trade hubs, where diverse people gathered, provided fertile ground for the growth of Christian teachings. The movement grew from house gatherings to organized communities, eventually reaching far-flung regions of the empire from Asia Minor to North Africa and Europe.

Despite its rapid expansion, the rise of Christianity was far from smooth. As the movement grew, it became increasingly visible to Roman authorities who did not fully understand this new faith. Unlike the polytheistic religions of the empire, Christianity was monotheistic and exclusive in worship, a stance that caused concern among the Romans, who valued loyalty to the emperor and adherence to the traditional gods as central to maintaining social and political order.

Persecution of Christians by the Roman Empire

Early Christians found themselves in a precarious position within the empire. While Judaism was tolerated as a long-established religion with certain legal protections, Christianity, viewed as a new and somewhat radical sect, was perceived with suspicion. Christians refused to participate in Roman religious practices, including sacrifices to the gods and the imperial cult, which honoured the emperor as a divine figure. This refusal was seen as disloyal and dangerous, challenging the stability of the state and the authority of the emperor.

The first major outbreak of persecution occurred under Emperor Nero in 64 AD. Following a devastating fire that swept through Rome, Nero sought to divert blame from himself and instead accused the Christians, a minority group in the city, of arson. As a result, many Christians were arrested, tortured, and executed in horrific ways, some being burned alive or thrown to wild animals in the arena. This marked the beginning of what would be centuries of periodic persecution against Christians.

Subsequent emperors also enacted measures against Christianity, though persecution varied in intensity depending on the ruler. Emperors like Domitian and Marcus Aurelius viewed Christians as threats to the traditional Roman values and sought to suppress the faith. Christians were often accused of atheism (due to their rejection of the Roman gods) and even treason, as they would not participate in state rituals.

In the 3rd century, Emperor Decius issued one of the most systematic persecutions of Christians. In 250 AD, he decreed that all citizens of the empire must make sacrifices to the Roman gods and obtain a certificate proving their loyalty. Many Christians refused to comply, choosing to face imprisonment, torture, or death rather than renounce their faith. This period of persecution was among the most intense and saw many Christians, including bishops and other leaders, martyred for their faith.

One of the most brutal persecutions occurred under Emperor Diocletian in 303 AD. Known as the "Great Persecution," this campaign aimed to eradicate Christianity from the empire. Churches were destroyed, scriptures were burned, and Christians were expelled from government positions. Those who refused to sacrifice to the gods were imprisoned, tortured, or executed. The Great Persecution marked the last and most severe wave of persecution before the eventual rise of Christianity to prominence within the empire.

Christian Martyrdom and Its Impact on the Faith

Despite; or perhaps because of; the persecution, the Christian faith continued to grow, with many Romans captivated by the dedication and resilience of Christian martyrs. Stories of martyrs such as Ignatius of Antioch, Polycarp of Smyrna, and Perpetua inspired others and demonstrated the power of faith, as these individuals often faced brutal deaths with unwavering conviction and peace.

The phenomenon of martyrdom became a significant aspect of early Christian identity. Martyrs were celebrated as heroes of the faith, and their stories were passed down in Christian communities, serving as both encouragement and a call to perseverance. Martyrs were seen as witnesses to the truth of Christianity, and their willingness to die for their beliefs was seen as proof of the faith's divine power.

The concept of martyrdom also fostered a sense of solidarity among Christians across the empire. Stories of martyrdom were shared in Christian gatherings and became a source of collective strength. Martyrs were honoured on the anniversaries of their deaths, which eventually evolved into the practice of venerating saints in the Christian tradition.

Christianity's Resilience and Transformation of Persecution

Rather than suppressing Christianity, persecution often led to a strengthening of Christian communities. The faithful saw themselves as followers of Christ, who had also suffered persecution and death. The sense of shared struggle and hope for eternal life became a central theme in Christian teaching, helping Christians to endure oppression and even attract new converts who were inspired by their courage and conviction.

In many ways, the persecution of Christians highlighted the unique nature of the faith within the Roman world. While other religious groups practiced their beliefs in private or made compromises to avoid trouble with the authorities, Christians boldly proclaimed their faith, even when faced with death. This dedication attracted many who felt disillusioned with the superficiality of Roman religious practices and were seeking a deeper sense of purpose and community.

The Christian message of love, forgiveness, and eternal life resonated with those who faced the harsh realities of Roman society, particularly the poor, enslaved, and marginalized. Through this, Christianity spread among various social classes, eventually reaching even the educated elite and members of the Roman aristocracy.

End of Persecution and the Path to Legalization

By the early 4th century, the resilience of the Christian faith had become undeniable, even to the Roman authorities. It was during the reign of Emperor Constantine that the fate of Christianity changed dramatically. In 312 AD, Constantine fought the Battle of the Milvian Bridge, where he reportedly saw a vision of a cross and heard the words, "In this sign, you will conquer." Interpreting this as a divine sign, Constantine adopted the Christian symbol and won the battle, marking a turning point in his life and the relationship between Rome and Christianity.

In 313 AD, Constantine issued the Edict of Milan, which granted religious tolerance to all religions, including Christianity. This marked the end of state-sponsored persecution and allowed Christians to worship openly. The edict was a groundbreaking change that transformed Christianity from a persecuted sect into a legally recognized religion within the empire.

Constantine's conversion and the subsequent legalization of Christianity had a profound impact on the faith. Christianity soon found itself in a position of influence, with Constantine and future emperors supporting the construction of churches, the convening of councils, and the establishment of Christian doctrine.

With the newfound freedom, Christianity grew rapidly, attracting converts from all levels of society, including those in positions of power. Christian bishops and leaders gained influence in Roman political and social affairs, marking the beginning of a complex relationship between the Church and the state that would shape the course of Western history for centuries to come.

The early rise of Christianity within the Roman Empire is a testament to the strength of conviction held by early Christians, who endured extreme persecution for their faith. Despite the attempts to suppress it, Christianity's appeal to people across social boundaries and its message of hope, love, and redemption allowed it to thrive and grow, eventually influencing the very empire that had sought to destroy it.

With the Edict of Milan, Christianity entered a new phase, shifting from a persecuted faith to one on the path toward becoming the official religion of the Roman Empire. This journey of resilience, persecution, and ultimate acceptance set the stage for the transformative role Christianity would play in the centuries to follow, as it spread beyond the Roman Empire and became a guiding force in the moral and spiritual life of Europe and the broader world.

Emperor Constantine's Conversion, the Edict of Milan, and the Establishment of the Catholic Church

By the early 4th century, the Roman Empire was a vast, complex territory under severe pressure. Internal strife, threats from external forces, and a complicated religious landscape caused frequent tension. The Roman emperors held on to power tightly, often enforcing loyalty through military strength and religious conformity. But in the early 300s, an unprecedented shift occurred under Emperor Constantine, who would become known as "Constantine the Great." His conversion to Christianity, his enactment of the Edict of Milan, and the subsequent establishment of the Catholic Church laid the groundwork for Christianity to become the dominant religious force in Europe and for the Church to grow into one of the most influential institutions in history.

Constantine's Conversion to Christianity

Constantine's journey toward Christianity is rooted in a significant military conflict. In 312 AD, Constantine was locked in a power struggle with Maxentius, his rival for control over the Western Roman Empire. The decisive confrontation came at the Battle of the Milvian Bridge, near Rome. According to historical accounts, on the eve of battle, Constantine experienced a powerful vision: he reportedly saw a cross of light in the sky, accompanied by the words *"In this sign, you will conquer"* (*In hoc signo vinces* in Latin). That night, he dreamt that Christ instructed him to mark his soldiers' shields with the Christian symbol known as the Chi-Rho (a combined Greek symbol of the first two letters of "Christ"). Taking this as a divine sign, Constantine ordered his troops to paint the symbol on their shields.

Constantine emerged victorious in the Battle of the Milvian Bridge, a victory he attributed to the Christian God's intervention. This triumph led to Constantine's increasing curiosity and affinity toward Christianity, though he did not immediately renounce the traditional Roman gods. Historians note that his "conversion" was a gradual process rather than a single moment, as he navigated his own beliefs and the political complexities of ruling a polytheistic empire. Nonetheless, Constantine became the first Roman emperor to favor Christianity, seeing it as not only a personal faith but a possible unifying force within the empire.

The Edict of Milan and Religious Tolerance

In 313 AD, a year after his decisive victory, Constantine and his co-emperor, Licinius, issued the Edict of Milan, a proclamation that granted religious tolerance throughout the Roman Empire. The Edict of Milan declared that individuals were free to practice any religion they chose, including Christianity. It effectively ended state-sponsored persecution of Christians and returned confiscated Christian property.

The Edict of Milan marked a radical shift in the Roman Empire's approach to religious practice. For nearly three centuries, Christians had been marginalized, discriminated against, and, at times, subjected to brutal persecution for their faith. Now, they were free to worship openly without fear of reprisal. The significance of the Edict was profound: it was the first formal recognition by the Roman government of Christianity's legitimacy, and it set a precedent for religious freedom in Western history.

Constantine's support of Christianity did not mean he imposed the religion on his subjects; rather, he adopted policies to promote unity and peace among the empire's diverse religious groups. Nonetheless, the emperor's growing favor toward Christianity led to increased conversions and marked the beginning of Christianity's influence on Roman political and social life.

Constantine's Role in the Establishment of the Catholic Church

As Christianity gained prominence, Constantine began working toward a more unified and organized Church. Prior to Constantine's rule, Christianity had developed as a loosely organized collection of beliefs and practices. Local communities often had their own interpretations of Christian doctrine, leading to theological differences and disagreements, including some beliefs considered heretical by the larger Christian community. Constantine saw this lack of unity as a potential threat to his empire, fearing that religious division could foster political instability.

In 325 AD, Constantine convened the First Council of Nicaea, the first ecumenical council of Christian bishops, held in the city of Nicaea (modern-day İznik, Turkey). This council was a defining moment for Christianity, as it sought to address and resolve significant theological disputes, particularly concerning the nature of Jesus Christ. The Arian controversy; named after the teachings of Arius, a priest who argued that Jesus was not divine in the same way as God the Father ; was a central issue. Arius's teachings, which challenged the traditional belief in Jesus's divinity, had created division within the Church.

Constantine, seeking unity, urged the bishops to come to a consensus. The council ultimately rejected Arianism and affirmed the belief in the Trinity; the doctrine that God exists as three persons in one essence: the Father, the Son (Jesus Christ), and the Holy Spirit. This theological stance became foundational to mainstream Christianity and was enshrined in the Nicene Creed, a formal statement of faith that remains central to Christian liturgy. The Council of Nicaea established a precedent for the Church's role in establishing orthodoxy and suppressing heresy, signalling, the beginning of the Catholic (meaning "universal") Church's formal organization and unity.

Development of the Catholic Church and Constantine's Influence

Constantine's support extended beyond theology. He commissioned and funded the construction of Christian churches throughout the empire, including the famous Church of the Holy Sepulchre in Jerusalem, which commemorated the site of Jesus's crucifixion and resurrection. He also built the Old St. Peter's Basilica in Rome and the Hagia Sophia in Constantinople, which later became one of the most significant churches in Christendom. These monumental structures symbolized the new status of Christianity and solidified its physical and spiritual presence in the empire.

Constantine also integrated Christian clergy into the political fabric of the empire. He exempted bishops and other clergy from certain taxes and military service, creating a privileged class within the Christian Church that could focus on spiritual and administrative duties. These privileges, along with Constantine's favor, granted the Church significant political and social influence. The integration of Christian leaders into the state apparatus helped solidify the Church's role not only as a religious institution but as a powerful entity within the Roman Empire.

Despite his active promotion of Christianity, Constantine remained officially neutral regarding other religions. He retained the title of *Pontifex Maximus*, the chief priest of Roman polytheism, and continued to allow the worship of traditional Roman gods, understanding that a swift and complete imposition of Christianity might lead to unrest. This tolerance reflected his pragmatic approach, as he aimed to foster unity without enforcing abrupt changes that could destabilize the empire.

After Constantine's death in 337 AD, his sons and subsequent emperors continued his legacy of supporting Christianity, though with varying levels of commitment. By the end of the 4th century, Emperor Theodosius I took Constantine's vision further by making Christianity the official state religion of the Roman Empire and prohibiting pagan worship. This marked the beginning of an era in which the Catholic Church would dominate European religious, political, and social life for centuries to come.

Legacy of Constantine and the Catholic Church

Constantine's conversion, the Edict of Milan, and the establishment of the Catholic Church left an indelible mark on Western civilization. By aligning himself with Christianity, Constantine not only changed the trajectory of the Roman Empire but also influenced the future of Europe and the world. His policies fostered an environment in which Christianity could flourish and spread beyond the empire's borders, becoming a dominant force that shaped societies, cultures, and governments.

The establishment of the Catholic Church as a structured, hierarchical institution under Constantine laid the foundation for the Church's role in European history. It introduced a model of centralized authority that influenced both religious and secular governance, as the Church became intertwined with state affairs. Constantine's influence on Christian theology and the organization of the Church helped standardize Christian beliefs, which provided cohesion within the diverse Christian communities.

Moreover, Constantine's reign highlighted the beginning of a new era in which religion and politics were inseparably linked. His legacy influenced the development of Christendom; a society where Christian values, laws, and authority shaped public and private life. The Catholic Church grew to become not just a religious institution but a central authority that wielded immense power over medieval kings, governed land, and influenced the lives of millions.

Constantine's conversion, his advocacy for Christianity, and his support in formalizing the Catholic Church marked a turning point for the Christian faith and Western civilization. His reign transformed Christianity from a persecuted minority faith to a powerful and respected institution that would play a dominant role in the centuries that followed. Constantine's vision of a Christian empire paved the way for a Europe deeply rooted in Christian beliefs and traditions, setting the stage for the medieval era and the continued influence of the Catholic Church on world history.

Tension Between the Growing Christian Faith and Pagan Rome, Setting the Stage for Religious Power Dynamics

As Christianity gained ground within the Roman Empire, it began to challenge the deeply ingrained pagan beliefs that had formed the foundation of Roman religious and cultural life for centuries. This shift from polytheism to monotheism introduced an entirely new framework for understanding the divine, one that threatened to undermine the traditional structures of Roman society. This tension marked the beginning of a long struggle between Christianity and the pagan traditions of Rome, setting the stage for a profound transformation of the empire's spiritual and political landscape.

The Pagan Foundations of Roman Society

Roman society had long been rooted in pagan polytheism, with a vast pantheon of gods and goddesses that represented various aspects of life, nature, and the state. Central to this belief system was the idea that Rome's success and prosperity depended on the favor of these gods, who required sacrifices, rituals, and reverence. Temples were dedicated to gods like Jupiter, Mars, Venus, and Minerva, and festivals celebrating these deities played a significant role in the lives of Roman citizens. This belief in divine support for the empire was further reinforced by the concept of *religio*, a Roman term that expressed loyalty to the gods as essential to the prosperity and stability of Rome.

The emperor himself held the title of *Pontifex Maximus*, meaning "chief priest," which designated him as the supreme religious authority in Rome. Emperors were seen as semi-divine figures whose role included upholding and protecting the empire's religious traditions. This authority included overseeing public sacrifices, priestly appointments, and ensuring the proper observance of Roman festivals and rituals. Roman religion was thus deeply intertwined with the state, and any challenge to its traditions was seen as a threat to Rome's social order and unity.

Christianity as a Radical Departure

Christianity's monotheistic message stood in stark contrast to Roman polytheism. Christians worshiped a single God and believed that Jesus Christ was the only way to salvation, rejecting the legitimacy of other gods. This belief alone challenged the very basis of Roman religious and political order, which depended on the idea of multiple gods and deified emperors. For Romans, religious observance was a communal duty meant to sustain the empire, while Christians considered their faith a personal, spiritual journey with loyalty to God above all earthly powers, including the emperor.

In addition, early Christians refused to participate in Roman rituals, including making sacrifices to the gods or honouring the emperor's divinity. This defiance was seen as both irreverent and seditious. Romans often viewed Christians with suspicion, branding them as atheists or traitors who rejected Rome's traditions. The refusal to conform to the empire's expectations created resentment and fear among the Roman populace and ruling class, who worried that Christianity's influence could erode the unity and power of the empire.

The Period of Persecution

The growth of Christianity continued despite its unpopularity among the Roman authorities, eventually leading to a period of intense persecution. Between the 1st and 4th centuries AD, Roman emperors enacted multiple waves of persecution to suppress the spread of Christianity. Among the most notorious of these were the persecutions under Emperor Nero, who blamed Christians for the Great Fire of Rome in 64 AD, and Emperor Diocletian, whose reign saw one of the most brutal crackdowns on Christian communities, known as the Great Persecution (303-311 AD).

During this time, Christians were systematically imprisoned, tortured, and executed for their faith. Public executions and spectacles of martyrdom were intended to demonstrate the empire's power and discourage conversion to Christianity. Many of the early saints and martyrs of Christianity, such as Saints Peter and Paul, were killed during this period, and their stories of unwavering faith under torture inspired future generations of Christians. Far from stifling the faith, these persecutions often strengthened Christian resolve, turning martyrs into heroes and reinforcing the movement's sense of purpose and unity.

The persecutions highlighted a deeper conflict: while Christianity preached peace, charity, and a vision of a world beyond the material, the Roman Empire valued power, conquest, and a pantheon that glorified both divine and human authority. Christianity's promise of eternal life and moral salvation offered hope to those who felt oppressed or disenfranchised within the rigid structures of Roman society, particularly slaves and lower-class citizens. This inclusiveness, along with the message of divine love, provided a stark alternative to Rome's often violent and hierarchical world.

The Gradual Shift Toward Acceptance

Although Christianity was a minority religion and subject to persecution, it continued to spread throughout the empire. This growth persisted partly due to the faith's appeal across social classes, ethnicities, and geographic boundaries, including its emphasis on compassion, charity, and forgiveness. Even within Roman high society, certain elites began to convert, which contributed to Christianity's legitimacy and reach.

By the early 4th century, the Roman Empire was undergoing profound challenges, with pressures from foreign invasions, economic instability, and political division. Constantine's rise to power and his subsequent conversion to Christianity (circa 312 AD) marked a turning point in this religious struggle. Constantine's support for Christianity gave the religion newfound status and protection, and the Edict of Milan (313 AD) formally ended the persecution of Christians, granting religious tolerance across the empire. For the first time, Christians were able to worship openly, allowing their communities to grow and organize without fear of reprisal.

The Power Dynamics of a "Christianized" Empire

Constantine's reign introduced a new dynamic: the incorporation of Christian values and beliefs into the Roman political structure. Under his rule, Christianity transformed from an underground movement into a public faith with state backing. Constantine established a precedent for the fusion of church and state, a union that would define much of European history. The emperor's patronage gave Christianity access to state resources and elevated its leaders, allowing for the construction of churches, the dissemination of Christian texts, and the establishment of Christian clergy as a social class with unique privileges.

However, this integration also meant that Christianity was increasingly shaped by the political needs of the Roman state. With the official endorsement of Constantine and his successors, the Christian Church began to adopt hierarchical structures mirroring those of the Roman government. This included the establishment of regional bishops with authority over specific territories, culminating in the rise of the bishop of Rome (later the Pope) as a central figure of Christian leadership. In return, the church offered the empire a moral and ideological foundation, aligning Christian doctrine with Roman authority and providing a unifying identity for a divided empire.

The Formation of the Catholic Church and Pagan Resistance

The growing prominence of Christianity led to tension with traditionalists who remained loyal to Rome's pagan gods. As Christianity took root, pagans saw their own religious practices, once central to the empire's identity, increasingly marginalized. In 380 AD, Emperor Theodosius I took the final step in the empire's religious transformation by declaring Christianity the official state religion and banning pagan worship. Temples were closed, and traditional practices were either restricted or abolished, bringing centuries of Roman polytheism to an official end.

This move sparked resistance among Roman pagans, many of whom were entrenched in the aristocracy and military. Pagan intellectuals and philosophers like the writer Symmachus argued that abandoning Rome's ancestral gods would lead to the decline of Roman power and tradition. This resistance was evident in the late 4th century as factions of the Roman aristocracy attempted to preserve their beliefs and practices. Though some pagans continued their rituals in private, the influence of the traditional gods was gradually eclipsed by the growing authority of the Christian Church.

Legacy of the Tension Between Christianity and Paganism

The tension between Christianity and Roman paganism was a defining moment in history, marking the end of one era and the beginning of another. Christianity's rise within the Roman Empire marked a shift from a religiously diverse society to a dominantly Christian one, creating a new religious and cultural unity that outlasted the empire itself. This process, however, was not without internal conflict; Christianity's establishment as the state religion led to new challenges, including debates over orthodoxy, the suppression of heretical movements, and the centralization of religious power.

The Church's dominance was also marked by compromises and adaptations, as it absorbed certain aspects of Roman culture and governance. This process of syncretism allowed the Church to survive beyond the fall of the Western Roman Empire in 476 AD, evolving into a central authority that shaped the medieval world. The transition from a pagan empire to a Christianized Rome laid the foundations for Western Christendom, setting up the Church as a powerful institution that would influence Europe's religious, political, and cultural landscapes for centuries.

The tension between Christianity and paganism within the Roman Empire represents a significant shift in the history of Western civilization. It reflects not only the resilience of the early Christian movement but also the transformative power of faith to redefine societal values, unify diverse groups, and establish new norms. The religious power dynamics forged during this period set the stage for the future of the Christian Church and the cultural legacy of the Roman Empire, which would echo through the Middle Ages and beyond.

Collapse of Empires and Early Apocalyptic Visions (476-632 AD)

The collapse of empires following the decline of the Western Roman Empire brought about a time of social upheaval, cultural transformation, and a renewed sense of apocalyptic anticipation. Christianity had begun to establish itself as the central religion in the former Roman territories, and the early medieval period saw a mingling of hope and fear regarding the end times. The Christian worldview during this period was marked by a complex blend of faith, superstition, and survival in a world reshaped by invasions, warfare, and the fall of ancient political structures.

The Fall of the Western Roman Empire (476 AD) and Its Aftermath

The official collapse of the Western Roman Empire in 476 AD was marked by the deposition of Romulus Augustulus, the last Roman emperor in the West, by the Germanic chieftain Odoacer. This event is widely considered the end of ancient Rome as a political entity in the West, though the Eastern Roman Empire, or Byzantine Empire, continued to thrive for nearly a thousand more years. The end of the Western Empire left a power vacuum that various tribes, kingdoms, and local rulers sought to fill, resulting in a fractured political landscape and widespread uncertainty.

After the fall, many Roman institutions, such as governance, infrastructure, and military organization, deteriorated, leading to a period known as the "Dark Ages." Roads and trade routes were no longer maintained, city populations dwindled, and a largely agrarian economy emerged as centralized systems of administration disappeared. Although Roman culture, architecture, and language left an enduring legacy, everyday life became more localized, with communities relying on their own resources and leadership for survival.

For the Christian Church, however, this period was both a challenge and an opportunity. While the collapse of the empire removed the organized protection once offered by the state, the Church was able to step into the role of a stabilizing force, offering spiritual guidance, education, and even political leadership where secular rulers were absent. Bishops and clergy became influential figures, often acting as de facto leaders within their communities and helping to preserve aspects of Roman learning, literacy, and administration. The Church became a unifying institution in an increasingly fragmented society.

Early Christian Eschatology and Apocalyptic Expectations

With the collapse of Rome, a wave of apocalyptic thought spread across the Christian world. The early Christians, guided by the teachings of Jesus and the writings of the apostles, had already been predisposed to apocalyptic thinking. This was reinforced by the destruction of the Jerusalem Temple in 70 AD, which many saw as a fulfilment of Jesus' prophecies regarding the end times. Now, with the fall of the once-mighty Roman Empire, a sense of dread and expectation swept through Christian communities.

Many Christians believed that the fall of Rome signalled the beginning of the end times, as foretold in biblical prophecies. The book of Revelation, along with passages from Daniel and other apocalyptic texts, became a focus of study, prayer, and interpretation. Christian scholars and theologians debated the meaning of these texts, with many interpreting the fall of Rome as a divine punishment for sin or as the fulfilment of prophecies regarding the rise and fall of earthly kingdoms.

In the absence of a stable, unifying political force, these apocalyptic visions took on new significance. The image of Rome as the "Fourth Beast" in the book of Daniel, representing the final worldly kingdom before the establishment of God's eternal reign, became a common interpretation. Christian eschatology saw the world as approaching a final reckoning, where Christ would return to judge humanity and establish a new, divine order. This anticipation shaped much of the thinking and writing during this period, as monks, scholars, and clergy speculated on the unfolding of God's plan for the world.

Rise of Barbarian Kingdoms and the Formation of New Societies

In the absence of Roman rule, new kingdoms and societies began to emerge across Europe, many of them led by the so-called "barbarian" tribes, including the Goths, Vandals, Franks, and Lombards. These groups, which had once been considered enemies of the empire, now filled the power vacuum and established their own territories. They brought their own customs, languages, and warrior traditions but also adopted many aspects of Roman culture and governance, incorporating Latin, Roman law, and, increasingly, Christianity.

One of the most prominent examples of this was the Frankish Kingdom, led by the Merovingian dynasty. Clovis I, the Frankish king who ruled from 481 to 511 AD, converted to Christianity, establishing the Franks as the first major Germanic kingdom to embrace the Christian faith. Clovis' conversion marked a significant milestone in the spread of Christianity among the barbarian tribes, laying the groundwork for the later unification of Western Europe under the banner of Christendom.

However, the process of cultural integration and Christianization was gradual, and many regions continued to observe pagan traditions alongside Christian practices. The Church worked to convert these populations through missionary efforts and by gradually integrating certain pre-Christian customs and festivals into the Christian calendar. The incorporation of barbarian rulers into the Christian fold brought stability to the Church, as it gained new allies who were committed to promoting the faith among their own people.

Religious Struggles and Schisms Within the Empire

While the Western Roman Empire had fallen, the Eastern Roman Empire, or Byzantine Empire, continued to thrive. This era marked an important period for the development of Christian theology, as the Byzantine Empire became a center for theological debate and ecclesiastical authority. However, religious tensions and theological disputes often arose, especially regarding the nature of Christ, the Trinity, and the role of images in worship.

One of the most significant controversies was the Monophysite controversy, a theological debate about whether Christ had one divine nature or two natures; divine and human. This controversy led to schisms and conflict within the Christian community, as different regions and churches held opposing views. The Council of Chalcedon in 451 AD attempted to settle the dispute, declaring that Christ possessed two natures in one person. However, the debate continued to create divisions within the Christian world, particularly between the Eastern and Western branches of the Church.

The rise of new kingdoms and the spread of Christianity among the Germanic tribes also led to variations in Christian practice and theology. The Pope in Rome, the Patriarch of Constantinople, and other regional bishops often held differing views on theological and ecclesiastical matters. Over time, these differences would grow more pronounced, ultimately contributing to the Great Schism of 1054, when the Eastern Orthodox and Roman Catholic Churches formally split.

Rise of Apocalyptic Thought and the Legacy of Rome's Collapse

The collapse of the Western Roman Empire left a lasting impact on Christian thought, particularly in the area of eschatology. Many Christians interpreted the fall of Rome as a sign of the impending apocalypse, an expectation that was heightened by the turbulence and instability of the period. Monasteries became centres of prayer, contemplation, and eschatological speculation, as monks sought to prepare for the coming end times through rigorous spiritual discipline.

This sense of imminent judgment and divine intervention led to the establishment of various monastic communities, where individuals devoted themselves to prayer, study, and asceticism in anticipation of the end. The monastic tradition emphasized a withdrawal from worldly pursuits, focusing instead on the cultivation of virtue, spiritual purity, and a deep relationship with God. These communities sought to embody the teachings of Christ and to prepare their souls for the coming judgment, setting an example for the wider Christian community.

In addition, many Christian texts and writings from this period reflect an apocalyptic worldview, with authors and theologians interpreting contemporary events as signs of the times. The barbarian invasions, political fragmentation, and social upheaval were often seen as evidence of a world in decline, one that was approaching its final days. Writers like Augustine of Hippo, in his work *City of God*, provided a theological framework for understanding the fall of Rome as part of a larger divine plan, one that would ultimately culminate in the triumph of God's eternal kingdom.

The collapse of the Western Roman Empire and the rise of new kingdoms set the stage for a transformative period in European history. Christianity emerged as a stabilizing force amidst the chaos, offering hope, guidance, and a sense of purpose to a world in turmoil. Apocalyptic expectations flourished as people grappled with the loss of the ancient world and sought to understand their place in God's unfolding plan.

The Christian faith became a unifying element across different regions and cultures, even as it adapted to local traditions and political realities. The integration of barbarian tribes into the Christian community brought new strength and vitality to the Church, which now played an increasingly central role in the lives of people throughout Europe. The era that followed would be shaped by the spread of Christianity, the rise of new kingdoms, and a deep-rooted expectation of divine intervention; a worldview that continued to shape the course of Western civilization for centuries to come.

Rise of Islam and Religious Wars; Prophecies in Both Christianity and Islam Foretelling Judgment

The Birth of Islam and Its Rapid Spread (610-632 AD)

In the early 7th century, a new monotheistic religion; Islam; emerged in the Arabian Peninsula, centered around the teachings of the prophet Muhammad, who Muslims believe was the final prophet sent by God. Muhammad began receiving revelations around 610 AD, which were later compiled into the Quran, Islam's holy book. These revelations emphasized strict monotheism, social justice, compassion, and submission to the will of Allah (God). Islam quickly spread in the Arabian Peninsula, initially within Mecca and Medina, two of the religion's holiest cities, and expanded as tribes and individuals converted to the new faith.

By 632 AD, the year of Muhammad's death, Islam had united the tribes of Arabia under a single religious and political framework. This new unity fostered rapid military and social expansion, with the first Caliphs (successors to Muhammad) leading campaigns to spread Islam beyond Arabia. Within a century, Islam had expanded across the Middle East, North Africa, and parts of Europe and Asia, marking one of the most remarkable religious expansions in history.

The spread of Islam brought significant changes to the social, political, and religious landscape of the time, especially in areas that were once part of the Eastern Roman (Byzantine) and Persian Empires. This expansion was not only military but also cultural and intellectual, as Islamic scholars began to engage with Greek, Persian, and Indian knowledge, leading to an era of scientific and philosophical advancements. Yet, the rapid rise of Islam and its divergence from Christianity set the stage for centuries of conflict, religious wars, and competing eschatological beliefs.

The Prophetic and Apocalyptic Elements in Islam and Christianity

From its beginnings, Islam included an apocalyptic dimension similar to the one found in Christianity. The Quran contains many verses that address the end times, judgment, and the afterlife. Prophetic teachings in Islam (known as *hadiths*) elaborate further on these themes, with descriptions of the Day of Judgment (*Yawm al-Qiyamah*), when all souls will be resurrected and judged by Allah based on their deeds. Islam teaches that righteous believers will be rewarded with paradise, while sinners and non-believers will face eternal punishment. Key figures and events in Islamic eschatology include the coming of the Mahdi, a messianic figure who will establish justice, and the return of Jesus (known as *Isa* in Islam), who is believed to play a role in defeating the forces of evil.

In Christianity, the book of Revelation and other apocalyptic texts had long warned of a final battle between good and evil, the rise of an Antichrist figure, and the eventual triumph of God's kingdom. This period of expectation was fuelled by both the fall of the Western Roman Empire and the rise of external threats. By the time Islam emerged, Christians were already anticipating events that could signify the coming end times, including wars, persecution, and moral decline. Many viewed the rapid expansion of Islam and the conquests that followed as a potential fulfilment of these apocalyptic warnings, leading to increased tension between Christians and Muslims.

In both faiths, the concept of judgment; individual and collective; was central. Christians believed in the final judgment as depicted in the Bible, where Christ would return to judge the living and the dead. Islamic teachings likewise anticipated a final reckoning in which each person's deeds would be weighed. These shared eschatological themes added a deeper layer to the rivalry and conflict between the two faiths, each viewing the other's presence and actions through the lens of their own prophetic teachings.

Religious Conflicts and Wars

With the expansion of Islam, conflicts inevitably arose between the Muslim and Christian worlds, especially as Muslims moved into territories traditionally dominated by Christians, including parts of the Byzantine Empire and territories surrounding the Mediterranean. These conflicts were not merely political but also took on religious significance, as each side viewed the other as a rival faith.

The Byzantine-Muslim Wars (7th-11th centuries):

Following the death of Muhammad in 632 AD, the Islamic Caliphate rapidly expanded, coming into direct conflict with the Byzantine Empire. A series of wars ensued, with Muslims seizing key Byzantine territories, including Jerusalem, Syria, and Egypt. Jerusalem, a city of profound religious significance to both Christians and Muslims, became a focal point of conflict. In Christian eschatology, the city held a special place as the site of Jesus' ministry, crucifixion, and resurrection. For Muslims, it was home to the Al-Aqsa Mosque, believed to be the location of Muhammad's ascension to heaven during the Night Journey.

This clash between the Byzantine and Islamic forces marked the beginning of centuries of religiously charged warfare. Despite intermittent truces and periods of coexistence, the Byzantine-Muslim Wars intensified religious tensions and fostered the perception on both sides of a cosmic struggle between Christianity and Islam. In Christian eyes, the Muslim forces represented a threat to the "Kingdom of Christendom" and even, potentially, a manifestation of apocalyptic prophecies regarding foreign invaders.

The Conquest of Spain (711 AD):

Islam's expansion continued westward, with the conquest of Spain in 711 AD by Muslim forces under Tariq ibn Ziyad. Known as Al-Andalus under Muslim rule, Spain became a flourishing centre of Islamic culture, philosophy, science, and architecture. For Christians in Western Europe, however, the loss of Spain signified a major setback and was seen as a challenge to the Christian world order. The Reconquista, the centuries-long struggle by Christian kingdoms to reclaim Spain, was driven by both political and religious motives, as leaders sought to restore Christian rule to the Iberian Peninsula.

The Islamic presence in Spain brought about a unique cultural exchange but also fuelled apocalyptic fears among Christians. Some Christian thinkers interpreted the Muslim presence in Europe as a punishment or test sent by God, reflecting the Christian view of Islam as both a military threat and a theological challenge.

The Crusades (1095-1291):

The culmination of centuries of Christian-Muslim conflict was the series of military campaigns known as the Crusades. These wars, initiated by the papacy in 1095, aimed to reclaim Jerusalem and other holy sites from Muslim rule. Pope Urban II called for the First Crusade in response to reports of Christian persecution in the Holy Land and to ensure safe pilgrimage routes to Jerusalem. The Crusaders, composed of knights, nobles, and commoners, set out with religious fervour, viewing the campaign as a sacred duty to protect and recover Christian lands.

The Crusades became a turning point in Christian-Muslim relations. While initially focused on reclaiming Jerusalem, the Crusades also fostered deep animosities, as atrocities were committed by both sides. The Crusaders captured Jerusalem in 1099, establishing a series of Christian states in the Levant. However, Muslim leaders like Saladin eventually recaptured the city, leading to ongoing conflicts until the final defeat of the Crusader states in the 13th century.

The Crusades were seen by many Christians as fulfilling the prophetic warnings of conflict and struggle that would precede the end times. Likewise, in the Islamic world, the Crusades were viewed as a defense against foreign invaders, with the battle for Jerusalem symbolizing a broader defense of the Islamic faith.

Apocalyptic Prophecies and Interpretations During This Period

As Islam rose to prominence and engaged in wars with Christian states, religious leaders and believers on both sides interpreted these events through apocalyptic lenses. Christian theologians like Joachim of Fiore, a medieval mystic, saw the spread of Islam and the conflict with Christians as part of the end-times struggle between good and evil, with Islam often depicted as an agent of divine punishment or as a prelude to the Antichrist's arrival. These interpretations were bolstered by the hardships of the period, as plagues, famine, and warfare were frequently interpreted as signs of the approaching apocalypse.

In Islamic eschatology, meanwhile, wars against the "Romans" (interpreted as Byzantines or Christians) were also seen as part of the events leading up to the end times. Hadiths spoke of battles between Muslim and Christian forces, with prophecies of a final confrontation in the Levant region. This conflict would lead to the emergence of the Mahdi, a messianic figure, and the return of Jesus, who would defeat the Antichrist figure known as *Dajjal*. These prophecies, like those in Christianity, fostered a sense of urgency and divine mission among Muslim warriors and rulers, who saw their efforts as part of a larger cosmic plan.

A Period of Religious Tension and Apocalyptic Expectation

The rise of Islam and the ensuing religious wars fundamentally shaped the medieval world, influencing politics, culture, and religious thought for centuries. Both Christianity and Islam carried a sense of divine mission, seeing their struggles as fulfilling sacred prophecies and as signs of the approaching end times. For Christians, the rise of Islam represented a test of faith and a challenge to the Christian world order, often interpreted as part of the apocalyptic struggle foretold in the Bible. For Muslims, their victories and the expansion of Islamic rule were seen as evidence of divine favor and as part of the preparation for the final judgment.

This period of intense religious rivalry set the stage for further conflicts, cultural exchanges, and theological developments in both faiths. The centuries that followed would witness continued wars, conversions, and coexistence between Muslims and Christians, all under the shadow of apocalyptic expectations and the hope for divine resolution. These dynamics not only shaped the course of history but also deepened the eschatological beliefs that continue to influence both religions to this day.

The Jewish Struggle for Identity Amid the Scattering of Their People: An Apocalyptic Dispersion

Historical Background: The Jewish Diaspora and Its Causes

The Jewish diaspora, or scattering of the Jewish people, began centuries before the birth of Christianity and the rise of Islam, marked by several key events. One of the earliest diasporas was triggered by the Babylonian Exile in the 6th century BCE when the Babylonian Empire under King Nebuchadnezzar conquered Jerusalem, destroyed the First Temple, and exiled a large portion of the Jewish population to Babylon. Although many Jews returned to Judea after the Persian Empire, under King Cyrus, allowed them to rebuild the Temple in Jerusalem, this period set a foundation for further dispersion and the development of a distinct Jewish identity shaped by hardship and survival.

Following the Roman occupation of Judea in the 1st century BCE, Jewish society faced ongoing challenges under Roman rule. Tensions boiled over in 66 CE, leading to the First Jewish-Roman War, also known as the Great Revolt. The Romans crushed the rebellion in 70 CE, destroying the Second Temple, which was the spiritual center of Jewish life and worship. This destruction deeply wounded the Jewish people and altered the course of Jewish history, as thousands were killed, enslaved, or dispersed. A second major uprising, known as the Bar Kokhba Revolt (132-136 CE), was also brutally suppressed by Rome. Following the failure of this revolt, Jews were systematically expelled from Jerusalem and faced prohibitions on worship within their own land. The Bar Kokhba Revolt solidified the dispersion, known as the "apocalyptic dispersion," in Jewish consciousness as an epoch of suffering and exile, prophesied by their ancestors.

These traumatic events led the Jewish people into a period of exile that would last for millennia. While some Jewish communities remained in the region, large numbers moved to various parts of the Roman Empire and beyond, spreading into North Africa, the Middle East, and Europe. This scattering became a defining feature of Jewish existence, as their identity became intrinsically tied to living as a people in exile, waiting for the restoration of Israel and the coming of the Messiah.

An Identity in Exile: The Spiritual and Cultural Challenges

The forced exile and dispersion raised complex questions for Jewish communities about maintaining their identity and faith in foreign lands. The Jewish experience of diaspora included adapting to various host cultures, languages, and political realities while staying true to the laws and teachings of the Torah. Jews faced pressure to assimilate but developed strategies to maintain their identity. Synagogues and local rabbis became central to their religious life, replacing the central authority of the Jerusalem Temple. The role of the rabbi and community leader gained importance, as each local synagogue served as a microcosm of the Jewish community.

Jewish scholars also adapted their religious practices and interpretations to their diaspora context. For example, the creation of the Talmud; comprising the Mishnah and the Gemara; codified Jewish oral traditions and teachings, enabling a more flexible practice of Judaism that could be followed regardless of location. The Talmud became a vital source of religious guidance and legal interpretation, helping Jews adapt and retain their religious identity under varied circumstances.

In addition to the struggle to maintain religious practices, the diaspora imposed constant political and economic pressures. Jews often lived as a marginalized minority, facing discrimination, restricted rights, and the threat of expulsion or violence. They also experienced periods of tolerance and prosperity, as in Moorish Spain, where Jewish communities flourished under Islamic rule, or later in Poland and the Ottoman Empire, where Jews were granted a degree of autonomy. Yet, despite periods of relative peace, the underlying feeling of displacement persisted, creating a shared identity based on survival and resilience in the face of adversity.

Apocalyptic Significance of the Dispersion

For many Jews, the dispersion carried profound theological and apocalyptic implications. Some viewed it as punishment for sins, aligning with the warnings of ancient prophets like Isaiah, Jeremiah, and Ezekiel, who had foretold suffering and exile if Israel strayed from God's laws. These prophets emphasized the idea of *Teshuvah* (repentance), urging the Jewish people to return to God's covenant to regain His favor. The dispersion and suffering were therefore seen not only as a political and social challenge but as part of a divine plan that demanded introspection, repentance, and faith.

The experience of exile also intensified the Jewish hope for the coming of the Messiah, a central theme in apocalyptic thought. The Messiah, in Jewish belief, was expected to restore Israel, rebuild the Temple, and establish an era of peace and justice. For many, the trials and suffering of the diaspora were a precursor to this messianic redemption, and each hardship, persecution, or moment of suffering was seen as bringing them closer to the eventual restoration of Israel. This belief provided resilience and unity across diverse Jewish communities, as the hope for the Messiah acted as a common thread connecting Jews scattered across the globe.

Jewish-Christian Tensions and Messianic Anticipation

During this period, Jewish communities also encountered rising tensions with the emerging Christian faith. Christians, who believed that Jesus of Nazareth was the promised Messiah, saw the Jewish rejection of Jesus as a failure to recognize God's fulfillment of His promises. This theological division led to misunderstandings and hostility between Jewish and Christian communities, with Christians sometimes viewing the Jewish diaspora as punishment for their rejection of Christ.

Jewish communities, meanwhile, maintained their distinct identity and continued to await their own Messiah. While some early Jewish sects interpreted apocalyptic writings like the Book of Daniel as foretelling events of the Roman destruction, mainstream Jewish thought held fast to the belief that the true Messiah had yet to come. This messianic hope distinguished Judaism from Christianity and reinforced the Jewish commitment to a future restoration that had not yet been realized.

Diaspora, Survival, and Apocalyptic Resilience

Jewish communities across the Roman Empire and beyond developed a unique resilience and survival strategy in response to the ongoing challenges of the diaspora. Laws and customs were passed down orally, and later written, to guide generations, emphasizing charity, community solidarity, and family as central pillars of Jewish life. This emphasis on community enabled Jewish people to preserve their culture and identity in the face of adversity. The daily rituals, Sabbath observance, dietary laws, and festivals served as markers of Jewish faith and identity, reminders of their covenant with God and the hope for redemption.

The Jewish diaspora became a "living prophecy," a people in waiting, anticipating an end to exile and a return to their homeland. This collective hope transcended generations, creating an apocalyptic expectation that unified Jews from different lands and languages. The scattered Jewish communities, while separated by geography, held onto a shared narrative of suffering, perseverance, and ultimate redemption. This anticipation remained central to Jewish identity, fueling the belief that their current struggles were part of a larger cosmic plan leading toward a divine resolution.

A People Defined by Hope and Resilience

The Jewish struggle for identity amid the scattering of their people became an enduring testament to resilience, cultural adaptation, and spiritual strength. The apocalyptic dimension of the Jewish diaspora colored the way Jews saw their displacement, transforming it into a divine test or preparation for the coming of the Messiah. Every hardship, every persecution, and every expulsion became a reminder of the covenant they had with God, as well as the promise of restoration and renewal.

Throughout the centuries, Jewish communities held fast to the idea that their suffering was part of a divine plan. Their continued existence in exile, combined with the hope for an eventual return to their homeland, gave rise to a uniquely apocalyptic identity: a people who, despite centuries of dispersion and hardship, saw themselves as playing an integral role in a divine story that would one day culminate in the fulfillment of God's promises.

Crusades, Plagues, and the Shape of Darkness

The Crusades and the Blood of Nations (1095-1291 AD)

The Call to Arms and the Crusading Spirit

The Crusades were a series of religious wars sanctioned by the Latin Church during the medieval period, primarily aimed at reclaiming Jerusalem and other sacred sites from Muslim control. The First Crusade was launched in 1095 after Pope Urban II delivered a passionate sermon at the Council of Clermont, calling upon Christians to take up arms and embark on a holy mission. This appeal to piety and religious zeal sparked a wave of fervour across Europe, leading to a mass mobilization of knights, peasants, and clergy.

The Crusades can be viewed as a significant intersection of faith, politics, and culture, as they were fuelled by a desire to secure access to holy places, foster Christian unity, and expand European influence. However, they also marked a dark chapter in history, characterized by violence, bloodshed, and the clash of civilizations. The conflict over Jerusalem; the Holy City for Jews, Christians, and Muslims; became the focal point of these wars, setting the stage for centuries of religious strife.

The First Crusade: An Outpouring of Faith and Violence (1096-1099)

The First Crusade began in 1096, driven by the belief that Christians had a divine mandate to liberate Jerusalem from Muslim rule. Thousands of people, including knights, peasants, and nobles, answered the call, embarking on a perilous journey that would lead them through unfamiliar territories and harsh conditions. Many were motivated by a mix of religious zeal, a desire for adventure, and the promise of spiritual rewards, including the forgiveness of sins and the prospect of eternal life.

As the Crusaders travelled through Europe, they encountered significant obstacles, including hostile territories and dwindling supplies. Despite these challenges, they persevered, forming various armies and engaging in battles along the way. In 1097, they captured Nicaea, a key city in Anatolia, and pushed further into the heart of the Muslim territories.

The siege of Jerusalem in 1099 marked a climactic moment in the First Crusade. After a gruelling and brutal siege lasting over a month, the Crusaders breached the city's defences. Upon entering Jerusalem, they engaged in widespread slaughter, killing many of the city's inhabitants, both Muslim and Jewish. The capture of Jerusalem was hailed as a monumental victory, and the Crusaders established the Kingdom of Jerusalem, marking the first significant Christian foothold in the Holy Land.

Religious Fervour and the Justification for Violence

The Crusaders viewed their actions as divinely sanctioned, interpreting their military campaigns as a form of holy warfare. This perception of religious duty permeated the ranks of the Crusaders, who believed they were fighting not just for territory but for the salvation of souls. The notion of *just war* gained traction, as leaders justified their violent conquests as necessary actions to reclaim land believed to belong to Christians.

This religious fervour fuelled a sense of righteousness among the Crusaders. It was not uncommon for warriors to display crosses on their armour, symbolizing their commitment to the Christian faith. The idea of martyrdom took root, as many believed that dying in battle against non-believers would guarantee them a place in heaven. This zealous mindset blinded many to the moral implications of their actions, as the brutality of warfare was framed as an expression of divine will.

The aftermath of the First Crusade saw the establishment of several Crusader states in the region, including the County of Edessa, the Principality of Antioch, and the Kingdom of Jerusalem. These new territories were marked by tension and conflict, as Crusaders struggled to maintain control over lands surrounded by Muslim populations.

Subsequent Crusades: The Expansion of Conflict

The initial success of the First Crusade sparked a series of subsequent Crusades, each characterized by varying degrees of military success and religious fervour. The Second Crusade (1147-1149) was launched in response to the fall of the County of Edessa to Muslim forces, but it ended in failure, demonstrating the challenges of sustaining momentum in such a distant and hostile environment.

The Third Crusade (1189-1192), led by prominent European monarchs such as Richard the Lionheart of England, Philip II of France, and Frederick Barbarossa of the Holy Roman Empire, aimed to reclaim Jerusalem after it fell to the Muslim general Saladin in 1187. This crusade was marked by famous battles, including the Siege of Acre and the Battle of Arsuf. Although Richard secured several victories and negotiated access for Christian pilgrims to Jerusalem, the ultimate goal of retaking the city remained unfulfilled.

The Fourth Crusade (1202-1204) took a dramatic turn when the Crusaders diverted their mission to Constantinople, leading to the sacking of the city in 1204. This deviation from the original purpose of reclaiming the Holy Land shocked many and contributed to a deepening rift between the Eastern Orthodox and Roman Catholic churches.

The Role of Religious Orders and the Concept of Chivalry

The Crusades also saw the rise of religious military orders, such as the Knights Templar and the Knights Hospitaller. These orders were formed to protect pilgrims and defend the Christian territories in the Holy Land. They blended the ideals of knighthood with religious devotion, establishing a culture of chivalry that emphasized bravery, loyalty, and honour.

Chivalry became an essential part of the Crusader identity, influencing the behaviours and attitudes of those who fought. Knights were expected to uphold virtues such as courage, generosity, and protection of the weak. However, this concept was often overshadowed by the violence of war, as the harsh realities of the Crusades led to brutal acts against both combatants and non-combatants alike.

Conflict Over Jerusalem: The Holy City at the Centre of Tension

Jerusalem's significance as a religious centre for Jews, Christians, and Muslims fuelled intense conflicts. For Christians, the city represented the site of Jesus' crucifixion and resurrection, while for Jews, it was the location of the First and Second Temples, central to their faith. Muslims revered Jerusalem as the site of the Al-Aqsa Mosque and the Dome of the Rock, believed to be where the Prophet Muhammad ascended to heaven.

Control over Jerusalem thus became emblematic of larger religious and political struggles. Each religious group saw its claim to the city as paramount, leading to escalating tensions and violence. The Crusades intensified these conflicts, as the desire to control the Holy City morphed into a broader struggle for dominance in the region.

Consequences of the Crusades: Cultural Exchange and Lasting Divisions

The Crusades had far-reaching consequences, including significant cultural exchanges between the East and West. Crusaders encountered new ideas, technologies, and goods from the Islamic world, which would eventually influence European society and contribute to the Renaissance. However, the Crusades also entrenched animosities between Christians and Muslims, leading to centuries of mistrust and conflict.

The fall of the Kingdom of Jerusalem in 1291 marked the end of the Crusading era in the Holy Land, but the legacy of the Crusades endured. The tensions and divisions created during this period would continue to resonate through history, shaping future interactions between different religious communities.

A Legacy of Faith and Conflict

The Crusades, marked by fervour and bloodshed, exemplified the complexities of faith, identity, and conflict. They reflected the profound desire to reclaim sacred spaces while simultaneously exposing the dark potential of religious zeal. As the blood of nations stained the landscape, the Crusades served as a reminder of the intricate relationship between faith and violence; a theme that would echo throughout history and into the modern age. The struggle for Jerusalem and the legacy of the Crusades laid the groundwork for ongoing tensions between Christians and Muslims, shaping a narrative of conflict that would endure for centuries to come.

Clashes Between Christians and Muslims: Crusaders' Apocalyptic Motivations

The Crusades were motivated by more than the desire to reclaim Jerusalem; for many Crusaders, they were part of a larger apocalyptic narrative. The belief that their battles were a prelude to the End Times infused the Crusades with a sense of cosmic purpose, positioning their struggle against Islam as a spiritual war of ultimate importance. This vision was shared by both sides, as Muslims saw the Crusaders as foreign invaders encroaching on sacred Islamic lands, igniting fierce and prolonged conflicts.

Apocalyptic Beliefs and Christian Motivations

In medieval Europe, Christianity carried a pervasive apocalyptic outlook. Biblical texts like the Book of Revelation and prophetic writings were studied widely, and religious leaders often interpreted current events as signs of an approaching apocalypse. This heightened sense of urgency contributed to the idea that the Crusades were not only wars for land or power but also a cosmic struggle between good and evil.

Pope Urban II's call to arms for the First Crusade in 1095 used language that resonated deeply with apocalyptic imagery. He described the mission as a holy war to save Christian lands from "infidels," painting Muslims as agents of darkness in contrast to the Crusaders, who saw themselves as champions of the Christian faith. Crusaders believed they were fulfilling a prophecy, one that would bring them spiritual reward and perhaps usher in the Kingdom of God on Earth. Fighting in this holy war was presented as a path to salvation, and those who died were often promised an eternal reward. This promise of absolution and the heavenly rewards for martyrdom spurred many Crusaders forward, convinced that their mission was part of a divine mandate.

Muslim Resistance and the Concept of Jihad

Muslim leaders viewed the Crusades not only as a territorial threat but also as a religious affront. While Crusaders invoked the apocalyptic narrative on their end, Muslims also perceived the conflict as a struggle of existential importance. This led to the rallying of forces under the concept of *jihad*, or "striving in the way of Allah." Muslim leaders encouraged fighters to defend their lands and their faith with the same spiritual and religious zeal that the Crusaders felt.

The term *jihad* in this context was often associated with a "just war," as Islamic leaders framed their resistance as a defense against Christian invaders. Saladin, the famous Muslim general and sultan, became a legendary figure for his role in uniting the Muslim world against the Crusaders. Under Saladin's leadership, Muslims rallied with the belief that they were resisting an existential threat to Islam, leading to a reassertion of Muslim control over the Holy Land. Saladin's victories, particularly his recapture of Jerusalem in 1187, were seen as divine vindications for the Muslim cause.

Cycles of Retribution: Apocalyptic Zeal on Both Sides

The intensity of apocalyptic beliefs on both sides fuelled a cycle of violence. As each side suffered defeats or losses, they interpreted these events as tests of faith or signals of divine will, often leading to intensified efforts to fight back. Crusaders who failed in their missions felt a renewed sense of urgency to purify themselves and attempt again, while Muslims saw each successful repulsion as a sign of God's favor, fueling their commitment to resist further invasions.

The Second and Third Crusades were direct responses to perceived apocalyptic defeats suffered by the Crusaders. After the fall of Edessa in 1144 and Jerusalem's recapture by Saladin in 1187,

European Christians were stirred into action by religious leaders who interpreted these losses as signs of divine displeasure. Pope Eugenius III's call for the Second Crusade and the charismatic preaching of figures like Bernard of Clairvaux painted these setbacks as moments requiring renewed faith and commitment. With each failure or victory, apocalyptic motivations were reinforced, adding a sense of prophecy-driven purpose to the bloodshed.

Religious Rivalries and the Quest for Jerusalem

Jerusalem was the focal point of the apocalyptic narratives driving the Crusades. Both Christians and Muslims regarded it as a holy city, integral to their respective religious identities. For Christians, it was the place of Christ's crucifixion and resurrection, while for Muslims, it held significance as the site of the Al-Aqsa Mosque and the Dome of the Rock. Both sides saw their control over Jerusalem as a symbol of divine favor.

For Crusaders, the city's symbolic weight added an urgency to their mission, and they often imagined themselves as participants in a cosmic drama with apocalyptic stakes. Many believed that by capturing Jerusalem, they could hasten the return of Christ, fulfilling biblical prophecies. Muslims, on the other hand, believed that defending the city was a matter of honor and faith, as well as an obligation to protect a key symbol of Islamic heritage.

The Enduring Legacy of Apocalyptic Crusading

The religious conflicts of the Crusades left a lasting impact on Christian-Muslim relations and contributed to centuries of mistrust and hostility. Each side saw the other as the embodiment of existential threat, which added fuel to apocalyptic narratives. The Crusades embedded these apocalyptic motivations deep into the collective memories of both Christian and Muslim communities, leading to a legacy of mutual suspicion that resonated through the medieval period and into modern history.

Ultimately, the apocalyptic zeal of the Crusaders and the fervent defense by Muslim forces turned the Holy Land into a battleground of ideologies, cementing an image of the Crusades as both a holy mission and a catastrophic clash of cultures. The passion with which these wars were fought remains emblematic of humanity's drive to see ultimate meaning in conflict; a theme that would echo in future religious and apocalyptic movements.

Rise of Prophecy-Laden Sects and Visions Among Christian and Islamic Believers

As the Crusades intensified, so did the religious fervour that fuelled them. Both Christian and Islamic communities began experiencing an upsurge in prophetic visions, end-time predictions, and the formation of sects focused on the approaching apocalypse. In these tumultuous centuries, believers on both sides of the conflict interpreted the events around them; wars, plagues, and natural disasters; as signs of the imminent end of days. This apocalyptic intensity created new religious movements and sects centered around visions and prophecies, reshaping the religious landscape of both Christianity and Islam.

44

Apocalyptic Sects and Prophetic Visions in Christianity

During the Crusades, many Christians, especially those who participated in the brutal battles or witnessed the carnage, began experiencing vivid visions of apocalyptic scenarios. The Book of Revelation became increasingly significant as it offered a blueprint for interpreting the signs of the times. Christian mystics, monks, and lay believers reported dreams and visions of the Second Coming, the Antichrist, and the Kingdom of God. These apocalyptic interpretations often coincided with the militaristic spirit of the Crusades, adding religious intensity to the fighting spirit.

Certain monastic orders, such as the Knights Templar and the Knights Hospitaller, were not only military orders but also deeply influenced by religious zeal and apocalyptic undertones. The Knights Templar, for example, saw themselves as warriors of God, tasked with reclaiming the Holy Land for the arrival of the Kingdom of Heaven on Earth. The Templars and other groups fostered a climate where apocalyptic teachings and eschatological themes became interwoven with military objectives.

Many preachers and leaders who inspired these apocalyptic sects focused heavily on themes of purification, urging believers to reject the world's sins and prepare for judgment. Peter the Hermit, for instance, became well-known for his charismatic sermons that painted the Crusades as a God-ordained mission to reclaim the Holy Land and prepare for Christ's return. Such leaders used apocalyptic rhetoric to motivate armies and masses alike, emphasizing themes of penance, martyrdom, and divine judgment.

Rise of Prophecy and Mysticism in Islam

In the Islamic world, the Crusades were also seen as a cosmic struggle, and apocalyptic beliefs began to flourish in response. The Qur'an and the Hadith (traditions of the Prophet Muhammad) contain several passages and sayings about the end times, and during this period, these teachings became a source of comfort, guidance, and mobilization for many Muslims. Islamic prophecy foretells the emergence of figures like the Mahdi (a messianic figure) and Isa (Jesus), who would defeat the forces of evil and establish justice before the Day of Judgment. These teachings led to widespread anticipation and, in many cases, a sense of duty among Muslims to fight against the perceived forces of darkness.

Muslim mystics and scholars, such as those influenced by Sufi traditions, often experienced visions and dreams concerning the end of days. Sufism, with its focus on spiritual introspection and closeness to God, became a channel for prophetic experiences and a source of eschatological insights. This period also saw the growth of Sufi orders, which encouraged believers to pursue an inner spiritual journey while remaining vigilant against external threats. Many Sufi leaders saw the Crusades as a signal of the nearing end times and used the struggle as a teaching tool to help followers prepare spiritually for the Last Day.

Several Muslim leaders, such as the famous Saladin, were seen as figures potentially fulfilling apocalyptic prophecies. Saladin's unification of the Muslim world against the Crusaders and his victory in Jerusalem in 1187 were interpreted by many as divine signs, marking him as a hero of Islam in the cosmic battle between good and evil. His successes were widely regarded as partial fulfilments of prophecy, reinforcing Muslim resilience and inspiring future generations to uphold the faith in the face of adversity.

The Impact of Prophetic Sectarian Movements

Both Christian and Islamic prophetic sects had lasting impacts on the broader religious and social landscape. For Christianity, the emergence of sects and movements with prophetic visions set a precedent for future apocalyptic movements that would flourish in Europe. It contributed to the idea that wars and crises were part of a divine plan, reinforcing the belief that earthly conflicts had heavenly significance. These beliefs continued into the late medieval period, influencing later conflicts, particularly as new prophetic movements emerged, often tied to political or social unrest.

In Islam, the apocalyptic fervour fostered a strong sense of unity and resilience. The concept of *jihad* as a spiritual struggle became deeply rooted, with many Muslim believers viewing their actions as part of a larger cosmic struggle. This outlook continued to play a role in future centuries, especially during times of conflict. Apocalyptic expectations fostered unity and a sense of purpose among Muslim populations, contributing to the resilience of Islamic civilization amid external pressures.

Shared Apocalyptic Expectations and Their Cultural Legacy

Despite their differences, both Christian and Muslim apocalyptic visions shared common themes: a battle between forces of light and darkness, the coming of a messianic or prophetic figure, and the final judgment. This period of intense conflict and religious fervour fostered an atmosphere where people expected that the world was moving toward a decisive, divine climax. These shared expectations left a lasting cultural legacy, embedding apocalyptic themes into literature, art, and folklore in both Christian and Muslim societies.

The Crusades were a catalyst for the rise of apocalyptic sects and prophetic visions in both the Christian and Islamic worlds. These movements emphasized the cosmic struggle of good versus evil and anticipated an approaching end of days. The resulting legacy not only impacted the religious beliefs of the time but also laid the groundwork for future apocalyptic movements in both traditions, forever linking the Crusades with visions of prophecy and the apocalypse.

The Black Death and European Collapse (1346-1353 AD)

The Apocalyptic Scale of the Bubonic Plague, Millions of Dead, Societal Collapse

In 1346, Europe was struck by a catastrophe that would reshape its social, economic, and spiritual fabric: the arrival of the bubonic plague, later known as the Black Death. This disease, one of the deadliest pandemics in human history, swept through Europe, Asia, and North Africa, leaving an indelible mark on the world. By the time it subsided around 1353, the Black Death had killed an estimated 75 to 200 million people, wiping out as much as 60% of Europe's population. To people living at the time, the sheer scale of the devastation felt nothing short of apocalyptic.

Origins and Spread of the Black Death

The bubonic plague originated in Central Asia and made its way westward via trade routes like the Silk Road. In 1346, it reached the Crimean Peninsula, where it was spread by fleas carried on black rats, which were common aboard merchant ships. When a Genoese ship returned to Sicily in 1347, it unknowingly carried the plague to Europe. From there, the disease spread rapidly, carried by both land and sea as infected rats and fleas moved along established trade and military routes.

The spread of the Black Death was swift and unrelenting. From Sicily, it travelled to mainland Italy, then northward into France, Spain, England, and beyond. Within a few years, the entire European continent was under siege. Cities that were once vibrant centres of trade and culture became epicentres of death and despair. The disease's rapid progression gave people little time to react, and as it spread from one city to another, it left death, fear, and chaos in its wake.

Symptoms and the Horror of the Plague

The bubonic plague had horrifying symptoms, unlike any disease people of the time had seen. It began with a sudden onset of fever and chills, followed by excruciating pain and swelling of the lymph nodes, commonly in the armpits, groin, and neck. These swollen lymph nodes, called "buboes," turned black and often burst, leaking pus and blood. Other symptoms included severe headaches, muscle aches, and vomiting. As the infection worsened, victims would sometimes develop a secondary form known as pneumonic plague, which attacked the lungs, making it even more contagious through airborne transmission.

People infected with the plague faced almost certain death, with mortality rates ranging from 60% to 100% depending on the form of the disease. Most victims died within a week of the first symptoms, and the pace of the disease overwhelmed families, communities, and entire regions. Mass graves and "plague pits" were dug to bury the countless dead, with bodies often piled one on top of another. In cities, the smell of death and decay filled the air, heightening the terror.

Societal Collapse: The Breakdown of Order

The scale of death led to widespread societal collapse. Cities, towns, and villages lost entire generations within months, and the absence of a significant portion of the population disrupted every aspect of society. Skilled laborers, farmers, and craftsmen died in large numbers, leading to a breakdown in the workforce. Fields went unplowed, crops rotted, and livestock wandered unchecked as there was simply no one left to tend to them. The resulting food shortages compounded the crisis, leading to famine in many regions.

Religious and civic institutions, overwhelmed by the need for last rites, burials, and care for the sick, were also brought to the brink. Many clergy, who were expected to minister to the dying, succumbed to the plague themselves, leading to a loss of spiritual leadership and leaving communities adrift. In some cases, priests refused to perform last rites out of fear for their own lives, shaking people's faith in the Church and leading to resentment and disillusionment. The resulting spiritual crisis would have long-lasting effects on the religious and social landscape of Europe.

A Widespread Apocalyptic Panic

The Black Death seemed to fulfill apocalyptic prophecies described in biblical texts, especially the Book of Revelation, which speaks of death, pestilence, and widespread suffering. Many Europeans believed they were witnessing the end times, as described in scripture. There was a belief that the plague was divine punishment for the sins of humanity, a view reinforced by religious authorities who preached repentance and penance. Processions, prayers, and religious rituals increased, as people sought to appease an apparently wrathful God. Yet, despite fervent pleas, the plague continued, leading some to question their faith or view the plague as a harbinger of the final judgment.

In response to the overwhelming death and suffering, certain groups adopted extreme religious practices. One notable example was the Flagellants, a group of wandering bands of penitents who roamed from town to town, publicly whipping themselves to atone for humanity's sins. They believed that only through such suffering could they hope to avoid divine retribution. The Flagellant movement gained popularity quickly, attracting followers who saw their acts as a path to salvation. However, their presence often disrupted public order, and the Catholic Church eventually condemned their practices as heretical.

The Impact on Art, Culture, and Worldview

The Black Death left a deep imprint on art, culture, and society. Artists began depicting scenes of death, decay, and the macabre, giving rise to themes like *memento mori* ("remember you will die") and the "Dance of Death" motif. These images reflected the overwhelming presence of mortality in everyday life and served as reminders of life's fragility. Literature, too, captured the despair and devastation, with works like Boccaccio's *The Decameron* exploring how individuals from different backgrounds sought to escape the horrors of the plague.

The Black Death also led to shifts in Europe's worldview. The catastrophic loss of life created a shift in social and economic power dynamics. With labour scarce, surviving workers demanded higher wages, and peasants found new leverage in a society where their labour was in high demand. This shift weakened the feudal system and set the stage for future social changes, including the rise of a middle class and increased social mobility.

Religious Impact and Seeds of Reform

Spiritually, the plague's devastation led to a crisis of faith. People questioned the Church's ability to intercede with God on their behalf, as prayers and rituals failed to stop the death toll. Corruption within the Church, combined with its inability to provide comfort or explanations, fostered resentment and disillusionment. This discontent would later play a crucial role in setting the stage for the Reformation, as people began seeking alternative spiritual paths and questioning traditional religious authority.

The Black Death's traumatic impact on the medieval psyche cannot be overstated. It shattered existing structures, reshaped social order, and created an atmosphere of profound fear and uncertainty. For those who survived, life after the plague was forever changed. The belief that the world was nearing its end permeated society, as people wrestled with questions of sin, divine judgment, and survival. Europe would never be the same, as the plague left a scar that reverberated through generations, shaping not only society but also the apocalyptic expectations that would colour European thought for centuries to come.

The devastation of the Black Death, seen as an apocalyptic event in its own right, is one of history's most powerful examples of how disease can alter the course of humanity, leaving a legacy of death, fear, and transformation.

Impact on Faith and Questioning of Divine Will: Apocalyptic Sermons and Fear of Judgment

The Black Death's arrival sent shockwaves through medieval Europe's faith and social structure, challenging deeply held beliefs and provoking widespread fear of divine retribution. As the plague ravaged communities, claiming lives without regard to age, class, or devotion, people increasingly questioned why God would allow such suffering. The Catholic Church, which had been the primary spiritual and moral authority, was faced with a massive crisis as individuals struggled to understand how an all-powerful, just God could bring or allow such devastation.

The Church's Role and Strain on Clergy

The initial response of the Catholic Church to the plague was to emphasize penance, prayer, and ritual. Priests, monks, and nuns devoted themselves to providing spiritual comfort to the sick and dying, administering last rites and funerals at an unprecedented pace. However, as the plague spread and clergy members succumbed to the disease alongside their parishioners, the Church was soon overwhelmed, unable to keep up with the sheer volume of suffering and death. Clerics often abandoned their posts to escape infection, leaving many communities spiritually and emotionally isolated.

The Church's apparent helplessness began to shake people's faith in its authority. Witnessing priests, monks, and nuns fall to the disease at the same rate as ordinary people was deeply unsettling for believers who saw them as closer to God and thus more protected. Many interpreted the loss of clergy as evidence that divine protection had been withdrawn or that God's judgment was so final that even holy servants were not exempt.

Questioning Divine Will and Theological Shifts

The seemingly indiscriminate nature of the plague's destruction led many to question the purpose and nature of divine will. Some began to believe that the plague was a direct punishment from God, sent to punish humanity for its sins. This belief gained traction as priests and laypeople alike sought to explain why so many lives were being taken in such a violent manner. Commonly cited sins included greed, pride, lust, and a general turning away from spiritual devotion, often targeting behaviours seen as morally or socially corrupt, such as the rise in materialism or moral laxity.

Some saw the plague as a reminder of the sinful nature of humanity, a punishment that could only be mitigated through repentance. Yet, as prayers, fasts, and penance failed to stop the spread of the disease, others grew frustrated and disillusioned. A sense of hopelessness set in, leading some to doubt God's goodness or even His existence altogether, an early seed of skepticism that would influence later generations.

Apocalyptic Sermons: Fear of Judgment and Visions of the End Times

As the death toll climbed, apocalyptic sermons became increasingly common across Europe. Priests and preachers, seeking to make sense of the tragedy, turned to the Bible's apocalyptic passages, particularly those found in the Book of Revelation, which spoke of death, pestilence, and punishment. These sermons painted vivid pictures of God's impending judgment, drawing from imagery that depicted the Four Horsemen of the Apocalypse: conquest, war, famine, and death.

Many preachers framed the Black Death as a precursor to the final judgment, and towns and cities echoed with fearful warnings that the world was on the verge of its end. Apocalyptic sermons urged people to repent while there was still time, as salvation might soon become inaccessible. This focus on impending doom resonated with those who saw the plague as a punishment but also served to deepen a sense of despair among those who felt powerless to avoid God's wrath.

The Flagellant Movement: A Radical Attempt to Appease Divine Wrath

One of the more dramatic responses to the Black Death was the rise of the Flagellant movement, a radical sect that emerged in 1348. Flagellants believed that the only way to avert God's wrath was through public acts of penance. They travelled from town to town, marching in processions where they would whip themselves bloody, chanting prayers and songs as they went. Their displays were often accompanied by apocalyptic messages, reinforcing the belief that the end of days was near unless humanity repented.

The Flagellants attracted large crowds and followers, who saw them as holy penitents attempting to save everyone from destruction. However, the movement quickly spiralled out of control, with some Flagellants adopting extreme beliefs that included rejecting Church authority, condemning clergy, and proclaiming themselves to be closer to God. In 1349, Pope Clement VI condemned the Flagellant movement as heretical, fearing that their actions would disrupt society and further weaken the Church's control. However, by then, they had already left a deep impact on public perception, reinforcing apocalyptic fears and underscoring the sense of divine punishment.

The Rise of Alternative Beliefs and Apocalyptic Visions

The Church's inability to halt the plague and the disillusionment it created led some people to explore alternative beliefs and practices. Folk religion, superstitions, and heretical sects gained popularity as people sought answers outside the traditional framework. Prophets, mystics, and visionaries emerged, claiming to receive divine revelations about the nature of the plague and what people could do to survive. Many of these figures warned of an impending apocalypse and called on followers to change their ways in preparation.

Apocalyptic visions became more common, with some claiming to see the Virgin Mary, angels, or even Jesus, all foretelling greater destruction to come if humanity did not repent. These visions spread among communities desperate for hope and guidance, and they often included detailed descriptions of fire, judgment, and the collapse of earthly kingdoms. People found both terror and comfort in these visions, believing them to be signs from God or the saints, affirming that they were living in the last days.

Impact on Belief in Judgment and the Afterlife

The plague's catastrophic impact led many to question what happened after death. As entire families and communities were wiped out, the idea of an afterlife became a more immediate concern, and people worried about whether their souls would find rest or face eternal punishment. Fear of purgatory and hell grew, with many seeking to secure their places in heaven through donations to the Church, acts of penance, and other pious acts. These efforts reinforced the apocalyptic mood, as people increasingly saw life on earth as brief and uncertain, with eternal consequences waiting on the other side.

Some of the more cynical saw the Church's emphasis on judgment and penance as a means of profiteering off people's fear. Certain members of the clergy encouraged donations or indulgences, promising that financial offerings could help secure salvation for deceased loved ones. This practice would fuel a deeper resentment toward the Church, which ultimately contributed to the desire for reform that erupted a century later with the Protestant Reformation.

Lasting Effects on Faith and Apocalyptic Belief

The Black Death created a lasting shift in Europe's spiritual landscape, reinforcing the idea that divine punishment could come at any time and without warning. This widespread exposure to death and suffering left a generation acutely aware of life's fragility and the unpredictability of fate, fostering a collective expectation that the apocalypse was near.

Jewish Persecution During the Plague and the Scapegoating of Minorities

The Black Death not only brought unimaginable death and suffering to Europe but also led to a wave of fear, distrust, and anger that found a tragic outlet in the scapegoating of Jewish communities and other minorities. As the plague spread rapidly and killed millions without any apparent cause, people became desperate to identify an explanation for the suffering. This search for a scapegoat led to widespread, violent persecution of Jewish communities, who were often blamed for "causing" the plague.

Misguided Beliefs and Accusations Against Jewish Communities

Many believed that the plague was a punishment from God, but as the devastation continued, rumours arose that the disease was actually the result of human malice. Anti-Semitic ideas were already deeply rooted in medieval Europe, and longstanding prejudices painted Jewish people as outsiders with practices and beliefs different from the Christian majority. The mysterious nature of the plague heightened these existing fears, and Jews were accused of poisoning wells and food supplies to spread the disease intentionally.

The rumour that Jews had conspired to cause the plague spread quickly. In 1348, local authorities in Switzerland claimed that Jews had poisoned wells, and this accusation soon spread to France, Spain, and beyond. Even though the Pope, Clement VI, issued papal bulls in 1348 and 1349 condemning these accusations and protecting the Jewish community, his statements had little impact on the deeply ingrained prejudices and rising hysteria across Europe.

Violent Persecutions and Massacres

In response to these baseless accusations, mobs across Europe attacked Jewish communities. Pogroms, or violent massacres, occurred in many cities, with people driven by the belief that purging their communities of Jews would end the plague. In some regions, local authorities sanctioned these attacks, while in others, mobs took matters into their own hands.

One of the worst episodes occurred in Strasbourg on February 14, 1349. Despite an initial attempt by city authorities to protect the Jewish community, the local council eventually allowed an enraged mob to carry out a massacre. Around 2,000 Jewish people were burned alive, while those who managed to escape were forced into exile, leaving behind their homes and possessions. Similar atrocities took place in Basel, Cologne, and other cities, with entire Jewish communities slaughtered or forcibly expelled.

In Germany, anti-Semitic violence became widespread as Jews were blamed for the Black Death. The belief that Jews were behind the pandemic also led to the confiscation of their wealth and properties. In some cases, local leaders used the situation as an opportunity to seize Jewish assets, benefiting financially from the forced expulsions and executions. The fear and anger caused by the plague were thus exploited to justify widespread looting and violence.

Expulsions and Forced Conversions

In addition to physical violence, Jewish communities across Europe faced expulsions and forced conversions. In some cases, Jewish people were given the choice of converting to Christianity or facing death. Many Jewish families chose exile, fleeing to regions where they might find more tolerance and safety, though they often faced harsh conditions and extreme poverty in their new homes.

For example, in France, Jewish communities that had once lived in relative peace were expelled from towns and villages. The Kingdom of Spain, which had a significant Jewish population, also saw a wave of expulsions. Many of these refugees sought asylum in Poland and other parts of Eastern Europe, where Jewish communities were given relative freedom and protection for a time.

Wider Implications and Legacy

The persecution of Jewish communities during the Black Death had lasting effects on European society. The violent actions taken against Jews deepened the cycle of fear and prejudice, reinforcing an environment of mistrust and xenophobia that would endure for centuries. The Black Death served as a powerful, tragic reminder of how fear could easily be twisted into hatred, leading to the scapegoating of innocent people. This scapegoating was fuelled not only by ignorance and superstition but also by existing anti-Semitic sentiments and economic motives, as the possessions of Jewish families were often seized and redistributed among local populations and authorities.

The trauma and displacement from these persecutions would echo across generations. Jewish families who fled to other parts of Europe faced the challenge of rebuilding lives in unfamiliar and often hostile territories. The Jewish communities of Western Europe, especially those in Germany and France, were significantly weakened, leaving a legacy of pain and memory that would resonate through the centuries.

The Papal Effort and Limited Support

Pope Clement VI was one of the few leaders to publicly speak against the persecution, stating that the Jewish people were not responsible for the plague and that the disease was a result of God's will, beyond human control. In his papal bulls, he condemned the violent attacks against Jewish communities and attempted to protect them from mob violence. However, his voice carried little weight with local leaders and the general populace, who were overcome with panic and prejudice. In many regions, his efforts were ignored or directly contradicted by secular and religious authorities who chose to scapegoat the Jewish people as a way of channelling public fear and frustration.

The Rise of Mystical and Apocalyptic Beliefs

The widespread violence and persecution of Jewish communities during the Black Death era also fuelled mystical and apocalyptic beliefs. Christian and Jewish communities alike were immersed in narratives about divine punishment, signs of the end times, and mystical interpretations of suffering. Many Jewish communities began to see their suffering as a test of faith, a trial that had been foretold in apocalyptic texts and prophecies from the Old Testament. These events deepened the Jewish people's anticipation of a messianic deliverance, a belief that God would one day rescue them from persecution and restore their dignity and land.

Similarly, in Christian communities, preachers framed the persecution of Jews as part of the broader apocalyptic signs of the time. Some believers viewed the violence as a necessary purging of "evil," while others saw the acts of mob violence as a fulfillment of biblical prophecies that anticipated the end of days. This intense period of persecution marked a painful chapter in the history of European Jews and added a sense of urgency and darkness to the apocalyptic worldview that was emerging in Europe.

The Jewish persecution during the Black Death set a tragic precedent that would echo into the future. By using Jewish communities as scapegoats, European society entrenched a pattern of blaming minorities during times of crisis. The hatred, fear, and violence that Jewish communities endured during the Black Death would resurface in subsequent centuries, during both religious conflicts and other pandemics.

Ultimately, the persecution of Jewish communities during the Black Death reinforced Europe's longstanding patterns of anti-Semitism, fear, and distrust of minorities. This devastating time period left a legacy of grief, displacement, and a painful memory for Jewish communities, embedding their experience of persecution deeply into the history of both Judaism and European society.

Renaissance and the Warning Signs of Change (14th-17th Centuries)

Revival of Ancient Knowledge and Philosophical Exploration in Europe

The Renaissance, spanning from the 14th to the 17th centuries, was a transformative period in European history, characterized by a rediscovery and revival of classical knowledge, art, and philosophy. This era, whose name literally means "rebirth," marked a transition from the medieval worldview, dominated by religious dogma and superstition, to a renewed interest in the achievements of ancient Greek and Roman civilizations. The Renaissance not only reshaped art and science but also laid the groundwork for modern Western philosophy, religious reform, and the emergence of individualism.

Rediscovery of Classical Texts and Knowledge

The Renaissance began in the city-states of Italy, particularly Florence, Venice, and Rome, where a prosperous merchant class and ruling elites invested in art and intellectual pursuits. One of the pivotal events that triggered the Renaissance was the rediscovery of classical texts that had been preserved by Islamic scholars during the European Dark Ages. Manuscripts by ancient philosophers like Aristotle, Plato, and Hippocrates had been maintained in the libraries of the Islamic world, especially in places like Baghdad, Cordoba, and Alexandria, where scholars studied and translated Greek and Roman works into Arabic.

The Crusades and increased trade between East and West brought many of these texts back into European hands, where they were translated into Latin and widely distributed. As scholars studied these works, they were struck by the sophisticated approaches to science, philosophy, and art found in the classical writings. The reintroduction of Aristotle's writings on logic and ethics, for example, sparked renewed interest in empirical observation and human reasoning. Plato's philosophy, with its emphasis on abstract ideas and spiritual exploration, inspired Renaissance thinkers to delve into questions of existence, reality, and the divine.

Humanism and the Rise of Secular Philosophy

Out of this rediscovery of ancient knowledge emerged a philosophical movement known as Humanism, which centered on the study of human nature, experience, and potential. Humanists were inspired by the classical ideal of the well-rounded individual who could excel in multiple areas of knowledge and skill, embodying the "Renaissance Man" archetype. They believed that human beings possessed the ability to understand the world around them, to shape their own destinies, and to seek knowledge beyond religious doctrine.

The Italian poet and scholar Francesco Petrarch is often credited as one of the fathers of Humanism. Petrarch believed that studying ancient literature and philosophy would cultivate virtues such as wisdom, courage, and civic responsibility, which could help individuals lead meaningful lives. This focus on human potential and secular achievements was a radical shift from the medieval view of humanity as inherently sinful and wholly dependent on divine grace.

Humanist scholars sought to reconcile ancient philosophy with Christian beliefs, but they also emphasized rationality and moral autonomy. Figures such as Erasmus of Rotterdam and Thomas More became proponents of a blend of Christian and classical ideals, stressing the importance of critical thinking, moral integrity, and a balanced life. The Humanist emphasis on the individual's ability to seek truth through reason and observation gradually shifted intellectual authority from religious institutions to individuals, marking a step toward the modern secular worldview.

Advances in Science, Medicine, and Exploration

The Renaissance was also a period of unprecedented scientific exploration and medical advancements, as scholars applied Humanist principles to understand the natural world. Scientists such as Nicolaus Copernicus, Galileo Galilei, and Johannes Kepler challenged the geocentric view that placed Earth at the centre of the universe, proposing instead a heliocentric model where the Earth revolved around the sun. These ideas were revolutionary, as they directly contradicted the teachings of the Catholic Church and traditional interpretations of the Bible.

In medicine, figures like Andreas Vesalius conducted detailed dissections of the human body, creating more accurate anatomical diagrams and challenging the medical theories of Galen, a Greek physician whose ideas had dominated for centuries. Vesalius's work laid the foundations for modern anatomy and surgery. Another significant figure, Paracelsus, introduced the use of chemicals in medicine, moving away from medieval herbal treatments and emphasizing the idea of curing diseases based on empirical knowledge rather than superstition.

Invention of the Printing Press and Dissemination of Knowledge

A key invention of the Renaissance that accelerated the spread of ideas was Johannes Gutenberg's printing press, developed around 1440. Before its invention, books were copied by hand, making them rare and expensive. The printing press allowed for the mass production of books, making literature, scientific texts, and philosophical works more accessible to a wider audience.

The Bible was one of the first major books printed, which helped disseminate Christian teachings and allowed people to interpret the scriptures independently of the Church's authority. This accessibility also facilitated the spread of Humanist literature, scientific research, and classical philosophy. People across Europe gained access to knowledge, and intellectual networks began to form as ideas could now circulate rapidly, leading to lively debates, challenges to existing beliefs, and the formation of a more educated public.

Art as a Reflection of Renaissance Thought

Renaissance art is one of the most visible and celebrated aspects of this era. Artists such as Leonardo da Vinci, Michelangelo, and Raphael sought to reflect human beauty, emotion, and divine harmony in their work. They pioneered techniques like linear perspective, which created depth and realism in painting, and chiaroscuro, which used light and shadow to give figures a lifelike quality. Art moved away from purely religious subjects to also embrace classical mythology, human anatomy, and secular themes, reflecting the Humanist focus on the human experience.

Leonardo da Vinci, with his scientific sketches of anatomy and mechanical inventions, embodied the Renaissance ideal of the "universal man." Michelangelo's depiction of the human form in his sculptures and paintings, such as the Sistine Chapel ceiling, celebrated the beauty and strength of humanity, resonating with the Humanist belief in human dignity and potential.

Impact on Religion and the Church's Influence

While the Renaissance encouraged exploration of secular themes and individual potential, it also raised questions about the role of the Church in society. The rediscovery of classical philosophy, which often contradicted religious dogma, created intellectual tension between scholars and religious authorities. Humanism encouraged people to question the Church's authority and seek personal understanding of the divine, laying the groundwork for the Protestant Reformation, which would challenge the Church's teachings, practices, and power.

This questioning attitude did not go unnoticed by the Church, and religious authorities viewed certain Renaissance ideas as a threat. The Church sometimes responded by sponsoring Renaissance art and scholarship, hoping to channel these achievements to reinforce its influence. The Vatican commissioned works by Michelangelo, Raphael, and other renowned artists, seeking to align the artistic achievements of the Renaissance with religious devotion. However, the seeds of independent thinking planted during this period would eventually contribute to the Reformation and significant shifts in the religious landscape of Europe.

The Renaissance and Apocalyptic Thought

Amidst this intellectual revival, there was also a sense of impending change, with some seeing the Renaissance as a sign of the approaching apocalypse. Renaissance thinkers and artists often interpreted their achievements as part of a divine mission to understand God's creation more fully, but some viewed the era's social upheavals, plagues, and political conflicts as indications of coming judgment. In religious and philosophical circles, the revival of ancient knowledge was sometimes seen as the last flowering of human achievement before an anticipated end of days. Apocalyptic preachers emerged, warning that the prosperity and knowledge of the Renaissance would give way to God's final judgment.

Legacy of the Renaissance in Shaping Modern Thought

The Renaissance set the stage for the scientific, philosophical, and religious transformations that would define the modern world. By promoting a return to classical learning, encouraging individual exploration, and questioning established beliefs, the Renaissance fundamentally reshaped European society. The values of reason, exploration, and artistic expression would inspire future generations, while the tensions it stirred with the Church set the stage for centuries of religious, scientific, and philosophical conflict.

The Renaissance was thus not only a period of artistic and intellectual rebirth but also a pivotal moment in humanity's moral and spiritual journey. It introduced ideas that would challenge traditional views of God, authority, and the cosmos, paving the way for an era of questioning, discovery, and profound change that would echo across history.

Decline of Strict Church Control: Enlightenment and Spiritual Decay

As the Renaissance unfolded, the Church's hold on society began to loosen, ushering in a complex era marked by both intellectual enlightenment and moral ambiguity. This period witnessed an emerging duality; while intellectual freedom and new philosophies blossomed, the weakening grip of religious structures also gave way to social, spiritual, and ethical instability.

Erosion of the Church's Authority

The authority of the Catholic Church, once the bedrock of European social and moral life, began to wane as a result of several intersecting factors. The humanistic ideals of the Renaissance encouraged individuals to look beyond religious doctrine and question the Church's control over knowledge and truth. This growing emphasis on critical thinking and the study of secular subjects led many to challenge the Church's teachings, as well as its role as the sole guardian of moral and intellectual authority. With the invention of the printing press in the mid-15th century, knowledge became more widely available, weakening the Church's long-standing monopoly on education and scripture interpretation.

The political landscape also contributed to this shift. As nations and empires became more consolidated, secular rulers grew more assertive and independent from the Church. Monarchs and political leaders began to see the Church not only as a spiritual authority but as a rival for power and resources. This new tension between Church and state diminished the Church's influence and paved the way for the rise of nation-states with their own secular identities.

Corruption within the Church and Public Disillusionment

Internal corruption further eroded the Church's image and influence. Clerical abuses, such as the sale of indulgences (payments made to the Church in exchange for forgiveness of sins) and the accumulation of wealth among the clergy, became widely known and were met with public resentment. The lavish lifestyles of some high-ranking clergy were seen as contradictory to the values of humility and piety they preached. As these abuses came to light, common people began to view the Church with skepticism, perceiving it as morally compromised and, in some cases, hypocritical.

This perception of corruption led to growing calls for reform, especially from figures within the Church who were disillusioned by its practices. These reformers questioned not only the Church's moral authority but also its theological foundations. Among these reformers was Martin Luther, whose 95 Theses in 1517 publicly denounced the Church's abuses and sparked the Protestant

Reformation. Luther's challenges to Church doctrine further weakened the institution's hold on the public, as he encouraged people to read and interpret the Bible for themselves, without reliance on clergy.

The Protestant Reformation and Diversification of Christianity

The Protestant Reformation, which began with Luther's criticisms, became a seismic religious movement across Europe, fracturing the unity of Christendom. New Christian denominations emerged, each interpreting the Bible in unique ways and developing distinct practices and doctrines. Protestant leaders, such as John Calvin and Ulrich Zwingli, promoted individual faith, simplicity, and a return to scriptural authority over traditional Church teachings.

As Protestantism spread, Catholicism faced competition for influence in communities where it had once been uncontested. In response, the Catholic Church launched its own internal reforms through the Counter-Reformation, an effort to address corruption and reaffirm Catholic doctrine. While the Counter-Reformation succeeded in revitalizing certain aspects of the Church, it could not halt the broader cultural shift towards religious diversity and individual interpretation of faith.

The fragmentation of Christianity fundamentally altered the religious landscape of Europe. With multiple denominations now coexisting, religious conflicts grew, sometimes erupting into violent clashes, as seen in the Thirty Years' War (1618-1648). This religious pluralism and discord contributed to a growing disenchantment with organized religion and authority, leading many to seek new sources of meaning and truth.

The Enlightenment: Reason as a New Guide for Humanity

The Enlightenment (17th-18th centuries) was the culmination of these intellectual shifts. Enlightenment thinkers, known as philosophers, emphasized reason, empiricism, and skepticism over tradition and religious dogma. Figures such as René Descartes, Voltaire, John Locke, and Isaac Newton explored human rights, the nature of reality, and the mechanisms of the universe, each challenging the authority of both Church and monarchy. Their works inspired a cultural shift where scientific inquiry, philosophical discourse, and political reform became paramount.

Enlightenment ideals celebrated human autonomy and reason, encouraging individuals to question established beliefs and authorities. The notion of an ordered, predictable universe, as described by Newtonian physics, suggested that natural laws; rather than divine intervention; governed existence. This view of the universe lessened the Church's role in explaining the world, as people increasingly looked to science to understand natural phenomena and social structures. Rationality and evidence-based thinking thus began to replace the theological and superstitious explanations that had once dominated society.

Spiritual Decay and Moral Ambiguity

Yet, as religious structures weakened and Enlightenment ideals spread, society experienced a moral shift that some perceived as spiritual decay. Traditional Christian teachings, which had long provided ethical guidance and a sense of accountability, lost their centrality. Without a unified moral authority, people found themselves navigating new ethical landscapes, often torn between emerging secular values and traditional religious beliefs.

Critics of the Enlightenment argued that reason alone could not provide a moral compass, and that, in dismissing spiritual authority, society risked embracing moral relativism. This concern was echoed in both religious and philosophical debates, with some contending that human reason, without divine guidance, was insufficient to address deeper existential questions and moral dilemmas.

This perceived moral ambiguity sparked apocalyptic warnings and foreboding sentiments, as some saw the decline of strict religious adherence as a sign of impending judgment or downfall. These fears were particularly pronounced among religious communities who interpreted the Enlightenment's secularism as a step away from God and towards a spiritually bankrupt society. Literature, sermons, and even artwork of the time often depicted themes of judgment and damnation, with some foreseeing the rise of a godless world as a precursor to the apocalypse.

The Dual Legacy: Enlightenment and Spiritual Decline

The decline of strict Church control, therefore, left a mixed legacy. On one hand, the weakening of religious authority and the rise of secular knowledge brought about unprecedented intellectual freedom, laying the groundwork for advances in science, human rights, and democratic governance. The Enlightenment's principles of equality and reason inspired political revolutions in America and France, reshaping modern Western thought and social structure.

On the other hand, the erosion of the Church's moral and spiritual authority also led to a search for meaning in increasingly secular terms, which for some represented a loss of moral and spiritual grounding. In religious circles, the Enlightenment era was often viewed as a descent into spiritual emptiness, where people abandoned God's guidance in favor of human-centered rationalism.

As the modern world took shape, the tension between secularism and spirituality persisted, shaping debates on ethics, governance, and human purpose. This era of enlightenment and spiritual decay is a critical chapter in humanity's journey; a time when people sought to balance reason and faith, grappling with the costs and freedoms of a world no longer under strict religious authority. It would ultimately set the stage for further conflict, reform, and the apocalyptic anxieties that would resurface in the centuries to come.

Seeds of Prophecy from William Branham and Modern Prophets Foretelling Moral Decay

In the 20th century, amid global wars, social upheaval, and technological change, certain figures emerged who claimed to have a prophetic message for the modern world. One of the most notable was William Marrion Branham, an American preacher who attracted a large following in the mid-20th century. Branham, along with a few other prominent religious leaders, claimed that he received direct revelations from God and warned of an impending apocalypse due to the world's moral and spiritual decline. His prophecies resonated with those who felt that modern society was straying further from the biblical principles that they believed should be its foundation.

William Branham: Background and Ministry

Born in 1909 in Kentucky, William Branham was raised in a humble, rural environment. His early years were marked by poverty, and he claimed to have had supernatural experiences from a young age. In the 1940s, Branham began a healing ministry that brought him national attention. He was known for his "gift of discernment," where he claimed to know details about individuals' lives and illnesses through divine insight. This attracted large crowds and helped to fuel the Pentecostal and Charismatic movements in the United States and abroad.

However, it wasn't only Branham's healing ministry that captivated his followers; it was also his emphasis on apocalyptic prophecy. Branham preached that he had been given visions that revealed God's impending judgment on a world that had fallen into spiritual decay and rebellion against God's commandments. He spoke out against societal issues such as moral laxity, materialism, the breakdown of family values, and the rise of secularism; all of which he saw as signs of humanity's spiritual decline.

Key Prophecies of William Branham

Branham's prophetic ministry focused on several specific themes that he believed were indications of the approaching apocalypse:

Seven Visions of the End Times (1933): Branham claimed to have received a series of seven visions in 1933 that outlined future events leading to the end of the world. Among these visions were the rise of specific political powers, advancements in technology, and moral decay. Branham's visions included a prediction of the rise of Nazi Germany, the ascent of Communism, the emergence of powerful machines and cars with "egg-shaped" designs, and the moral decline he believed would plague the United States, eventually leading to its destruction.

The Fall of Morality: Branham spoke often about what he perceived as the erosion of traditional moral values, particularly in the West. He condemned the "modern" lifestyles that he saw emerging, such as increasing immodesty in clothing, the breakdown of the family unit, and sexual immorality. For Branham, these trends were not merely social changes but signs of deeper spiritual decay. He warned that such behaviours were leading society toward divine judgment, and he often referenced scriptures that called for repentance.

The "Laodicean" Church Age: Branham believed that the world was in the "Laodicean" church age, a term he borrowed from the Book of Revelation, where Jesus addresses the "lukewarm" church in Laodicea. According to Branham, this represented an age of spiritual indifference and complacency. The Laodicean Church Age was characterized, he said, by churches that were more interested in wealth and social status than in true devotion to God. He warned that, because of this lukewarm spirituality, many churches were no longer leading people towards salvation but rather towards a superficial, worldly Christianity that would be unable to withstand the coming judgment.

A Woman Leader in America: Branham also predicted that a powerful woman would rise to a position of influence in the United States before its downfall. He didn't clarify whether this woman would be a political figure or a spiritual one, but he viewed her as a symbol of the moral decay that he believed was already corrupting American society.

Branham's Apocalyptic Influence

William Branham's messages resonated with those who felt alienated by the rapid cultural shifts of the 20th century. As society experienced dramatic changes, including the liberalization of social values, the civil rights movement, the sexual revolution, and growing secularism, many people saw Branham's prophecies as a warning that modern society was headed for a collision with divine justice. He called for a return to biblical principles, urging people to prepare for the Second Coming of Christ, which he believed would soon occur.

His influence continued beyond his lifetime, as his sermons and teachings were widely circulated, and his brothers remained committed to his message. Today, a global network of believers continues to view Branham's prophecies as a lens through which to interpret current events, particularly the perceived decline in morality and spirituality in modern culture.

Other Modern Prophets and Apocalyptic Warnings

While Branham was among the most notable, he was not alone. Throughout the 20th century, other preachers and religious leaders echoed similar warnings:

David Wilkerson: The American pastor and author of *The Cross and the Switchblade* spoke out against what he saw as the moral decay of America and warned of coming judgments, including financial collapse and natural disasters, as consequences of the nation's sins.

Billy Graham: Though he did not claim prophetic visions, Billy Graham often spoke in apocalyptic terms, urging people to prepare for the return of Jesus and warning that society's increasing secularism and moral relativism were signs that the end times were near.

Hal Lindsey: Author of *The Late Great Planet Earth*, Lindsey wrote about prophecy in terms of contemporary politics, arguing that the Cold War and Middle Eastern conflicts were signs of the apocalypse. His work popularized a form of apocalyptic Christianity focused on current events.

Themes of Moral Decay and Impending Judgment

The recurring theme in these prophecies was that the modern world was witnessing a "falling away" from traditional values and divine truths. Many saw the rise of materialism, increasing secularization, and shifting social norms as indicators of humanity's rebellion against God. Prophetic voices warned that such moral decline would not go unchecked and that a reckoning was inevitable.

These modern prophecies found resonance especially among conservative Christians who viewed them as fulfilling biblical predictions of a time when people would "call evil good and good evil"

(Isaiah 5:20). The concept of a "moral decay" thus became central to the apocalyptic narrative; an idea that humanity's abandonment of godly values would hasten divine judgment.

Today, William Branham's teachings continue to shape certain sects of Christianity, particularly within Pentecostal and Charismatic movements. His prophecies are studied as indicators of both historical and future events, with many of his brothers believing that modern-day immorality, secularism, and global crises are signs of the impending apocalypse that Branham foresaw.

Branham's message has also had an enduring impact on how some Christians interpret current events. In a world marked by complex social issues and shifting moral landscapes, his prophecies offer a framework through which to view such changes as confirmation of an unfolding divine plan. Branham's legacy thus lives on as a sobering reminder of the perceived consequences of turning away from traditional values and divine guidance. His teachings continue to fuel apocalyptic beliefs and underscore the fear that humanity's moral decay may eventually lead to its downfall.

Reformations, Revolutions, and Shadows of the Antichrist

The Protestant Reformation and Rise of Antichrist Fears (1517-1648 AD)

Martin Luther's Rebellion Against the Catholic Church and the Rise of Protestant Denominations

The Protestant Reformation was a watershed event in Western history, redefining religious belief, political power, and social structure in Europe. The movement began in 1517 with the actions of Martin Luther, a German monk who, disillusioned with the corruption he perceived within the Catholic Church, launched a protest that would spark religious, political, and social upheaval across the continent. Luther's objections to the Church's practices, particularly the selling of indulgences, as well as his belief in the authority of Scripture over papal power, led him to write his famous *Ninety-Five Theses*; a manifesto that openly criticized the Catholic Church's doctrines and practices.

Luther's ideas quickly spread, gaining support from those who felt oppressed by the Church's dominance and who resented the wealth and power it wielded. This movement soon coalesced into what became known as Protestantism, a collective of new Christian denominations that broke away from Catholic orthodoxy. Luther's rebellion did more than fracture the Church; it ignited a fervour of apocalyptic thought, with both Catholics and Protestants accusing each other of embodying the spirit of the Antichrist.

The Context of Corruption and the Selling of Indulgences

By the 16th century, the Catholic Church had long been the central religious and political institution in Europe, wielding significant influence over monarchs and nations. However, with this power came widespread corruption. Many church leaders, including some popes, lived in opulence, and church positions were frequently bought and sold. This period of ecclesiastical corruption became especially contentious over the Church's practice of selling indulgences; a system in which the faithful could pay money to have their sins absolved or reduce the time they or a deceased loved one would spend in purgatory.

Luther condemned this practice, seeing it as a direct violation of the Bible's teachings on salvation, which he believed came through faith alone, not through monetary payment. His *Ninety-Five Theses*, nailed to the door of Wittenberg's Castle Church in 1517, served as a formal protest against these practices, and its language questioned the validity of the Church's authority. Luther argued that indulgences could not save souls and that the pope had no authority to grant forgiveness. He asserted that true repentance could only come from personal faith and a relationship with God, which could not be mediated by the Church.

The *Ninety-Five Theses* and the Spread of Reformation Ideas

Luther's *Ninety-Five Theses* ignited a firestorm. The invention of the printing press, a relatively recent development, allowed his ideas to spread with unprecedented speed. Soon, Luther's criticisms were being read by ordinary people, scholars, and clergy alike. His writings resonated with those who were frustrated with the Church's hold on society and who yearned for a simpler, more personal faith. Many were drawn to his calls for a return to Scripture as the highest authority, a principle that would become central to Protestant theology.

As Luther's ideas gained traction, he continued to refine his beliefs, rejecting the authority of the pope and questioning many traditional Catholic teachings. His teachings emphasized *sola scriptura* (Scripture alone), *sola fide* (faith alone), and *sola gratia* (grace alone) as the pillars of true Christian faith. These principles became foundational to Protestantism, which sought to strip away what Luther saw as the corrupting influences of the Church's bureaucracy and excesses.

The Rise of Protestant Denominations

Luther's actions emboldened other reformers, and soon, new leaders emerged, each with their own theological interpretations and ideas. In Switzerland, Ulrich Zwingli and later John Calvin led reformation efforts that emphasized predestination and a strict moral code. Calvin's teachings, in particular, led to the formation of Calvinism, which spread to France, Scotland, and the Netherlands. Calvinist ideas also influenced Puritanism, which would later play a significant role in the settlement of North America.

The Reformation fractured Europe into a series of Protestant denominations, each interpreting Christian doctrine differently. While Luther had hoped to reform the Church from within, the movement took on a life of its own, resulting in the formation of various Protestant sects, including Lutherans, Calvinists, and Anabaptists. Each of these groups interpreted Scripture uniquely, diverging from both the Catholic Church and from each other.

Apocalyptic Fears and the Concept of the Antichrist

The Reformation stirred an undercurrent of apocalyptic thought, with each side accusing the other of representing the Antichrist. In Catholic tradition, the Antichrist was expected to be a figure who would deceive and lead the faithful astray before the final judgment. With both Catholics and Protestants identifying each other as manifestations of this sinister force, the Reformation became steeped in prophetic language, heightening tensions and fears of impending doom.

Luther himself believed that the papacy might be the Antichrist foretold in the Book of Revelation. He argued that the pope's position, which he saw as claiming authority over all of Christendom, matched the characteristics of the Antichrist who would set himself up as a ruler above all. Luther's bold assertions caused outrage within the Catholic Church, as he openly denounced the pope and the papacy as corrupting forces leading people away from true faith.

Meanwhile, Catholic authorities viewed the spread of Protestantism as a form of heresy that threatened the unity of the Christian world. The Catholic Church responded by launching the Counter-Reformation, a movement aimed at reaffirming Catholic doctrine and curtailing the influence of Protestant ideas. The Inquisition intensified, targeting Protestant reformers and leaders, whom the Catholic Church deemed heretical and dangerous.

Religious Conflicts and the Political Fallout

The Reformation's theological disputes soon spiralled into violent conflicts, as religious divisions became intertwined with political ambitions. The Protestant Reformation fractured the once-unified Christian Europe, as various rulers chose sides, either embracing Protestantism or remaining loyal to the Catholic Church. German princes, in particular, used the Reformation as an opportunity to assert their independence from the Holy Roman Empire and the pope.

The Holy Roman Emperor Charles V, a staunch Catholic, viewed the Reformation as a direct challenge to his authority and fought to suppress Protestantism within his territories. However, the movement gained too much momentum to be contained, leading to decades of warfare and political instability across Europe. The Treaty of Augsburg in 1555 attempted to bring peace by allowing rulers within the Holy Roman Empire to choose between Catholicism and Lutheranism for their regions, though this did not prevent future conflicts.

The Legacy of the Protestant Reformation

The Protestant Reformation reshaped the religious landscape of Europe and paved the way for a more fragmented Christian world. The Catholic Church, forced to respond to the growing Protestant movement, initiated its own reforms at the Council of Trent (1545-1563), which clarified Catholic doctrines and corrected some abuses. The Counter-Reformation aimed to restore the Church's moral authority and curb the spread of Protestantism, but it also led to increased persecution of Protestants and other dissenting groups.

This period of religious upheaval fostered a new age of theological debate, religious freedom, and, for some, a growing apocalyptic expectation. The divisions and animosity created by the Reformation fuelled the belief that the world was nearing an era of great trials and judgment, reinforcing fears of the Antichrist and setting the stage for centuries of religious conflict.

The Protestant Reformation's legacy continued to shape the modern world, influencing the development of democracy, individual rights, and the separation of church and state. The movement away from centralized religious authority encouraged personal interpretations of Scripture and a broader questioning of traditional institutions, values that would eventually influence the Enlightenment and the modern age. However, the Reformation also left a trail of sectarian divisions and an enduring sense of religious urgency, as both Protestants and Catholics grappled with what they saw as signs of an impending apocalypse.

Apocalyptic Warnings in Luther's Teachings; Vision of the Church as a Potential Antichrist Figure

As Martin Luther's critique of the Catholic Church developed, he began to perceive apocalyptic significance in the Church's power structure and practices. His writings not only challenged the doctrinal authority of the Church but also painted a stark and prophetic picture of the Church itself as a potential Antichrist; a vision that resonated deeply with the apocalyptic fears of the time. Luther's warning about the corruptive potential of religious institutions influenced a generation of believers who viewed the Church's actions as a deviation from Christ's teachings and an ominous sign of the approaching end times.

Luther's Interpretation of the Antichrist and the Corruption of the Church

Luther's theological views led him to believe that the Antichrist could manifest as a corrupt authority within Christianity itself. He argued that the "spirit of Antichrist" was embodied by the Church hierarchy, specifically the papacy, which he viewed as abusing its authority to control and deceive the faithful. In Luther's mind, this kind of corruption was a dangerous threat to true Christianity. He saw the pope's power as a self-serving rule that rivalled Christ's authority and led people away from a genuine relationship with God.

Luther's writings, particularly in works like *On the Papacy at Rome* and *Against the Roman Papacy, an Institution of the Devil*, were filled with apocalyptic language, often drawing from the Book of Revelation. He warned that the pope, as head of the Catholic Church, was not leading people to salvation but instead was guiding them down a path of spiritual decay. Luther associated certain papal actions, like the selling of indulgences and the accumulation of wealth and political power, with the traits of the Antichrist described in Scripture; someone who would deceive believers and turn them away from true faith.

Theological Basis for Viewing the Church as the Antichrist

Luther's view of the papacy as the Antichrist drew on specific biblical passages, primarily from the books of Daniel, Thessalonians, and Revelation, where figures of corruption, deception, and false authority are described. In the Book of Revelation, the "Beast" and the "false prophet" were figures believed to lead people astray and persecute true believers. Similarly, Paul's Second Epistle to the Thessalonians spoke of a "man of lawlessness" who would exalt himself and deceive many before the end of days. Luther interpreted these references as warning signs of a powerful entity that would lead a false church; one that prioritized human authority over God's truth.

In Luther's view, the Catholic Church's demand for obedience, the pope's claim of supreme authority, and the practice of indulgences represented a perversion of true Christianity. To Luther, this was not merely theological disagreement but a spiritual crisis that had apocalyptic consequences. His conviction that the Church was leading people astray was a call to resist what he saw as a counterfeit faith, one that symbolized a betrayal of Christ's teachings.

Impact of Luther's Apocalyptic Warnings on the Public

Luther's teachings gained traction across Europe, not only because they provided a path for spiritual independence but also because they resonated with a widespread fear of impending judgment. During this period, many believed they were living in the "end times," a notion fuelled by wars, plagues, and social unrest. Luther's warnings about the papacy as the Antichrist tapped into these anxieties, framing the Reformation as not just a theological movement but a battle between good and evil. The idea that the Church itself could be an agent of the Antichrist shook the foundations of European society and emboldened those who wished to resist Church authority.

For Luther's followers, his teachings provided a justification for breaking away from the Church's power. His warnings were not abstract theological musings but a call to resist what he saw as the ultimate deception. Luther's vision gave people a framework for viewing the Reformation as a cosmic struggle, a necessary upheaval to prevent further corruption. By casting the Church as a possible Antichrist, Luther positioned Protestantism as a purer, more direct path to salvation, contrasting it with the Catholic Church's hierarchical and ritualistic structure, which he believed had deviated from true Christianity.

Antichrist Prophecies and the Broader Reformation Movement

Luther was not alone in his apocalyptic interpretation of the times. Other reformers and radical sects took up similar themes, interpreting the Church's actions as signs of the Antichrist's influence. This sense of an impending end created a fertile ground for new religious movements that aimed to break away from traditional structures and prepare for a new era of faith. Many Protestants saw their resistance to Catholicism as part of a larger prophetic mission, a struggle to save the world from the false teachings they associated with the Antichrist.

As the Reformation spread, so did apocalyptic rhetoric. Protestant preachers across Europe painted vivid pictures of the Church as a deceptive institution leading people to spiritual ruin. This vision resonated with laypeople who had already grown wary of the Church's wealth and influence. Luther's association of the Church with the Antichrist provided a moral justification for questioning authority and embracing the Protestant cause, which emphasized personal faith and scripture over institutional loyalty.

The Long-Term Influence of Luther's Apocalyptic Warnings

Luther's warnings about the Antichrist became an enduring part of Protestant identity. Even after his death, his apocalyptic views on the Church continued to shape Protestant attitudes, fostering a wariness of centralized religious authority that would influence future religious movements and sects. In some areas, Luther's rhetoric fuelled hostility between Catholics and Protestants, each side viewing the other as an embodiment of end-time deception.

In the years to come, the idea of the Antichrist continued to influence Protestant theology, especially in regions like England and North America, where Protestant sects like the Puritans and later groups like the Methodists and Baptists carried forward an apocalyptic perspective that warned against spiritual corruption. Luther's teachings contributed to a lasting legacy of apocalyptic thought, one that associated institutionalized religion with potential spiritual deception. This suspicion of centralized authority would later fuel other reform movements, secular revolutions, and a more personal approach to religious faith.

In sum, Luther's apocalyptic warnings about the Church as the Antichrist figure not only catalysed the Reformation but also redefined how people viewed authority, faith, and the structure of Christian society. His views amplified a larger call to examine and question authority, laying the foundation for future movements that would continue to challenge established power structures in the name of truth and salvation.

Religious Wars (e.g., Thirty Years' War) as a Symbol of End Times

The early modern period was marked by intense religious conflicts, most notably the Thirty Years' War (1618-1648), which exemplified the deep-seated tensions between Protestant and Catholic states in Europe. This war became not only a brutal struggle for political power and religious supremacy but also a conflict imbued with apocalyptic significance. For many contemporaries, the bloodshed and chaos represented clear signs of the end times, echoing the prophecies of the Bible about conflict, judgment, and redemption.

Background: The Reformation's Influence on Political and Religious Landscape

The Protestant Reformation, which had started in the early 16th century with figures like Martin Luther and John Calvin, had significant implications for the political landscape of Europe. As Protestantism gained followers, various rulers embraced the movement to assert independence from the Catholic Church and the papal authority. The fragmentation of Christianity created a volatile environment where religious allegiances were closely tied to national identities, and political power was often contested along religious lines.

The Peace of Augsburg in 1555 attempted to address these tensions by establishing the principle of *cuius regio, eius religio*, allowing princes to determine the religion of their own territories. However, this compromise proved fragile as it did not resolve underlying tensions, particularly in regions with mixed populations or where Protestantism was gaining ground in traditionally Catholic areas. The lack of a lasting resolution set the stage for further conflict, particularly in the Holy Roman Empire, where religious divisions were sharp.

Outbreak of the Thirty Years' War

The Thirty Years' War began in 1618 with the Defenestration of Prague, an event where Protestant nobles threw two Catholic officials out of a window as a reaction against the Habsburgs' attempts to impose Catholicism in Bohemia. What started as a local conflict quickly escalated into a larger war involving most of Europe, as various powers took sides; Catholic versus Protestant; leading to a complex web of alliances and enmities.

The war can be divided into four main phases:

1. **The Bohemian Phase (1618-1625):** This phase saw the initial conflict in Bohemia, where Protestant nobles revolted against Habsburg rule. The defeat of the Protestants at the Battle of White Mountain in 1620 marked a significant Catholic victory.
2. **The Danish Phase (1625-1630):** King Christian IV of Denmark intervened to support the Protestant cause but faced defeats, leading to greater Catholic dominance in northern Germany.
3. **The Swedish Phase (1630-1635):** Led by King Gustavus Adolphus of Sweden, this phase saw renewed hope for Protestant forces. The Swedes achieved several victories, but Gustavus's death in 1632 shifted the war's momentum.
4. **The French Phase (1635-1648):** France, although a Catholic nation, entered the war on the side of the Protestants to counter Habsburg power. This phase saw extensive destruction and was marked by the war's transformation into a broader struggle for political control in Europe.

Apocalyptic Significance of the War

As the war dragged on, it became clear that it was not merely a battle for religious or territorial supremacy but also a catastrophic struggle that had apocalyptic implications. The staggering loss of life, with estimates ranging from 7 to 11 million people due to warfare, famine, and disease, led many to interpret the events through an eschatological lens. For contemporaries, the devastation appeared to fulfill prophecies found in the Book of Revelation and other biblical texts warning of wars, plagues, and tribulations as signs of the impending end times.

- **Interpretation of Signs:** Many people began to see the destruction wrought by the war as evidence of divine judgment. The suffering and chaos were interpreted as reflections of humanity's sinful nature and the consequences of turning away from God. Sermons and pamphlets circulated widely, depicting the war as a precursor to the Last Judgment, urging believers to repent and seek salvation before it was too late.
- **Religious Extremism:** The apocalyptic fervour fuelled by the war gave rise to various radical religious movements, some of which predicted imminent apocalyptic events. Groups such as the Anabaptists and other radical Protestants viewed the upheaval as a divine call to establish a new, pure community of believers in anticipation of Christ's return.

Consequences and Legacy of the Thirty Years' War

The Thirty Years' War resulted in tremendous political, social, and religious upheaval, leading to the decline of the Holy Roman Empire and the emergence of state sovereignty as a defining principle in European politics. The Peace of Westphalia in 1648 marked the end of the war and established a new framework for international relations based on the recognition of state sovereignty, allowing rulers to determine their own religious affiliations without external interference.

However, the war also left a legacy of destruction and disillusionment that contributed to the development of secularism in Europe. The massive loss of life and the failure of religious institutions to provide peace led many to question the efficacy of established religious authority, shifting the focus from divine intervention to human responsibility.

The apocalyptic interpretations that emerged during the Thirty Years' War also influenced later generations, contributing to a long-standing tradition of seeing current events as signs of impending judgment. The war's legacy continued to resonate, shaping religious thought, social movements, and even political ideologies in subsequent centuries, as people grappled with the implications of such catastrophic events and sought meaning in the face of suffering and loss.

The Thirty Years' War serves as a potent example of how religious conflicts can be perceived as manifestations of deeper spiritual struggles, revealing the tension between faith and human ambition. The war illustrated the profound impact of the Reformation on European society and the apocalyptic fears that can arise in times of crisis, reshaping both the religious landscape and the course of history.

Enlightenment and the Decline of Faith (17th-18th Centuries)

Enlightenment Ideals Reshaping Society, Focus on Reason Over Faith

The Enlightenment, spanning the late 17th to the 18th century, marked a profound transformation in Western thought and society. Characterized by a shift from traditional beliefs rooted in religion and dogma to an emphasis on reason, empirical evidence, and individualism, the Enlightenment played a pivotal role in reshaping various aspects of culture, politics, and philosophy. This period laid the groundwork for modern secularism and significantly impacted how humanity viewed itself and its place in the universe.

Roots of the Enlightenment

The Enlightenment emerged in Europe, particularly in France, England, and Germany, as a response to the rigid structures of the preceding medieval period and the authoritarian nature of religious institutions. Several key factors contributed to the rise of Enlightenment thought:

1. **Scientific Revolution:** The scientific advancements of the 16th and 17th centuries challenged traditional views of the universe. Figures like Galileo Galilei, Johannes Kepler, and Isaac Newton encouraged a reliance on observation, experimentation, and mathematics, fostering a belief that natural phenomena could be explained through reason rather than divine intervention.

2. **Humanism and Classical Knowledge:** The Renaissance had revived interest in classical texts and ideas from ancient Greece and Rome, emphasizing human potential and achievement. Enlightenment thinkers built upon this foundation, arguing for the value of human reason and the capacity for individuals to understand and improve their world.

3. **Political and Economic Changes:** The rise of nation-states, the decline of feudalism, and the growth of trade and commerce contributed to a shift in power dynamics. The emergence of the bourgeoisie (middle class) fostered new ideas about governance, liberty, and rights, leading to demands for greater political participation and individual freedoms.

Key Enlightenment Thinkers and Ideas

The Enlightenment produced a plethora of influential philosophers, writers, and scientists whose ideas shaped contemporary thought. Key figures included:

René Descartes: Often considered the father of modern philosophy, Descartes emphasized doubt and reason as the foundations of knowledge. His famous statement, "Cogito, ergo sum" ("I think, therefore I am"), underscored the significance of human consciousness and rational thought.

John Locke: A proponent of empiricism, Locke argued that knowledge comes from sensory experience. His ideas about natural rights and the social contract influenced political theory, particularly in the context of democracy and governance.

Voltaire: A vocal critic of religious intolerance and dogma, Voltaire championed freedom of speech, separation of church and state, and civil liberties. His works highlighted the need for reason and tolerance in society.

Jean-Jacques Rousseau: Rousseau explored the concepts of popular sovereignty and the general will, arguing that true freedom comes from participation in democratic governance. His ideas on education also influenced thoughts about human development and morality.

Immanuel Kant: Kant sought to reconcile reason and faith, arguing that while human understanding is limited, moral law and ethics can be derived through reason. He famously stated, "Sapere aude" ("Dare to know"), encouraging individuals to think for themselves.

Shift from Faith to Reason

The Enlightenment's emphasis on reason over faith led to a gradual decline in the authority of religious institutions and dogmas:

Questioning of Religious Beliefs: As Enlightenment thinkers promoted rational thought, many began to question established religious doctrines. The notion that faith should be grounded in reason gained traction, leading to challenges against religious orthodoxy and superstitions.

Rise of Secularism: Enlightenment ideals paved the way for secular governance and the separation of church and state. The authority of religious institutions diminished in public life, and rational thought began to shape laws, policies, and social norms.

Impact on Christianity: While some Enlightenment thinkers remained believers, many advocated for a more rational interpretation of Christianity. The emergence of Deism, which viewed God as a distant creator who does not intervene in the world, reflected this shift. Deists emphasized reason and morality over traditional religious practices.

Cultural and Social Changes

The Enlightenment also led to significant cultural and social changes, including:

Literacy and Education: The spread of Enlightenment ideas was facilitated by the growth of literacy and the establishment of educational institutions. Books, pamphlets, and newspapers became more widely available, allowing Enlightenment thought to reach broader audiences.

Art and Literature: The period saw a flourishing of literature and the arts, as writers and artists sought to explore human experience and challenge traditional narratives. Movements such as Romanticism emerged as reactions to the Enlightenment's rationalism, emphasizing emotion, nature, and individualism.

Political Revolutions: The principles of the Enlightenment inspired political revolutions, most notably the American Revolution (1775-1783) and the French Revolution (1789-1799).

Enlightenment ideas about liberty, equality, and the rights of individuals became foundational to these movements, challenging the established order.

Apocalyptic Underpinnings

Despite the Enlightenment's focus on reason and progress, the era was not devoid of apocalyptic thought:

Rethinking of End Times: Enlightenment thinkers often reinterpreted biblical prophecies and eschatological themes. Some viewed the decline of religious authority as a sign of a new age, while others saw the upheaval of society and politics as potential precursors to catastrophic events.

Societal Warnings: In the face of rapid changes and challenges to traditional values, some writers warned of moral decay and societal collapse. The fear that humanity might drift away from divine principles fostered a sense of urgency among certain groups, echoing apocalyptic themes from earlier periods.

The Enlightenment represents a crucial turning point in human history, reshaping societal norms and values. By prioritizing reason over faith, it facilitated a decline in the authority of religious institutions and encouraged a shift toward secularism and individualism. While it laid the groundwork for modernity, the Enlightenment also intersected with apocalyptic thinking, revealing humanity's ongoing struggle to reconcile reason, faith, and the quest for meaning in a rapidly changing world. This dynamic would continue to evolve, shaping the discourse around morality, spirituality, and the future of humanity in the centuries to come.

Shift Toward Secularism as a Sign of Moral Decay, Warnings of Approaching Wrath

The Enlightenment marked a significant shift in human thought, particularly regarding the relationship between reason, faith, and morality. As secularism gained prominence, many traditional religious beliefs were challenged, leading to concerns among the faithful about the moral implications of this transformation. This shift was often interpreted as a sign of impending moral decay, with apocalyptic warnings surfacing in various cultural and religious contexts.

Understanding Secularism

Secularism refers to the principle of separating religious institutions and beliefs from state affairs and public life. During the Enlightenment, this shift was fueled by several key factors:

1. **Intellectual Freedom:** The Enlightenment fostered an environment where individuals began to question established norms, including religious doctrines. The emphasis on rational thought and empirical evidence encouraged a more critical approach to religious beliefs.

2. **Rise of Scientific Understanding:** As scientific discoveries and advancements challenged supernatural explanations, many began to favor naturalistic explanations of the universe. This shift diminished the authority of religious interpretations of natural phenomena,

further promoting secular ideologies.

3. **Political Revolutions:** The rise of secular governance during revolutions, such as the American and French Revolutions, illustrated a move away from monarchies that claimed divine right to rule. These movements emphasized human rights, equality, and the importance of reason, leading to calls for secular laws and policies.

Moral Decay in the Face of Secularism

With the rise of secularism, many religious leaders and communities expressed concern over the perceived moral decay of society. This fear was rooted in several observations:

1. **Erosion of Traditional Values:** The declining influence of religious teachings was seen as leading to a breakdown of moral standards. Critics argued that secular ideologies prioritized individualism and personal freedom over collective ethical responsibilities.

2. **Increased Immorality:** Observers noted a rise in behaviours viewed as immoral or unethical; such as promiscuity, crime, and substance abuse; coinciding with secularization. Many attributed this to the absence of religious guidance and accountability.

3. **Disconnection from Spiritual Foundations:** Secularism was seen as a movement away from the spiritual and moral principles that had historically guided societies. This disconnection led some to believe that people were increasingly alienated from their sense of purpose and moral compass.

Apocalyptic Warnings and Prophetic Voices

In response to the perceived moral decline, various religious leaders and groups began issuing apocalyptic warnings, arguing that secularism signalled an approaching judgment from God. Key elements of this response included:

1. **Revival of Prophetic Literature:** Throughout the 17th and 18th centuries, many religious figures revived themes from biblical prophecy, emphasizing the connection between societal changes and divine judgment. They warned that humanity's abandonment of faith and morality would lead to catastrophic consequences.

2. **Interpretations of Biblical Texts:** Religious leaders often turned to prophetic texts, particularly from the Old and New Testaments, to underscore their warnings. For instance, passages from Revelation and the prophetic writings of the Hebrew Scriptures were frequently cited to illustrate the consequences of turning away from God.

3. **Theological Movements:** Various theological movements, including Puritanism and Methodism, emerged in response to the Enlightenment's secularizing trends. These

movements sought to rekindle religious fervor and moral discipline, viewing themselves as protectors of faith in a morally decaying world.

4. **Social Commentary:** Writers and theologians of the time often used literature and sermons to convey their concerns. Figures like Jonathan Edwards in America and John Wesley in England preached messages emphasizing repentance and the need to return to spiritual values to avert divine wrath.

Cultural Reflections of Moral Decay

The concerns about secularism and moral decay were not limited to religious circles; they permeated the broader cultural landscape:

Literature and Art: The era produced a wealth of literature reflecting fears about societal decay and moral ambiguity. Novels, poems, and plays often depicted characters grappling with the consequences of moral choices in a changing world.

Social Movements: The rise of social movements advocating for moral reform, temperance, and abolitionism emerged in part as a response to perceived societal decline. Activists sought to align social practices with what they believed to be divine moral standards.

Intellectual Critique: Philosophers and writers also critiqued the moral implications of secular thought. While some embraced Enlightenment ideals, others warned that an overemphasis on reason without spiritual grounding could lead to nihilism and despair.

The Legacy of Secularism and Moral Warnings

The shift toward secularism during the Enlightenment sparked an ongoing dialogue about morality, faith, and the human condition. While secularism contributed to significant social progress and advancements in thought, it also raised fundamental questions about humanity's ethical responsibilities and spiritual roots.

Ongoing Struggle: The tension between secularism and religious belief remains a central theme in contemporary discourse. The debates surrounding morality, ethics, and the role of faith in public life continue to shape societies across the globe.

Apocalyptic Resonance: As moral decay is often viewed through the lens of prophecy and apocalyptic literature, the theme of impending judgment has persisted throughout history, influencing the beliefs and actions of individuals and communities alike.

Cultural Reflection: Modern literature, film, and art continue to grapple with themes of morality and societal decay, echoing the concerns raised during the Enlightenment. The struggle between secular ideals and spiritual values remains relevant in discussions about humanity's future.

The shift toward secularism during the Enlightenment was a complex and multifaceted phenomenon that reshaped the landscape of faith, morality, and society. While it fostered intellectual freedom and significant societal progress, it also raised profound questions about the consequences of moving away from traditional religious values. The warnings of approaching wrath and moral decay, articulated by various prophetic voices, serve as a reminder of the enduring struggle to find meaning, purpose, and ethical grounding in a rapidly changing world. This dynamic would continue to influence humanity's moral journey as the narrative of faith, reason, and the consequences of secularism unfolded in the centuries to come.

Rise of Scientific Advancements, Devaluing Traditional Spiritual Beliefs

The period of the Enlightenment marked a significant turning point in human thought, characterized by a growing emphasis on scientific inquiry and rationality. This rise of scientific advancements had profound implications for traditional spiritual beliefs, leading to a gradual devaluation of religious frameworks that had long governed societal understanding of the world.

The Birth of Modern Science

Scientific Revolution (16th-18th Century): The Scientific Revolution, beginning in the late Renaissance, laid the groundwork for modern science. Pioneering figures such as Nicolaus Copernicus, Galileo Galilei, Johannes Kepler, and Isaac Newton challenged long-held beliefs about the natural world, leading to revolutionary discoveries that transformed humanity's understanding of the universe.

Empirical Method: The development of the empirical method, championed by thinkers like Francis Bacon, emphasized observation, experimentation, and evidence-based reasoning. This approach contrasted sharply with reliance on religious texts and traditions, which had previously been the primary sources of knowledge about the world.

Mechanistic Universe: The mechanistic view of the universe, popularized by Newton, portrayed the cosmos as a vast machine governed by natural laws. This perspective reduced the need for supernatural explanations, undermining the theological interpretations of natural phenomena.

Challenges to Religious Authority

As scientific advancements gained traction, they posed significant challenges to the authority of religious institutions and traditional spiritual beliefs:

Questioning Creation Narratives: The heliocentric model proposed by Copernicus and supported by Galileo undermined the geocentric view of the universe held by the Church. This scientific challenge to the creation narrative forced a reevaluation of scriptural interpretations and led to conflicts between science and faith.

Critique of Miracles: The rise of naturalistic explanations for events previously attributed to divine intervention diminished the perceived need for miracles. As scientists demonstrated that natural processes could explain phenomena such as disease, weather, and celestial events, faith in the miraculous waned.

Human Reason vs. Divine Revelation: Enlightenment thinkers emphasized human reason and intellect as the primary means of understanding truth. This focus on rationality often marginalized the role of divine revelation, leading to a belief that human intellect could achieve knowledge without the need for spiritual guidance.

Impact on Spiritual Beliefs

The growing influence of science had several consequences for traditional spiritual beliefs:

Decline of Dogma: As scientific reasoning gained prominence, dogmatic beliefs began to lose their grip on society. People started to question established doctrines and practices, seeking a more personal and individualized understanding of spirituality.

Secularization of Thought: The scientific worldview contributed to the secularization of thought, where spiritual and religious considerations were often deemed irrelevant in addressing practical, everyday concerns. The increasing focus on the material world further distanced individuals from religious practices.

Emergence of Rationalism: Philosophers such as René Descartes and John Locke championed rationalism, advocating for reason as the primary source of knowledge. This philosophical shift further devalued traditional spiritual beliefs, as individuals began to prioritize logical reasoning over faith-based understanding.

Skepticism and Atheism: The Enlightenment paved the way for rising skepticism toward religion and the emergence of atheistic thought. Figures such as Voltaire and David Hume openly critiqued religious institutions and questioned the existence of God, contributing to a broader cultural shift away from organized religion.

Cultural Reflections and Reactions

The scientific advancements and the accompanying decline of traditional spiritual beliefs sparked a variety of cultural responses:

Literature and Philosophy: Literature and philosophical writings of the time often grappled with the implications of scientific progress on human existence and spirituality. Thinkers explored themes of existentialism, humanism, and the search for meaning in a world increasingly dominated by rational thought.

Religious Revivals: In response to the perceived threat of secularism, various religious revivals emerged, seeking to rekindle spiritual fervor. Movements such as Methodism emphasized personal experiences of faith, often incorporating emotional expressions of spirituality to counterbalance the intellectualism of the Enlightenment.

Eclectic Spirituality: As traditional religions faced challenges, some individuals turned to eclectic spiritual practices, seeking alternative forms of meaning and connection. This trend included a blend of Eastern philosophies, mystical traditions, and nature-based spiritualities.

The Long-Term Legacy

The rise of scientific advancements during the Enlightenment reshaped the landscape of human thought, leading to a reevaluation of spiritual beliefs and practices. This transformation had several lasting implications:

Ongoing Dialogue: The tension between science and religion continues to be a topic of debate in contemporary society. Discussions surrounding evolution, climate change, and ethical implications of scientific advancements often reflect the ongoing struggle between empirical evidence and faith-based perspectives.

Integration of Faith and Reason: In the modern era, many individuals and religious groups seek to reconcile scientific discoveries with spiritual beliefs. This integration has led to the development of theological perspectives that embrace science as a means of understanding the divine.

Revitalization of Spirituality: The questioning of traditional beliefs has also led to a resurgence of interest in spirituality, with individuals exploring diverse paths to connect with the transcendent. This search often reflects a desire for meaning and purpose in a rapidly changing world.

Crisis of Faith: The decline of traditional spiritual beliefs has resulted in a crisis of faith for some, leading to disillusionment and a sense of loss in a world that increasingly prioritizes scientific reasoning over spiritual understanding.

The rise of scientific advancements during the Enlightenment marked a profound turning point in human history, challenging traditional spiritual beliefs and reshaping the landscape of knowledge. While science opened new avenues for understanding the world, it also raised essential questions about the role of faith, morality, and spirituality in human existence.

The Industrial Revolution and New Idols (18th-19th Centuries)

Industrialization, Materialism, and the "Idol" of Technological Progress

The Industrial Revolution, beginning in the late 18th century and continuing through the 19th century, transformed the fabric of society, economy, and culture in ways previously unimaginable. At the core of this transformation was an intense focus on technological advancement, production efficiency, and material wealth; elements that came to embody a new form of "idolatry." As human ingenuity unlocked unprecedented power over the natural world, the ideals of industrialization gave birth to a new age of materialism, fundamentally shifting how society viewed progress and success.

Roots of Industrialization

The Advent of Machinery: The invention of machines like the steam engine, spinning jenny, and power loom revolutionized manufacturing and labor. These innovations allowed for rapid production and ushered in factory-based economies, moving away from agriculture as the main source of income.

Urbanization: With the rise of factories, people flocked to cities for jobs, leading to massive urban growth. This urbanization created densely populated industrial centres where the values of hard work, efficiency, and technological progress became the driving forces of daily life.

Economic Transformation: The new economy based on factories and mass production replaced the slower, artisanal methods of production. Wealth became increasingly concentrated in the hands of industrialists and capitalists who owned the means of production, which often led to stark class divisions and social inequality.

Materialism and Economic Growth as the New Ideals

As the production and consumption of goods skyrocketed, material wealth and possessions became symbols of status and success:

Shift from Subsistence to Consumerism: People began to see value in possessions, with personal wealth and material comforts becoming the markers of success. The economy increasingly revolved around consumer goods, shaping societal priorities around accumulation and consumption.

Industrial Wealth and Class Divides: Industrialists and factory owners amassed immense wealth, often at the expense of the working class, who endured long hours and harsh working conditions. This concentration of wealth fostered resentment, social unrest, and a focus on material gain as both the measure and the purpose of life.

Pursuit of Technological Progress: As technology advanced, people came to view it as the ultimate solution to societal problems. Many placed faith in technological development as a force for good, believing it could "save" humanity and bring about a utopia of comfort, convenience, and control over nature.

Technology as the New "Idol"

The rapid progression of technology created a society that, in some ways, began to "worship" industrial achievements and technological advancement:

Mechanization as Salvation: Society placed immense faith in the power of technology to solve all human problems, a belief that often resembled religious fervour. People believed that machines, technology, and industrial efficiency could create an ideal society, free from traditional challenges.

Work as Purpose: The industrial age elevated work to a new level of importance. Factory life normalized long hours, and "the harder you work, the more successful you'll be" became a social doctrine, especially in urban areas. Hard work was exalted, and personal identity became closely tied to one's labour output and productivity.

Science and Technology over Religion: Traditional religious and spiritual beliefs began to take a back seat as science and technology were increasingly viewed as the primary means of understanding and shaping the world. Many began to believe that the wonders of science and engineering could replace the moral and ethical guidance once provided by religion.

Moral and Social Consequences

The industrial age's emphasis on materialism and technological "idolatry" brought about significant social and moral repercussions:

Loss of Spiritual Values: As society became more materialistic, spiritual and moral values began to erode. Success was measured in terms of wealth and productivity rather than virtue or piety, leading to a decline in the importance of religious and ethical teachings.

Exploitation and Dehumanization of Workers: Factory conditions were harsh, with long hours, low pay, and often dangerous environments. Workers, including children, were treated as mere components in the industrial machine, stripped of individuality and dignity. This dehumanization of the working class highlighted the moral costs of prioritizing efficiency over empathy.

Alienation from Nature: Industrialization promoted the conquest and exploitation of natural resources. Forests were cleared, rivers polluted, and the landscape transformed to support factories and cities. This disconnect from nature fostered a mindset where the environment was viewed merely as a resource to be used, undermining reverence for the natural world.

Religious Responses and Apocalyptic Fears

The Industrial Revolution also triggered a spiritual backlash, with some religious figures and groups interpreting the rise of materialism as a sign of moral decay and impending judgment:

Calls for Spiritual Revival: Some religious leaders warned that society's focus on wealth and technology was leading people away from God, resulting in a spiritual crisis. They called for a return to faith and morality, emphasizing that the pursuit of material wealth was empty without a moral foundation.

Apocalyptic Prophecies: The unprecedented changes brought by industrialization stirred fears of the end times among some religious communities. They interpreted the era's focus on materialism and exploitation as a departure from divine teachings, believing it could provoke God's wrath and bring about an apocalyptic reckoning.

Rise of Social Reform Movements: In response to industrial excesses, various religious and social reform movements emerged, seeking to address the exploitation and moral decay seen in industrial society. These movements, such as the Methodist revival and the Salvation Army, aimed to restore moral values, support the poor, and counteract the negative effects of industrialization.

Long-Term Legacy and Cultural Reflections

The Industrial Revolution set a new standard for societal values, cantering around production, consumption, and material success. The legacy of this period can be seen in various aspects of modern life:

Capitalism as a Global System: The industrial age cemented capitalism as the dominant economic system, prioritizing profit, competition, and individual gain. This has led to both prosperity and ongoing social issues, as the focus on wealth continues to shape modern values and policies.

Rise of Modern Secularism: The focus on technology and material progress contributed to the rise of secularism, as more people began to question religious narratives and sought answers in science and rationalism instead. This has fostered an increasingly secular culture, especially in the Western world.

Lasting Social Inequalities: The wealth divide that emerged during industrialization left a lasting impact on modern society. Economic inequality remains a pressing issue, as capitalism and industrialism have created significant disparities in wealth and opportunity.

Reflection in Literature and Art: The industrial era inspired a wave of literary and artistic works that critiqued the era's excesses and warned of the dangers of materialism. Works such as Charles Dickens's *Hard Times* and Mary Shelley's *Frankenstein* reflect anxieties about industrial progress, social injustice, and the loss of human empathy in the pursuit of technological advancement.

The Industrial Revolution reshaped society's priorities, elevating materialism, technological progress, and wealth as new idols that, for many, replaced traditional spiritual beliefs. This era not only brought unprecedented advancements but also sparked ethical, social, and spiritual concerns that continue to resonate today. The industrial age serves as a potent reminder of the potential costs of prioritizing progress and wealth at the expense of human connection, morality, and reverence for the natural world. As society grapples with the legacy of this period, it faces the ongoing challenge of balancing technological advancement with moral responsibility and spiritual depth.

Exploitation and Degradation of Humanity: Foreshadowing Apocalyptic Labor Struggles

The Industrial Revolution, while advancing technology and economic growth, also introduced a dark era of exploitation and human degradation. The rise of factory systems and unregulated labour created a world in which workers, including men, women, and children, were treated as mere tools for production, with little regard for their well-being or humanity. These conditions led to widespread suffering, social upheaval, and ultimately, labour movements that would foreshadow an impending social "reckoning." Many saw this environment of oppression as an apocalyptic warning; a sign that society was moving toward collapse if it did not correct its moral path.

Labor Conditions and Human Exploitation

Factory Work and Brutal Hours: Factories demanded that workers operate for excessively long hours; often 12 to 16 hours a day; with only minimal breaks. Work weeks often spanned six or seven days, leaving little time for family life, rest, or personal pursuits. In their pursuit of productivity, factory owners pushed workers to their physical and mental limits.

Harsh and Dangerous Conditions: Factory environments were typically hazardous. Workers operated heavy machinery without adequate training or safety measures, resulting in frequent accidents and severe injuries. Air quality was poor, with smoke, dust, and toxic fumes circulating in crowded spaces. In textile mills, workers often suffered respiratory illnesses due to constant exposure to cotton dust.

Child Labor: Children, some as young as five or six, worked alongside adults in factories, mines, and fields. Factory owners preferred children for certain tasks due to their small size, which allowed them to reach into machines or crawl into confined spaces. These children worked long hours for little pay, and the physical toll of the labour often led to stunted growth, injuries, and, in some cases, death.

Miserable Living Conditions: Factory workers often lived in overcrowded, unsanitary slums near the factories. Housing was cramped, poorly built, and lacked access to clean water, sewage systems, or sanitation facilities. Disease outbreaks were common, with cholera, typhus, and tuberculosis devastating communities, especially in growing industrial cities like Manchester, London, and New York.

Wage Exploitation and Class Divide: Wages for factory workers were meager, barely enough to survive. Many workers were trapped in poverty, unable to rise above the conditions imposed upon them by industrial capitalism. Meanwhile, factory owners amassed significant wealth, widening the class divide and creating a rigid social hierarchy.

Human Degradation and Moral Decline

The relentless pursuit of profit at the expense of human dignity was seen by many as a sign of society's moral decay:

Loss of Human Identity: Workers were often viewed as "cogs" in the industrial machine, valued only for their ability to produce. This mindset stripped individuals of their humanity, reducing them to units of labour rather than individuals with personal aspirations, families, or intrinsic worth.

Family and Social Breakdown: The intense demands of factory work disrupted family life. Parents were often too exhausted or preoccupied with survival to provide for their children emotionally or supervise them. Children, subjected to labor from an early age, were deprived of education, play, and normal childhood experiences, which disrupted family structures and social bonds.

Moral and Ethical Concerns: Many critics saw the mistreatment of workers as an ethical crisis. Writers, artists, and thinkers of the time, like Charles Dickens and Friedrich Engels, highlighted the harsh realities of industrial life, portraying it as a degradation of moral and social values. Religious leaders condemned the greed of factory owners and warned that such practices could not go unpunished, invoking apocalyptic imagery to call for reform.

Spiritual Crisis: Amid the industrial boom, spiritual teachings that emphasized compassion, community, and the sanctity of life seemed increasingly incompatible with society's values. Many felt that humanity's disregard for these principles in pursuit of material wealth was an affront to divine laws, signalling a moral crisis with apocalyptic implications.

Rise of Labor Movements: Foreshadowing Apocalyptic Struggles

The conditions faced by workers gave rise to organized labour movements, which sought to confront the injustices of the industrial system:

Unions and Collective Bargaining: Workers began to form unions to negotiate better wages, shorter hours, and safer conditions. While factory owners initially resisted these efforts, unionization grew, leading to a series of labour strikes and protests. Striking workers risked their livelihoods and faced intimidation, harassment, and sometimes violence from authorities.

Major Labor Strikes and Protests: Strikes like the Haymarket Affair in Chicago (1886) and the Pullman Strike (1894) in the United States, as well as similar movements across Europe, highlighted the intense struggle between the working class and the capitalist elite. These events were often marked by violent confrontations with police or military forces, resulting in deaths and injuries.

Socialist and Anarchist Ideals: Amid the suffering, radical ideas began to gain traction. Socialists, anarchists, and other reformers argued for a society that prioritized human welfare over profit. They viewed capitalism as inherently exploitative, promoting a vision of society where the wealth created by industrial labour would be distributed more equitably. These ideas fuelled further labour activism, often framed in terms of a righteous struggle against systemic oppression.

Calls for Revolution and Apocalyptic Warnings: Some saw the labour struggles as an inevitable clash between good and evil. Writers and preachers warned that the suffering of the poor and the exploitation of the working class would bring divine retribution. This rhetoric often invoked apocalyptic language, depicting labour struggles as signs of an impending reckoning if society failed to correct its moral trajectory.

Apocalyptic Interpretations of the Labor Struggles

The labour struggles of the Industrial Revolution were viewed by many as signs of an impending social apocalypse, reflecting society's self-destructive focus on wealth and power.

Warnings from Religious Leaders: Religious leaders began to denounce industrial exploitation as a departure from Christian teachings, warning that a society based on greed and oppression was doomed to collapse. They preached that if the world continued down this path, it would bring about God's wrath.

The Workers' Struggle as a Symbol of Good vs. Evil: For some, the labour movement symbolized a battle between good (the exploited, oppressed workers) and evil (the greedy, morally bankrupt industrialists). This binary view framed the class struggle as an epic contest with apocalyptic stakes.

Prophetic Writings and Sermons: Christian preachers and theologians warned that the injustices of industrial society were a sign of the "end times," linking contemporary labour exploitation to biblical prophecies of a world consumed by greed, oppression, and moral corruption. These messages resonated with the working class, who felt abandoned by society's traditional institutions and yearned for justice.

Philosophers' Vision of a Future Reckoning: Thinkers like Karl Marx and Friedrich Engels also predicted a form of societal collapse, although from a secular perspective. They saw the exploitation of workers as unsustainable, prophesying that the working class, if oppressed long enough, would rise up against their oppressors, leading to a radical reordering of society.

Long-term Impact and Legacy

The exploitation and degradation during the Industrial Revolution set the stage for future social upheavals.

Lasting Labor Reforms: The efforts of labour activists eventually led to significant reforms. Laws were passed to limit working hours, regulate child labour, and improve workplace safety. These reforms marked the beginning of a long journey toward workers' rights, with labour unions continuing to advocate for fair treatment.

Moral Reflection on Industrial Capitalism: The exploitation of workers during this period prompted society to question the values underpinning industrial capitalism. It raised debates about ethical business practices, social justice, and humanity's moral responsibilities, themes that still resonate today.

Inspiration for Social and Political Movements: The struggles of the working class inspired a wave of social reform movements, from the fight for fair labour standards to broader political campaigns for workers' rights and social equality. These movements provided a framework for future efforts to protect the vulnerable in society.

Industrial Capitalism and Modern Reflections: The degradation of humanity during the Industrial Revolution continues to serve as a warning about the moral costs of unbridled capitalism. The ongoing challenges of income inequality, labour exploitation, and the environmental impact of industrial practices echo the abuses of the past, reminding society of the need for vigilance against injustice.

The Industrial Revolution's exploitation and degradation of humanity cast a dark shadow over its technological achievements, illustrating the moral costs of progress pursued without ethical constraints. The brutal labour conditions and apocalyptic warnings that arose during this period served as a powerful indictment of industrial society, leading to a labour movement that would fight for basic human dignity. As society continues to grapple with the legacy of industrial capitalism, these events remain a potent reminder of the need to balance progress with humanity, compassion, and moral accountability.

Emerging Warnings about the Consequences of Unchecked Ambition and Greed

The late stages of the Industrial Revolution saw mounting warnings from thinkers, writers, religious leaders, and social activists about the consequences of unchecked ambition and greed. As society transformed under the influence of industrialization, the promise of progress came with severe consequences that could not be ignored. Exploitation, social inequality, environmental degradation, and the neglect of spiritual values were seen as inevitable byproducts of a world driven by profit and power. Many feared that this path would lead to societal collapse, an era of moral decay, and even divine retribution, marking the dawn of an apocalyptic age.

Philosophers and Writers Sound the Alarm

Charles Dickens and Social Critique: Authors like Charles Dickens used their work to critique the exploitation and moral decay fostered by industrial society. His novels, such as *Hard Times* and *Oliver Twist*, painted vivid pictures of the suffering of the working class and the hypocrisy of the wealthy elite. Dickens highlighted the spiritual emptiness of a society that valued material success over compassion and justice.

Thomas Carlyle and "The Gospel of Work": Carlyle, a Scottish philosopher, criticized the prevailing materialism and glorification of wealth. He argued that society had lost its moral compass, embracing a "cash nexus" that reduced human relationships to financial transactions. Carlyle believed that true fulfillment came from meaningful work and purpose, not wealth. His warnings stressed that a civilization obsessed with profit and productivity would eventually self-destruct.

Karl Marx and Friedrich Engels' Prophetic Warnings: Although rooted in economic theory, Marx and Engels' critique of capitalism resonated as a prophecy of societal collapse. They argued that the unchecked ambitions of capitalists to maximize profits would inevitably lead to the exploitation of workers, creating a class divide so vast it would result in revolutionary upheaval. In *The Communist Manifesto*, they foretold a future where the working class would rise up, seeing the ruling elite as oppressors to be overthrown; a vision of conflict that resonated with apocalyptic imagery.

John Stuart Mill and the Limits of Wealth: Philosopher John Stuart Mill was deeply concerned with the unchecked ambition of industrial society. He argued that the pursuit of wealth should have limits and that society's well-being should not be measured solely by economic growth. Mill's call for a "stationary state," where people focused on quality of life rather than accumulation, was a radical stance against the prevailing capitalist mindset. He warned that endless growth would lead to resource depletion, social decay, and eventually disaster.

Romantic Poets' Lamentations on Nature and Humanity: Poets like William Wordsworth and Lord Byron warned against the impact of industrialization on nature and the human spirit. They lamented how the pursuit of wealth and progress destroyed the natural world and disconnected people from their humanity. Wordsworth's poetry often invoked a longing for a simpler life, cautioning that the loss of nature and simplicity signalled a moral decline.

Religious Warnings and Apocalyptic Sermons

Religious Leaders on Greed and Divine Judgment: Christian leaders in Europe and America condemned the rampant greed and materialism that defined industrial society, framing it as a rebellion against God's will. They preached that such selfish ambition would bring divine judgment, warning that the quest for wealth would lead to God's wrath. Some preachers cited the Bible, comparing the world's trajectory to the destruction of Sodom and Gomorrah, invoking fear of a societal reckoning.

The Salvation Army and Social Salvation: Founded in the 1860s, the Salvation Army emerged as a Christian movement focused on uplifting the downtrodden and exposing the dangers of greed and moral decay. By addressing issues like poverty and addiction, the Salvation Army sought to offer both physical aid and spiritual salvation, challenging the indifference of wealthy industrialists toward the poor. They warned that the materialistic culture was corrupting society's soul and emphasized the need for repentance and charity.

The "Social Gospel" Movement: In the United States, the Social Gospel movement combined Christian ethics with social reform, advocating for fair labour practices, poverty alleviation, and ethical treatment of workers. Leaders of this movement argued that Christianity demanded a society that cared for all its members. Their teachings emphasized that if society continued to neglect the poor and exalt wealth, it would face moral and spiritual ruin.

Prophecies and Visions of Apocalyptic Punishment: Some Christian and Jewish preachers warned of apocalyptic consequences for the sins of industrial society. Citing biblical prophecies, they foretold that humanity's greed and disregard for God's teachings would lead to catastrophic events;

wars, plagues, and natural disasters. Such prophecies appealed to people's fear of divine punishment and reinforced the belief that society was heading toward a reckoning.

Social Activists and the Call for Reform

Labor Activists Warn of Social Collapse: Labor leaders and activists cautioned that the extreme inequality and oppression of workers would eventually destabilize society. Figures like Mother Jones and Eugene V. Debs rallied for workers' rights, arguing that without reform, the world would face violent class struggles. Their warnings spoke of a time when the "oppressed" would no longer tolerate exploitation and would take drastic action, echoing apocalyptic themes of justice and retribution.

The Muckrakers and Exposure of Industrial Corruption: Journalists known as "muckrakers" investigated and exposed the corruption, greed, and exploitation endemic in industrial society. Figures like Upton Sinclair, author of *The Jungle*, highlighted the appalling conditions faced by workers in the meatpacking industry, bringing public awareness to the need for social reform. Their reports stirred public anger, demanding change and warning that if society did not address these injustices, it would collapse under its moral failings.

Warnings Against Environmental Degradation: As industry continued to consume natural resources at an unprecedented rate, concerns about environmental degradation emerged. The pollution of rivers, destruction of forests, and blackened skies symbolized humanity's unchecked ambition. Some activists foresaw the long-term impacts of these actions, predicting that the relentless exploitation of nature would lead to disastrous consequences for both humanity and the planet, a warning echoed today as environmental concerns remain pressing.

Philosophical and Spiritual Reflections on Materialism

Existential Writings on Meaninglessness and Alienation: Thinkers like Søren Kierkegaard and later existentialists like Friedrich Nietzsche highlighted the alienation and spiritual void created by modern society's focus on wealth and production. They argued that a life driven by material gain alone was ultimately empty, leaving individuals disconnected from any deeper purpose. Nietzsche famously warned of a "God is dead" world, where traditional morals and values were replaced by a nihilistic pursuit of power and control; conditions he believed would lead to cultural collapse.

Critiques of Modern Idolatry: Many philosophers described the relentless pursuit of technology, wealth, and power as a form of idolatry. Max Weber spoke of the "iron cage" of rationality, where society became entrapped in a mechanical, profit-driven mindset that stripped life of meaning. These critiques argued that humanity had replaced spiritual values with secular idols of industry and ambition, a trend seen as dangerous and spiritually corrosive.

Warnings from Spiritual Leaders on the Path to Ruin: Eastern spiritual leaders, like Swami Vivekananda and other Indian mystics, also warned of the dangers of materialism. They saw Western society's focus on wealth as spiritually destructive, advocating instead for balance, simplicity, and inner peace. These spiritual leaders suggested that if humanity failed to pursue a higher path, it would suffer not only material but also spiritual decline.

Legacy and Long-term Implications

The warnings from this period left a lasting impact, influencing movements and ideologies that sought to counteract the materialistic culture of industrial society:

Emergence of Ethical Business Practices: Growing awareness of the consequences of unchecked ambition eventually led to more ethical business practices. Business owners and corporations began to consider the social and environmental impact of their actions, giving rise to concepts like corporate social responsibility, which focused on creating a more balanced and humane economic system.

Rise of Social and Environmental Movements: The concerns voiced by early thinkers, activists, and religious leaders provided a foundation for modern social and environmental movements. From labour rights to environmental conservation, these movements aimed to mitigate the consequences of industrial exploitation and protect society's most vulnerable.

Spiritual and Philosophical Re-evaluation: The existential and spiritual crises spurred by the Industrial Revolution continued to inspire new philosophical and religious reflections on materialism and the meaning of life. Thinkers, writers, and spiritual leaders urged people to seek fulfillment beyond wealth, fostering a modern emphasis on mindfulness, simplicity, and holistic well-being.

The Modern Environmental and Social "Apocalypse": Many contemporary warnings about environmental collapse, global inequality, and ethical consumption draw directly from the concerns raised during the Industrial Revolution. The "apocalyptic" language used today in discussions of climate change, social inequality, and economic injustice echoes the alarms first sounded in the 19th century.

The Industrial Revolution's legacy includes both its remarkable achievements and its darker aspects. The warnings against unchecked ambition and greed resonate as timeless lessons, underscoring the dangers of valuing material progress over moral integrity. As society continues to grapple with issues like inequality, environmental degradation, and spiritual disconnection, these early critiques serve as a reminder that a balance between ambition and compassion is essential for a just and sustainable world. If ignored, these warnings imply a future fraught with consequences that could irrevocably alter the fabric of society; an apocalyptic prospect for the world.

Twentieth Century Conflicts and the Prophecies of Destruction

World War I and the Birth of Global Conflict (1914-1918)

The Great War: A Global Scale of Death and Destruction Previously Unseen

World War I, known at the time as "The Great War," was a conflict on a scale of death and destruction never before witnessed. Spanning from 1914 to 1918, this war engulfed much of Europe, involving nations from across the world and fundamentally reshaping the social, political, and moral landscape of the 20th century. The war claimed the lives of approximately 17 million people, including civilians and military personnel, and left millions more wounded and traumatized. It introduced a new era of modern warfare, with devastating technological advancements and a ruthless efficiency in killing that shocked the world. This "war to end all wars" was characterized not only by its brutal tactics but also by the global sense of despair and hopelessness it unleashed, affecting generations to come.

Causes of World War I: A Tangle of Alliances and Rising Tensions

The roots of World War I lay in complex international alliances, imperial ambitions, and rising nationalist sentiments. Leading up to the war, European powers had formed two main alliance systems: the Triple Entente, comprising France, Russia, and Britain; and the Triple Alliance, including Germany, Austria-Hungary, and Italy. These alliances were intended to create a balance of power, but instead, they created a fragile, volatile system that meant any regional conflict could escalate quickly to involve multiple nations.

Nationalism and Imperialism: National pride and a sense of superiority fuelled by nationalist movements grew throughout Europe, creating tension among empires that sought to assert their power. Nations like Germany, eager to expand their influence, viewed Britain and France as competitors in both political dominance and colonial ambition.

Militarism and Arms Race: An unprecedented military buildup occurred among the major powers, resulting in massive armies and arsenals. The glorification of military strength and readiness, known as militarism, became the norm. Both Germany and Britain, in particular, were locked in an arms race, each building powerful navies, while other countries expanded their armies. The development of more advanced and deadly weapons, including machine guns, artillery, and chemical gases, set the stage for unprecedented casualties.

Assassination of Archduke Franz Ferdinand: The immediate spark that ignited World War I was the assassination of Archduke Franz Ferdinand of Austria-Hungary and his wife, Sophie, in Sarajevo on June 28, 1914. A Serbian nationalist named Gavrilo Princip carried out the assassination, driven by resentment toward Austria-Hungary's rule over Serbian populations. This event triggered a series of diplomatic crises, ultimatums, and mobilizations, eventually drawing in all the major powers due to their alliances and resulting in a chain reaction that quickly escalated into a full-scale war.

The Horrors of Trench Warfare and New Technology

World War I introduced the grim reality of trench warfare, a form of combat in which soldiers dug extensive networks of trenches along the Western Front, particularly in Belgium and northern France. Life in the trenches was harrowing, with soldiers enduring brutal conditions, exposed to mud, cold, and disease, often under constant threat from artillery shells, gas attacks, and snipers.

Stalemate and Attrition: Trench warfare created a brutal stalemate that made rapid movement nearly impossible. Opposing forces were often only yards apart, separated by a desolate area known as "no man's land." The strategy of each side was to wear down the enemy through attrition, resulting in countless battles where little ground was gained, and both sides suffered staggering casualties. Iconic battles such as the Battle of the Somme and the Battle of Verdun became infamous for their immense loss of life and minimal territorial gain.

Chemical Warfare and Machine Guns: World War I was the first major conflict to see the use of chemical weapons on a large scale. Poisonous gases like chlorine, phosgene, and mustard gas were deployed, causing horrific injuries and death. Soldiers were often left blinded, with severe respiratory damage or chemical burns. Machine guns also revolutionized the battlefield, capable of mowing down waves of soldiers in seconds. These weapons contributed to the sheer scale of carnage and marked the war as one of unprecedented brutality.

Artillery Barrages and Psychological Trauma: Artillery accounted for a significant proportion of battlefield casualties. Constant shelling created a psychological toll on soldiers, many of whom experienced "shell shock," now understood as a form of post-traumatic stress disorder. The unending explosions and devastation created an environment of unrelenting fear and helplessness, with soldiers often suffering mental breakdowns.

Aircraft and Tanks: Though still in their infancy, aircraft were used for reconnaissance and eventually aerial combat and bombing missions. The tank, introduced later in the war, was designed to overcome the stalemate of trench warfare, though early models were unreliable and vulnerable to breakdowns. These new technologies marked the beginning of mechanized warfare and foreshadowed even more devastating advancements in future conflicts.

Global Involvement and Devastation Beyond Europe

Although the majority of fighting took place in Europe, World War I was a global conflict that drew in countries from around the world. European empires, which controlled vast territories in Asia, Africa, and the Middle East, enlisted soldiers from their colonies, making the war truly global. Countries like India, Australia, and Canada provided troops for the British Empire, while French colonies also contributed significantly.

Involvement of the United States: Initially neutral, the United States entered the war in 1917, following repeated German attacks on American shipping and the infamous Zimmermann Telegram, in which Germany attempted to entice Mexico into an alliance against the United States. The entry of American forces gave the Allied powers a much-needed boost in manpower and resources, ultimately tipping the scales toward an Allied victory.

Fighting in the Middle East and Africa: The war extended to the Ottoman Empire, which had joined the Central Powers, leading to significant battles in the Middle East. In Africa, European colonies fought each other in the hopes of expanding their influence, often disregarding the lives of native populations.

Economic and Environmental Impact: The scale of destruction during World War I left much of Europe devastated. Cities, villages, and infrastructure were reduced to rubble, and agricultural land was scarred by trenches, shell holes, and unexploded munitions. Economies were strained to the breaking point, leading to shortages, inflation, and poverty among civilians. Environmental damage was widespread, with areas like the Somme and Verdun rendered nearly uninhabitable for years due to the contamination from chemicals and explosives.

Moral and Social Collapse: A World Left Traumatized

The war shattered traditional ideas about honour, heroism, and human decency. What had begun as a conflict framed in terms of national pride devolved into a prolonged bloodbath, leaving many disillusioned with notions of duty and patriotism. For millions of soldiers and civilians, the senseless slaughter and disregard for human life created a profound sense of hopelessness and moral decay.

Destruction of Faith in Institutions: Many lost faith in their governments, religious institutions, and even the idea of progress itself. The optimism of the 19th century, built on advancements in science, industry, and philosophy, gave way to a bleak, disillusioned worldview. Intellectuals, artists, and writers of the time reflected this shift, with works that captured the horror and futility of the conflict, such as Erich Maria Remarque's novel *All Quiet on the Western Front* and Wilfred Owen's war poetry.

The Lost Generation: World War I created what came to be known as the "Lost Generation," a term popularized by writers like Ernest Hemingway to describe those who were disillusioned and traumatized by the war. Many survivors found it difficult to reintegrate into civilian life, haunted by memories of the trenches and struggling with mental and physical scars. This generation experienced a loss of purpose and direction, grappling with existential despair in a world that seemed to have abandoned all moral and spiritual values.

Rise of Apocalyptic and Prophetic Thought: The scale of death and devastation in World War I led some to believe that the conflict was a sign of an impending apocalypse. Both religious leaders and secular thinkers spoke of the war as a divine judgment on humanity's sins. Prophecies, sermons, and publications at the time suggested that the war might be a precursor to an era of even greater suffering, an idea that gained traction as Europe was plunged into economic and political instability in the war's aftermath.

The Treaty of Versailles and the Seeds of Future Conflict

The Treaty of Versailles, signed in 1919, officially ended the war, but it laid the foundation for future conflicts. The treaty imposed harsh penalties on Germany, including massive reparations, territorial losses, and strict military limitations. While the intention was to prevent future aggression, these punitive measures fostered resentment and economic hardship in Germany, leading to political radicalization and the eventual rise of Adolf Hitler and the Nazi regime.

Economic Strain and Humiliation: The reparations demanded by the treaty crippled Germany's economy, leading to hyperinflation, unemployment, and widespread poverty. Many Germans viewed the treaty as an unjust humiliation, sowing the seeds of nationalist fervour that would later fuel World War II.

The League of Nations' Weakness: The League of Nations was established to prevent future wars, but it lacked real authority and the means to enforce its decisions. The United States, despite President Wilson's advocacy for the League, ultimately did not join, weakening the organization. Without the power to mediate effectively, the League struggled to prevent further aggression in the years leading up to World War II.

A Fragile Peace and Ominous Portents: The Treaty of Versailles ended the immediate fighting, but it did little to address the underlying tensions. Nationalist movements, economic instability, and unresolved resentments made the peace fragile, creating conditions ripe for future conflict. For many, the Great War was not just a horrific chapter of history but a sign of darker times to come; a harbinger of an apocalyptic struggle that would continue to haunt the 20th century.

Emerging Sense of Doom: The Beginning of "Wars to End All Wars"

The devastation of World War I left the world with a lingering sense of doom, as people began to recognize that this might not be the end of global conflict, but the beginning of a new, far darker era. The unprecedented loss of life, combined with the horrors of modern warfare, created a haunting atmosphere in which the very idea of civilization seemed fragile and threatened. The phrase "the war to end all wars," initially intended as an optimistic belief that humanity would never again repeat such violence, soon took on an ironic tone. Instead, people began to fear that World War I was merely the opening act of a series of increasingly devastating conflicts.

Disillusionment with Peace Efforts

The Treaty of Versailles, signed in 1919, aimed to establish a lasting peace, but it left many unresolved tensions. Though the treaty officially ended the war, its terms were so punitive toward Germany that they inadvertently planted the seeds for future aggression and resentment. Germans felt humiliated, economically strangled, and unjustly blamed for a war that involved multiple nations and complex causes. Across Europe, people recognized that the treaty had not fostered genuine reconciliation, and this fuelled a pervasive sense of unease.

League of Nations and Fragile Peace: The League of Nations, intended to maintain global peace, was a groundbreaking attempt to prevent future wars through diplomacy. However, the

League's lack of enforcement power, combined with the absence of key nations like the United States, meant it was largely ineffective. Many citizens across Europe, especially those who had suffered the most, doubted the League's ability to truly prevent another conflict, and the dream of lasting peace began to fade.

Economic Strain and Political Instability: The economic consequences of the war were devastating. Many European countries were left with massive debts, and postwar inflation caused suffering among the working classes. In Germany, hyperinflation led to poverty and despair, and political radicalization became more common as people searched for solutions to their worsening conditions. The economic instability weakened governments and set the stage for the rise of extreme ideologies, particularly in Germany and Italy, where fascism and ultranationalism took root.

Mistrust and Isolationism: The war made people wary of international alliances and treaties. Countries like the United States turned inward, adopting isolationist policies, while Europeans felt disillusioned by the idea of global cooperation. Instead of creating a sense of unity, World War I fractured trust between nations, and the fractured alliances made the international landscape more volatile.

The Phrase "War to End All Wars": Optimism Turned to Irony

When British author H.G. Wells popularized the phrase "the war to end all wars," it reflected a hopeful sentiment that World War I's destruction would shock humanity into ensuring that such horror would never happen again. Politicians and public figures echoed this sentiment, believing the war's impact was so extreme that no one would dare to repeat it. However, as the years passed, this optimism soured into bitter irony. People recognized that the nature of warfare itself had changed and that humans now possessed the capability to annihilate each other on a massive scale.

The Cynicism of a War-Torn Generation: Veterans and civilians alike found it increasingly difficult to believe that peace could last. A deep-seated cynicism took root, especially among the "Lost Generation," the men and women who had lived through the war. Many became disillusioned with previous notions of heroism and patriotism, instead seeing these values as mere propaganda that had led to senseless slaughter. This generation embraced a bleak view of the future, one that foresaw further conflicts rather than a newfound age of peace.

Literature and Art Reflecting a Darker Worldview: The cultural response to the war was immediate and profound. Writers, poets, and artists across Europe and America produced works that reflected the disillusionment, grief, and bitterness of the postwar period. Literature like Erich Maria Remarque's *All Quiet on the Western Front* and the poetry of Wilfred Owen and Siegfried Sassoon depicted the horrors of war and questioned the values that had led to such destruction. These works captured a collective sense of foreboding, an acknowledgment that humanity might be on a self-destructive path.

Rise of Apocalyptic Thought and Prophecy: The sense of doom sparked a resurgence in apocalyptic thinking. Religious leaders and secular thinkers alike began interpreting World War I as a harbinger of even greater destruction, perhaps even the prophesied end times. Many saw the war as a divine warning or judgment, believing that humanity was being punished for its sins and that future wars would only increase in magnitude and suffering. Books, pamphlets, and sermons circulated with themes of judgment and repentance, urging people to recognize the war as a sign of worse things to come unless they changed their ways.

Technological Advancements and the Potential for Total Destruction

World War I demonstrated the terrifying potential of industrial warfare, as new weapons and strategies brought unprecedented levels of destruction. For the first time, people saw how modern technology could be harnessed not for progress but for mass killing. The rapid advancement of military technology foreshadowed a future where humans could potentially destroy entire civilizations with a few devastating innovations.

The Threat of Chemical Weapons and Biological Warfare: The use of poison gas during World War I horrified soldiers and civilians alike, showing how science could be used to create weapons of mass destruction. The psychological scars left by gas attacks gave rise to fears of future chemical or biological warfare on a larger scale. People began to fear that technology itself had become an "idol" of sorts, a tool that, if unchecked, could lead to humanity's self-destruction.

Air Power and Strategic Bombing: Aircraft played a relatively minor role in World War I, but their potential was unmistakable. The war saw the first instances of bombing civilians from the air, a tactic that would later be employed on a terrifying scale during World War II. The idea of entire cities being targeted from the sky became a new and frightening possibility, making people question how humanity could control the forces it had unleashed.

The Beginning of Nuclear Thought: Although nuclear technology was still decades away from development, the war inspired scientific breakthroughs that would later lead to the splitting of the atom. Intellectuals, scientists, and some military strategists began to theorize about the potential of atomic energy and its implications for weaponry. Though this technology had not yet materialized, the idea of humanity harnessing such a destructive force hinted at an apocalyptic future where war could bring about total annihilation.

The Shift in Global Consciousness: A Dark Foreboding

The psychological impact of World War I was profound, altering how people viewed themselves, their nations, and the future. The war shattered the idealistic belief in progress and human perfectibility, replacing it with an awareness of humanity's capacity for evil and self-destruction. This shift in global consciousness would shape politics, culture, and religion throughout the 20th century, leaving an indelible mark on the way people approached future conflicts.

Rise of Authoritarianism and Fascism: The war's aftermath created a fertile ground for authoritarian leaders to seize power. People, weary of instability and hardship, sought strong leaders who promised order and security. In Germany, Italy, and other nations, fascist movements emerged, led by figures like Adolf Hitler and Benito Mussolini. These leaders capitalized on the sense of doom and loss of faith in democratic institutions, presenting themselves as saviours in a chaotic world. This marked the beginning of a new era of political extremism, which would ultimately lead to World War II.

Questioning of Morality and Purpose: In the war's wake, philosophers and intellectuals began to question the nature of humanity and the meaning of life. Existentialism, a philosophical movement that explored themes of absurdity, despair, and individual purpose, gained popularity. Thinkers like Jean-Paul Sartre and Albert Camus explored the idea that life might be inherently meaningless, and that individuals must create their own purpose in a world marked by violence and chaos.

Fear of Future Catastrophe: The fear of another war weighed heavily on the minds of people and leaders alike. Though some politicians and intellectuals tried to remain optimistic, the sense of foreboding was impossible to ignore. Many came to see World War I not as an isolated tragedy but as a precursor to even more horrific conflicts. The phrase "war to end all wars" became a grim prophecy rather than a hopeful assertion, as people began to understand that humanity might be trapped in an endless cycle of violence and retribution.

New Spirituality and Prophetic Movements: The war's psychological toll also spurred interest in new forms of spirituality, prophecy, and religious revival. People sought answers to explain the suffering they had endured, turning to religious leaders who preached about apocalyptic visions and divine judgment. Prophetic movements gained followers, particularly among those who believed the world was nearing an era of wrath and purification. This rise in apocalyptic thought would shape much of the 20th-century religious landscape, particularly as World War II loomed on the horizon.

World War I was a turning point in global history, marking the beginning of an age where the scale and potential for destruction were unprecedented. The sense of doom that emerged after the war was not merely the product of immediate trauma but a reflection of a world that had glimpsed its own capacity for annihilation. Humanity was now on a path toward "wars to end all wars," a dark prophecy suggesting that unless wisdom and restraint prevailed, future conflicts could bring about the end of civilization itself. This realization created a pervasive sense of dread that would echo through the 20th century and beyond, as humanity faced the reality of its own self-destructive power.

William Branham's Teachings and Prophecies on Coming Judgment and Redemption

Branham's ministry emerged during a period of great social and spiritual upheaval, following World War II and the early days of the Cold War, when many people sought spiritual answers to make sense of the rapid changes and global uncertainties. Through his sermons, visions, and claimed miracles, Branham warned of an impending period of divine judgment and prophesied a need for humanity to return to righteous, God-centered lives. His messages of coming judgment and redemption struck a chord with people who felt that society was straying from moral values and heading toward an apocalyptic end.

Branham's Early Life and Calling

William Branham was born in Kentucky in 1909 to a poor family and experienced what he described as supernatural occurrences from an early age. He recounted a vision at the age of three where he heard a voice calling him to a special mission, and these experiences intensified as he grew older. Throughout his ministry, Branham claimed that God had chosen him as a messenger to bring a final message to the world, a warning before the end times and a call to prepare for the return of Christ.

Branham's ministry took shape during the late 1940s, and his healing services attracted large crowds as people flocked to see and experience what they believed were miracles. He became one of the most prominent figures in the Pentecostal and Charismatic movements, which emphasized the gifts of the Holy Spirit, including healing, prophecy, and speaking in tongues. Branham, however, set himself apart with his unique claims about his mission, his visions, and the detailed prophecies he shared.

1. The Downfall of America

William Branham's prophecy about America's downfall stemmed from his belief that the nation was straying dangerously from its Christian roots. He warned that America's increasing pursuit of wealth, power, and individualism had replaced devotion to God. This shift was more than just a cultural change for Branham; it was a spiritual catastrophe, one that would bring divine judgment upon the country.

Branham often spoke about the spiritual consequences of materialism. To him, America's obsession with prosperity blinded people to spiritual truths, creating a society more focused on external success than internal devotion. He saw America as a land once founded on godly principles but now corrupted by greed, moral decay, and secular values.

In his vision of the future, Branham prophesied that America would face a severe downfall, not just economically or politically, but spiritually. He believed this collapse would come as a direct result of abandoning moral standards and turning away from the values that, in his view, once made America a "blessed" nation. He described this eventual judgment as both inevitable and catastrophic, urging Americans to repent and return to their faith.

2. The Seven Visions

In 1933, Branham experienced a powerful series of visions that would shape his ministry and prophetic outlook for the rest of his life. These seven visions, which he regarded as divine revelations, painted a foreboding picture of the future and became a central part of his teachings.

Vision 1: Branham saw Italian dictator Benito Mussolini invading Ethiopia. He predicted that Mussolini would suffer a terrible end, one marked by disgrace and public shame. This vision was significant because it symbolized the violent ambitions of men in power and how such pride would ultimately lead to destruction.

Vision 2: He saw Adolf Hitler rising to power in Germany and plunging the world into a devastating war. Branham interpreted Hitler's rule as a symbol of evil incarnate, reflecting humanity's susceptibility to charismatic but corrupt leaders. This vision foreshadowed the horrors of World War II and reinforced Branham's belief in the destructive potential of unchecked authority.

Vision 3: He saw a worldwide spread of communism and atheism, ideologies that Branham believed were opposed to God. He viewed the spread of these beliefs as part of a larger spiritual decay, representing society's turn away from divine truths. He warned that these ideologies would drive a wedge between humanity and God.

Vision 4: Branham envisioned a world where technological advancements, specifically in transportation, would astonish people. He foresaw driverless cars and bubble-like vehicles, predicting a time when human achievements would reach unparalleled heights. But he also cautioned that reliance on technology could lead people to pride and distraction from spiritual matters.

Vision 5: This vision depicted a powerful woman rising to influence in America. Branham speculated that she could symbolize either a literal leader or a spirit of deception within the church. He feared her influence would lead people astray from true faith, marking a dangerous period of spiritual confusion.

Vision 6: In this vision, Branham saw society collapsing morally, leading to a time of unprecedented violence and confusion. This vision mirrored his concerns about moral decay and painted a stark picture of humanity devolving into chaos due to spiritual neglect.

Vision 7: The final and most chilling vision depicted the end of America as we know it. Branham foresaw an apocalyptic scene in which America faced complete destruction. He suggested that this might occur through nuclear warfare or other catastrophic means. This vision was the culmination of his warnings, symbolizing the ultimate judgment that would come if society did not repent and return to God.

Together, these seven visions formed a narrative of warning and consequence, where Branham's prophetic insight aimed to alert people to the dangers of a world drifting away from divine principles.

3. Teachings on Modesty

Modesty, especially in dress and appearance, was a cornerstone of Branham's teachings. He viewed modesty as an outward expression of an individual's respect for God, a way to honour one's body and soul. In particular, he focused on the role of women, emphasizing that modesty in women's dress was essential to preserving purity and humility.

Branham was concerned that society's standards of beauty and fashion were becoming dangerously immodest, reflecting a deeper moral crisis. He warned against the influence of media and popular culture, which he felt promoted sensuality over spirituality. For him, dressing modestly was not simply a matter of personal choice but a spiritual discipline, one that helped protect the soul from worldly distractions.

He often spoke out against modern fashion trends, believing that they led people, particularly women, away from their true identity in Christ. Branham saw immodesty as symptomatic of a broader moral decay, with people valuing appearances over inner virtue. He urged his followers to reject societal norms that conflicted with biblical principles, seeing this as essential to maintaining a godly life.

4. Moral Decline as an Apocalyptic Sign

Branham believed that the world's moral decline was a clear indicator of the end times. He saw evidence of this decline in various aspects of culture; entertainment, politics, education, and even religious institutions. For him, the normalization of immorality, from promiscuity to dishonesty, was a sign that humanity was drifting further from God.

He was especially concerned with how entertainment and media glorified sinful behaviours, desensitizing society to values that were once seen as sacred. Branham warned that this moral decay would bring about divine wrath, as God could not tolerate humanity's indifference to righteousness forever. This shift in values, according to Branham, fulfilled prophecies about the end times, where society would become "lovers of pleasure more than lovers of God."

Branham's teachings on moral decay were rooted in his conviction that humanity was heading toward judgment. He saw the erosion of traditional morals as a prelude to apocalyptic events, a sign that the world was nearing its end.

5. The True Bride of Christ

Branham preached about a remnant of believers he called the "Bride of Christ." He believed that, in the last days, only a small group would remain truly faithful to God's teachings, resisting the influence of a morally corrupt society. This Bride, he taught, would be set apart from mainstream churches and would adhere strictly to biblical principles.

The Bride, in Branham's teachings, represented the true followers of Christ, those who would stand firm despite widespread deception and moral compromise. He viewed the larger Christian world as having lost its way, blending too much with secular values and traditions. In contrast, the Bride would remain pure and dedicated, untouched by the world's distractions.

For Branham, the Bride was not just a concept but a call to action for believers to recommit to their faith and avoid the compromises of mainstream religion. He saw this group as the only ones who would be saved in the end times, rewarded for their unwavering faith.

6. The Modern World's Misunderstanding of Life

Branham often spoke about the modern world's misguided understanding of life. He criticized society for focusing on wealth, success, and scientific progress, which he believed led to spiritual emptiness. For Branham, life's purpose was not found in material achievements but in devotion to God and adherence to biblical principles.

He warned that the modern emphasis on self-fulfillment and personal freedom had led people to believe they could live without accountability to God. This, he argued, created a culture where people misunderstood the true purpose of life, leading to confusion and a sense of meaninglessness.

Branham's message was that life's meaning could only be found in a relationship with God. He saw the world's rejection of this truth as a fundamental error, one that would have dire consequences. According to Branham, the modern world's inability to grasp this reality was a sign that humanity was moving toward judgment and would face the consequences of its spiritual neglect.

Teachings on The End of Days

William Branham's teachings on the end of days encapsulated a rich tapestry of prophetic insights, interpretations of scripture, and visions that he believed revealed the impending culmination of history. Here's a detailed overview of his views on the end times, encompassing his prophecies, interpretations, and the overarching themes he emphasized:

1. The Imminence of the End Times

Branham firmly believed that the end of days was imminent, suggesting that the signs foretold in the Bible were unfolding before the eyes of humanity. He often referenced Matthew 24, where Jesus spoke of wars, rumours of wars, famines, and earthquakes as precursors to His return. Branham interpreted the growing intensity of global conflicts and natural disasters as evidence that the end was near.

He articulated a sense of urgency, often calling on believers to be vigilant and prepared for the return of Christ. Branham's insistence on the immediacy of the end times was rooted in his conviction that the world was spiralling into moral decay and that God's judgment was about to be realized.

2. The Role of the Antichrist

Branham spoke extensively about the figure of the Antichrist, portraying him as a deceiver who would rise to power during the end times. He believed that the Antichrist would emerge from a corrupt religious system, deceiving many and leading them away from the true teachings of Christ.

He often connected this figure to the moral and spiritual decline of society, suggesting that the Antichrist would exploit humanity's weaknesses, promoting a false sense of peace while masking his true nature. Branham emphasized that many who identified as Christians would be misled, demonstrating the necessity for discernment and adherence to biblical truth.

Branham also warned that the Antichrist would utilize modern technologies and societal changes to gain influence, making it essential for believers to remain steadfast in their faith and vigilant against deception.

3. The Rapture and the True Bride

A cornerstone of Branham's eschatology was the belief in the Rapture, where true believers would be taken up to meet Christ before the great tribulation. He emphasized that only the "Bride of Christ"; those who had maintained faithfulness to God's Word; would be included in this event. This group was seen as distinct from the larger Christian population, which Branham believed had compromised its beliefs.

Branham's teachings posited that the Rapture would be a sudden and miraculous event, often accompanied by great signs and wonders. He spoke of the need for believers to be spiritually prepared, emphasizing personal holiness and a deep relationship with God as prerequisites for being part of the Bride.

4. Judgment and Tribulation

Branham warned of a time of great tribulation that would precede the end of days, characterized by suffering and turmoil. He described this period as a necessary purification for the world, where the consequences of humanity's rebellion against God would become manifest.

He often referenced prophetic scriptures that spoke of judgment, including the book of Revelation, which details the tribulations that would occur. Branham depicted these events not just as future occurrences but as spiritual realities that believers needed to confront in their lives today.

His perspective on tribulation was both cautionary and hopeful; while he warned of the severity of the times to come, he also emphasized that for believers, there was a promise of redemption and eternal life through faith in Christ.

5. The Second Coming of Christ

A pivotal aspect of Branham's eschatological views was the Second Coming of Christ. He taught that this event would not only mark the culmination of history but would also bring about a new order in which righteousness would reign.

Branham often emphasized the significance of Christ returning for His Bride, highlighting that His coming would fulfill the promises made in scripture. He described this event as one filled with glory and power, contrasting it with the current state of the world marred by sin and decay.

In his sermons, he articulated a vision of the end times where Christ would reign on earth, establishing a kingdom of peace and justice. This hope served as a motivating force for his followers, encouraging them to persevere through the trials of life in anticipation of this glorious return.

6. Signs of the Times

Branham was known for identifying various signs of the times, which he believed indicated the proximity of the end. He pointed to events like natural disasters, societal upheaval, moral decline, and political unrest as confirmations of biblical prophecy coming to fruition.

He placed significant emphasis on the moral state of humanity, viewing the abandonment of traditional values and the rise of immorality as direct indicators of the impending judgment. Branham believed that the spiritual condition of society was intertwined with the fulfillment of prophecies related to the end of days.

7. The Restoration of the True Church

Branham believed that the end times would also witness a restoration of the true church, one that would return to the fundamental teachings and practices of the early apostles. He emphasized that this restoration was necessary to counteract the corruption that had infiltrated mainstream Christianity.

He encouraged believers to seek a deeper understanding of their faith and to adhere closely to scriptural teachings. For Branham, this restoration was both a spiritual awakening and a call to action for believers to prepare for the return of Christ.

The Holocaust and the Rebirth of Israel (1933-1948)

Nazi rise and the systematic persecution of Jews, a near-extermination echoing biblical prophecy

The rise of the Nazi regime in Germany and the ensuing Holocaust is a story filled with tragedy, resilience, and profound implications for the Jewish people and the world at large. It is a narrative that intertwines with biblical prophecies and serves as a haunting reminder of humanity's capacity for both darkness and hope.

The Nazi Rise and Systematic Persecution of Jews

In the aftermath of World War I, Germany lay in ruins. The Treaty of Versailles had stripped the nation of its pride, leaving millions in despair and economic turmoil. As the country grappled with humiliation and hardship, whispers of blame echoed through the streets, coalescing around a singular target: the Jewish community. Once an integral part of German society, Jews found themselves increasingly marginalized, painted as the scapegoats for the nation's woes.

In this climate of fear and resentment, Adolf Hitler emerged, his voice resonating with those hungry for change. The charismatic leader of the National Socialist German Workers' Party (Nazi Party) channelled the nation's anger into a fervent ideology, one that placed blame squarely on the shoulders of Jews. Hitler's propaganda painted them as the enemy within, responsible for Germany's misfortunes, and the populace, weary of their suffering, began to rally around his vision.

With alarming speed, the Nazis seized control of the government. The Nuremberg Laws of 1935 marked a turning point, institutionalizing racial discrimination and stripping Jews of their rights. As the laws took effect, Jewish shops were vandalized, synagogues were set ablaze, and families found themselves increasingly isolated from their communities. The once-vibrant Jewish life in Germany began to dim, eclipsed by an ominous shadow.

Then came Kristallnacht, the Night of Broken Glass, in November 1938. Across Germany and Austria, a coordinated attack unfolded. Jewish businesses were smashed, homes invaded, and synagogues turned to ash. The sound of shattering glass echoed through the streets, a haunting prelude to the horrors that lay ahead. As families huddled in fear, they could not yet comprehend the full scale of the impending catastrophe.

When World War II broke out in 1939, the Nazis implemented their plan with ruthless efficiency. Jews were rounded up and herded into crowded ghettos, their lives reduced to mere survival amid squalor and deprivation. In these cramped quarters, fear and despair festered, yet the spirit of resilience flickered within many. Families clung to hope, sharing stories, celebrating traditions, and finding solace in their shared faith even as the world around them crumbled.

But hope was a fragile thing. The Nazis escalated their campaign, formalizing the "Final Solution" in 1942; a chilling euphemism for their intent to exterminate every Jewish person in Europe. Mobile killing units, known as Einsatzgruppen, followed the German army into Eastern Europe, conducting mass executions. In the quiet of the forests, the cries of innocent lives were silenced, buried in shallow graves.

Extermination camps, such as Auschwitz and Treblinka, became the face of this horror. Trains laden with unsuspecting Jews arrived daily, only to be met with the grim reality of gas chambers disguised as showers. The industrialized killing of millions unfolded with horrifying efficiency, reducing human lives to mere numbers in the eyes of their captors.

As the smoke rose from the crematoriums, the world outside began to take notice, yet too often, it was too late. The apathy and complicity of many allowed the horror to persist unchecked. Among those who remained silent were even some who professed faith, questioning how a just and loving God could allow such evil to unfold.

In the midst of this darkness, the Holocaust became a crucible for faith and identity. Jewish leaders sought to find meaning in their suffering, echoing the cries of the Old Testament prophets who had warned of judgment for the unfaithful. As they looked to their scriptures, they found a bitter resonance with their current plight, recognizing the historical cycles of persecution and redemption that had characterized their people.

Yet, even in this abyss of despair, the seeds of hope began to take root. The Holocaust's aftermath ignited a profound shift in Jewish consciousness. The world had witnessed the unthinkable, and from that devastation arose a renewed sense of purpose. The call for a Jewish homeland intensified, culminating in the establishment of Israel in 1948; a moment seen by many as a fulfillment of ancient prophecies.

As the new nation took shape, it symbolized not just survival but a powerful rebirth. Israel represented hope amid despair, a place where Jewish culture could flourish free from the shadows of persecution. It became a living testament to resilience and the enduring spirit of a people who had endured the worst humanity could offer.

The story of the Nazi rise and the Holocaust serves as a solemn reminder of the depths of human cruelty, but also of the heights of resilience and faith. It is a narrative that echoes through history, urging us to remember and learn from the past, to stand against hatred, and to nurture hope in the face of despair. As we reflect on this chapter, we are reminded that the quest for justice, peace, and understanding continues, woven into the fabric of our shared humanity.

Establishment of the State of Israel in 1948: A Fulfillment of Prophecy

In the aftermath of World War II and the Holocaust, the urgency for a Jewish homeland reached a fever pitch. The devastation of the Holocaust had left deep scars, with six million Jews murdered, and a staggering number of survivors left displaced and traumatized. The horrific realities of genocide fuelled the resolve of Jewish leaders and communities to secure a safe haven where they could live freely and preserve their culture and identity.

Throughout history, Jewish prayers and aspirations had always pointed towards a return to Zion, the ancient homeland. The prophetic words of the Hebrew Scriptures resonated deeply: from the promises made to Abraham, Isaac, and Jacob to the visions of the prophets like Isaiah and Ezekiel, who foretold the return of the Jewish people to their land. These texts became sources of strength and hope, reinforcing the belief that the Jewish people were destined to reclaim their homeland.

The international community began to recognize the need for a Jewish state. The Balfour Declaration of 1917 had initially expressed British support for a "national home for the Jewish people" in Palestine, a sentiment that gained momentum in the years that followed. In 1947, the United Nations proposed a partition plan to resolve the ongoing tensions between Jewish and Arab communities in the region, recommending the establishment of independent Jewish and Arab states.

On May 14, 1948, David Ben-Gurion, the head of the Jewish Agency, proclaimed the establishment of the State of Israel. The declaration was made in Tel Aviv, just before the expiration of the British Mandate in Palestine. In his address, Ben-Gurion spoke of the "suffering of the Jewish people" and the historical connection of Jews to the land, evoking the ancient promise that had sustained them through centuries of exile. "The State of Israel will be open for Jewish immigration and the Ingathering of Exiles," he declared, embodying the long-held dream of return.

The establishment of Israel was immediately met with resistance from neighbouring Arab states. Within hours, armies from Egypt, Jordan, Syria, Iraq, and Lebanon invaded, intent on thwarting the nascent state. The ensuing conflict, known as the Arab-Israeli War of 1948, saw fierce fighting as Israeli forces defended their newly declared sovereignty against overwhelming odds.

Despite being vastly outnumbered, the determination and resolve of the Jewish fighters turned the tide in several key battles. The war resulted in significant territorial gains for Israel, but it also led to the displacement of many Palestinians, a complex and painful chapter that continues to impact the region today. The term "Nakba," or "catastrophe," is used by Palestinians to describe this period, highlighting the deep-seated grievances that emerged from the conflict.

As the dust settled, Israel emerged not only as a state but also as a symbol of resilience and rebirth. For Jews around the world, the establishment of the state was seen as the fulfillment of biblical prophecies. Many viewed it as a sign that God had not forgotten His people, fulfilling promises made centuries earlier. The ancient words of the prophets echoed in their hearts, affirming that the return to Zion was not merely a dream but a divinely ordained reality.

In the years following its establishment, Israel became a refuge for Jews from all corners of the globe. Survivors of the Holocaust, Jews from Arab countries, and those fleeing persecution found safety and a new beginning in the land of their ancestors. The country's development was marked by both challenges and triumphs as waves of immigrants arrived, each contributing to the diverse tapestry of Israeli society.

Culturally and spiritually, the rebirth of Israel sparked a renaissance of Jewish life and identity. Synagogues, schools, and community centres flourished, creating a vibrant atmosphere where Jewish culture could thrive. The revival of the Hebrew language, which had remained dormant for centuries, became a symbol of national identity and pride.

However, the establishment of Israel was not without challenges. The ongoing conflict with the Palestinians and the broader Arab world cast a long shadow over the state's existence. Issues of territory, identity, and coexistence became central to the national discourse, raising complex questions that remain unresolved to this day.

For many religious Jews, the creation of Israel represented a fulfillment of the prophecies concerning the end of days. The gathering of Jews to their homeland was interpreted as a precursor to the Messianic era, a time of ultimate redemption and peace. The hope that this new state would be a beacon of light and a fulfillment of divine promise persisted in the hearts of many.

As we reflect on the establishment of the State of Israel, it is essential to acknowledge both the triumphs and the tragedies that accompanied its birth. It stands as a testament to the resilience of a people who endured centuries of suffering, maintaining hope for a homeland where they could thrive. Yet, it also reminds us of the complexities of history, the ongoing struggles for justice and peace, and the imperative to seek understanding and reconciliation amid the shadows of the past.

The establishment of Israel was not merely a political event; it was the culmination of a long journey marked by faith, prophecy, and the unyielding spirit of a people who refused to surrender their dreams. It serves as a powerful reminder of the cyclical nature of history, where hope and despair often coexist, and where the quest for peace continues to shape the narrative of humanity.

The aftermath of World War II and the establishment of the State of Israel were inextricably linked to a resurgence of apocalyptic fears, particularly among Jewish communities worldwide. The experience of the Holocaust had deeply scarred the Jewish psyche, instilling a profound sense of vulnerability and existential threat. In this context, the survival of the Jewish people and their return to Israel took on a dual significance: not only as a physical return to their ancestral homeland but also as a spiritual and prophetic fulfillment that would shape their future.

Growing Apocalyptic Fears Tied to Jewish Survival and the Return to Israel

As Jews navigated the immediate aftermath of the Holocaust, the collective memory of suffering, persecution, and near-extermination loomed large. The question of survival became paramount, and with it emerged a heightened awareness of the precariousness of their existence. For many, the establishment of Israel was seen as a divine intervention, a chance for safety and the revival of a nation long subjected to displacement and oppression. However, alongside this hope, there were also fears that history could repeat itself.

Many Jewish leaders and thinkers began to articulate a growing concern regarding the fragility of the Jewish state. The very existence of Israel was viewed as a fulfillment of biblical prophecy, yet it also felt like a double-edged sword. The return to the land was fraught with peril, as hostility from neighbouring Arab states was immediate and fierce, leading to the 1948 Arab-Israeli War. For those who had experienced the horrors of the Holocaust, this conflict evoked memories of vulnerability and the precariousness of life.

The resurgence of anti-Semitism globally added to these fears. Jewish communities in various countries faced rising hostility, raising questions about the safety and viability of their existence outside of Israel. The memories of pogroms, the Inquisition, and the Holocaust haunted them, leading to a belief that the Jewish people would always be at risk of annihilation unless they remained steadfast in their commitment to their homeland.

Prophetic interpretations emerged that framed the establishment of Israel as a harbinger of the end times. Many saw the gathering of Jews to their homeland as a sign of the approaching Messianic age. However, with these hopes came apprehensions. The concept of survival intertwined with apocalyptic thought; was the establishment of Israel a signal that the end of days was imminent? Would the return of Jews to the land culminate in a divine judgment or an ultimate confrontation between good and evil?

These fears were amplified by religious leaders and thinkers who viewed current events through the lens of scripture. They interpreted ongoing conflicts in the Middle East as precursors to the apocalyptic battles foretold in the Bible, particularly the Battle of Armageddon, where it was believed that the forces of good would clash with those of evil. The tension between Israel and its neighbours became a focal point for these interpretations, reinforcing the idea that the survival of the Jewish state was essential for the fulfillment of prophetic events.

The theological implications were profound. Many began to link their personal and communal survival with the fate of the state of Israel. The belief that the return to the land was necessary for the coming of the Messiah deepened this connection. Religious narratives emphasized that a strong, unified Israel was vital for Jewish survival and for fulfilling God's promises to His people. This intertwining of faith, survival, and prophecy fostered a heightened sense of urgency among Jewish communities.

The rise of apocalyptic fears also sparked a renewed commitment to Jewish identity and continuity. The establishment of Israel not only provided a homeland but also invigorated Jewish culture, religious practice, and community cohesion. The return to Zion inspired a wave of Jewish immigration, known as Aliyah, as Jews from around the world sought to contribute to the new state. The hope of building a society rooted in justice, morality, and faith became a rallying cry for many.

However, the ongoing conflicts with Palestinians and the broader Arab world continued to exacerbate fears. Each outbreak of violence or political tension was interpreted as a sign of impending doom, leading to a cycle of anxiety and hope intertwined with the belief that Israel's survival was contingent on divine favor. The question loomed: would the Jewish state endure the challenges it faced, or would it be consumed by the very forces that sought its destruction?

This apocalyptic lens through which Jewish survival and the return to Israel were viewed created a complex narrative that spanned generations. It instilled a sense of resilience among Jews while also perpetuating the anxiety of potential calamity. The notion that they were living in prophetic times, facing existential threats yet holding onto hope for ultimate redemption, became a defining aspect of Jewish identity in the post-war era.

As the decades unfolded, the intertwining of apocalyptic fears with Jewish survival and the return to Israel would continue to shape the narrative of both the Jewish people and the broader Middle Eastern landscape. It would remind them of the fragility of existence, the weight of history, and the unyielding hope for a future defined by peace, justice, and fulfillment of ancient prophecies. In this way, the establishment of Israel was not only a geopolitical event but also a profound moment in the spiritual journey of a people longing for safety, meaning, and the ultimate promise of redemption.

World War II and the Antichrist Figure (1939-1945)

Fascist regimes and Adolf Hitler as an "Antichrist" figure; mass destruction on an unprecedented scale

In the chaos and brutality of World War II, Adolf Hitler emerged as a figure embodying unchecked power and evil, leading many to see him as a manifestation of the Antichrist. Under Hitler's reign, fascist ideology spread, drawing nations like Germany, Italy, and Japan into a militaristic, authoritarian alliance that sought domination over large portions of the world. Hitler's fervent speeches, his charismatic sway over the German people, and his ruthless actions against those he deemed inferior became synonymous with the ultimate expression of hatred and destruction. For many religious observers and theologians, the characteristics of Hitler's regime closely mirrored biblical warnings about a powerful, destructive figure who would rise in opposition to God and humanity, fitting the description of the Antichrist from prophecy.

The Rise of Fascist Regimes and Adolf Hitler

The foundation for Hitler's ideology began with the Treaty of Versailles, which placed heavy burdens on Germany following World War I. The harsh penalties, economic reparations, and territorial restrictions left Germany struggling with national humiliation and economic hardship. Many Germans felt a deep resentment, and Hitler, an obscure political agitator in the early 1920s, capitalized on this bitterness. Through his speeches, he promised a resurgence of German power, pride, and dominance, capturing the despair of the German people and turning it into a unified fervour for change.

As Hitler rose to power, he propagated the idea of an Aryan master race, elevating the notion of German purity while demonizing Jews, Roma, Slavs, disabled individuals, and anyone deemed "undesirable" by the Nazi regime. His propaganda machine painted these groups as the enemies of society, poisoning the "natural" order, and thus justifying their elimination. This racial ideology became the core of Hitler's ambitions for a "pure" empire and laid the groundwork for the mass exterminations that would follow.

The Antichrist Archetype and Hitler's Actions

The figure of the Antichrist has deep roots in Christian apocalyptic literature, depicted as an individual who would rise with charisma and influence to lead humanity astray, oppose Christ, and embody ultimate evil. Hitler's personality and actions resonated with this description. He was a figure who, through charm and coercion, led millions to follow his vision, blinding them to the cruelty that his plans would unleash. His speeches created an intense fervour, instilling a sense of mission and superiority within his followers that justified unspeakable acts of violence.

Under Hitler's leadership, Germany initiated a campaign of invasion across Europe, beginning with Poland in 1939 and eventually engulfing most of the continent in war. These invasions were marked by unprecedented levels of brutality and destruction, as entire cities were bombed and civilians massacred. Hitler's vision extended to global domination, with plans that stretched far beyond Europe. His ideology was inherently apocalyptic, aiming to reconstruct the world according to his twisted ideals, a world where only his notion of the "strong" could survive.

The Holocaust: Genocide as Mass Destruction

One of the darkest facets of Hitler's rule was the Holocaust; the systematic extermination of six million Jews, along with millions of others, including Poles, Russians, LGBTQ individuals, and political dissidents. This genocide was carried out with cold precision and was a level of destruction unseen in history. Hitler's "Final Solution" sought to eliminate Jews from Europe entirely, marking the Holocaust as a horrifying fulfillment of an almost apocalyptic vision, where life was destroyed on a previously unimaginable scale.

The concentration camps, ghettos, and mass shootings orchestrated by the Nazi regime were scenes of unimaginable suffering and horror. Jews were forced into ghettos, separated from society, and ultimately sent to concentration and extermination camps where most were systematically murdered. The sheer brutality, the industrial scale of killing, and the callous disregard for human life cemented Hitler as a figure that many saw as the Antichrist incarnate; a leader who embodied the height of human evil.

Christian Views of Hitler as the Antichrist

Many Christians saw Hitler's actions and ideology as clear signs of the Antichrist's work. He led a movement that was profoundly anti-Christian in spirit, devaluing human life, promoting hatred, and seeking global power. His disdain for Christianity, although carefully hidden from the public during his rise, was evident in his private statements, where he mocked Christian values as weak and saw them as obstacles to his vision of a dominant, ruthless Germany.

For those familiar with biblical prophecies, Hitler's character and ambitions fit into the apocalyptic framework. He was seen as the embodiment of the spirit of the Antichrist; a figure of immense evil who thrived on destruction and led millions astray. The Bible warns of a time when such figures will rise, creating suffering and despair on an unprecedented scale, and Hitler's war and genocide seemed to fulfill this vision precisely.

Unprecedented Scale of Destruction

World War II was marked not only by the genocide of the Holocaust but also by catastrophic destruction across Europe, Asia, and parts of North Africa. Entire cities were decimated by bombings, and countries were left in ruins. The sheer scale of loss; over 70 million dead, both soldiers and civilians; left a scar on humanity. Nations were shattered, economies collapsed, and a sense of profound despair and helplessness spread worldwide. For those living through this era, it felt as though the end times had indeed arrived, fulfilling Jesus' words in Matthew 24:6-8, where he spoke of wars and rumours of wars as signs of the end.

The horrific weapons and tactics employed during the war; mass bombings, gas chambers, and the atomic bombs dropped on Hiroshima and Nagasaki; further reinforced the idea that humanity had reached an apocalyptic turning point. The "wars to end all wars" was a phrase that resonated with people, as it felt that the darkness of human capability had been fully revealed.

Aftermath and Lasting Legacy

The end of World War II did not bring peace, but rather a haunting awareness of humanity's capacity for evil. The collective trauma experienced left survivors questioning the future and grappling with the implications of what they had witnessed. The devastation brought forth a reckoning with themes of morality, justice, and the divine.

Hitler's regime, his ideology, and the global destruction he caused left a powerful impression that would linger in apocalyptic thought for decades to come. People sought to understand how such evil could arise and how to prevent it from occurring again, while also fearing that such devastation could indeed recur. The conflict's impact on humanity, combined with the rising tensions of the Cold War that followed, instilled an anxiety that the prophecies of ultimate destruction and judgment might soon come to pass.

For the generations that followed, Hitler's image as an Antichrist figure remained a stark reminder of the thin line between civilization and chaos, good and evil. The fear of another leader rising with similar destructive ambitions continued to haunt humanity, and many wondered if this was but a foretaste of what the true Antichrist could bring. Thus, Hitler's legacy as an "Antichrist" figure became a sobering reminder of the need for vigilance, morality, and the relentless pursuit of peace and justice in the face of potential darkness.

The revelation of atomic power, a tool for the ultimate end-of-world scenario

In the final stages of World War II, humanity unlocked a force that would forever alter the course of history: atomic power. The revelation of this nearly incomprehensible energy, with the power to both create and annihilate on an unprecedented scale, became a stark symbol of the potential for an end-of-world scenario. The discovery and deployment of atomic energy began as a scientific endeavour, led by prominent physicists of the day, who sought to understand the atom's immense power. However, as the global conflict intensified, this scientific breakthrough quickly transformed into a military tool with catastrophic potential.

The Development of the Atomic Bomb: A Scientific and Military Race

During the 1930s, nuclear physics was advancing rapidly, with scientists discovering that atoms could be split to release vast amounts of energy. The concept of nuclear fission captivated physicists around the world, and soon it became apparent that if harnessed, this energy could produce an explosion far beyond anything humanity had ever created. As World War II progressed, there was a growing fear that Nazi Germany might be pursuing nuclear weapons. In response, the United States launched the Manhattan Project in 1942; a secret military research project dedicated to creating an atomic bomb.

Under the leadership of physicist J. Robert Oppenheimer and General Leslie Groves, the Manhattan Project became a massive operation involving thousands of scientists and engineers working at various sites across the U.S. By 1945, the team had achieved what was once thought impossible: they developed two atomic bombs, each capable of obliterating entire cities. Their successful testing of the bomb in the New Mexico desert; known as the Trinity Test; marked the dawn of the Atomic Age and the emergence of a force that many would view as apocalyptic in nature.

The Bombings of Hiroshima and Nagasaki: The World Witnesses Atomic Power

On August 6, 1945, the United States dropped the first atomic bomb on Hiroshima, Japan. The immediate aftermath was a scene of unimaginable destruction: buildings crumbled, fires erupted, and within moments, tens of thousands of people were killed. The bomb created an intense heatwave, followed by a shockwave that flattened much of the city. Survivors of the blast endured severe injuries, burns, and radiation exposure, many of them succumbing to the effects in the days and weeks that followed.

Three days later, on August 9, a second atomic bomb was dropped on Nagasaki, resulting in similar devastation. By the end of these bombings, over 200,000 people had lost their lives. The bombings effectively ended the war, as Japan soon surrendered, but they also exposed humanity to the horrifying reality of atomic power. For the first time, it was clear that human beings possessed the capability to bring about mass extinction through technology alone, without reliance on nature's forces.

Apocalyptic Parallels and Prophecies

The unprecedented destruction of Hiroshima and Nagasaki led many to draw apocalyptic parallels. Religious and secular observers alike saw atomic energy as a manifestation of ultimate destruction; a kind of "fire from the heavens" that echoed the biblical prophecies of the end times. Many Christians, in particular, viewed the revelation of atomic power as a sign that the world was entering a period where prophecies about global destruction could become reality. The imagery of fire, devastation, and the power to wipe out entire nations matched descriptions of divine judgment and the fiery end-of-world scenes depicted in the Book of Revelation.

For figures like William Branham and other prophetic voices of the time, the advent of atomic energy was viewed as a harbinger of judgment. Branham spoke about humanity's increasing technological advancements, particularly in the realm of warfare, as signs that mankind was on a path toward self-destruction. He saw atomic power as a warning that humanity was tampering with forces it could not control; forces that could ultimately bring about divine wrath if misused.

The Cold War and the Shadow of Nuclear Annihilation

The impact of atomic power extended beyond the war, shaping the world's geopolitical landscape for decades to come. With the onset of the Cold War, a tense standoff emerged between the United States and the Soviet Union, as both nations amassed vast arsenals of nuclear weapons. This period became marked by the "arms race," with each superpower aiming to maintain a balance of power through the accumulation of atomic bombs and the development of even more powerful hydrogen bombs.

The doctrine of "Mutually Assured Destruction" (MAD) was born; an understanding that if one superpower launched a nuclear attack, the other would retaliate with equal or greater force, leading to the annihilation of both nations and potentially the world. The knowledge that a single decision could trigger global destruction created an atmosphere of constant anxiety and existential dread. People lived with the persistent fear that the world could end at any moment due to a nuclear miscalculation or conflict.

During this period, many individuals turned to religion and philosophy, seeking to understand the moral implications of atomic power. It was as if humanity was being confronted with the ultimate test: having created a tool of apocalyptic potential, would people find the wisdom to control it, or would it eventually lead to their undoing?

Atomic Power and the Moral Dilemma

The revelation of atomic power not only introduced a potential end-of-world scenario but also forced humanity to confront profound ethical questions. What right did any nation have to wield such power? Could atomic energy be used for good, or was it an inherently destructive force? These questions were deeply unsettling, as the power unleashed by splitting the atom seemed almost divine, a capability that should have been beyond human reach.

In the years following the bombings, scientists like Albert Einstein, who had once advocated for the development of atomic weapons, spoke out against their use. Einstein famously stated, "I am become Death, the destroyer of worlds," a quote from the Bhagavad Gita that captured the terrifying responsibility associated with atomic power. His and other scientists' warnings highlighted the moral dilemma of atomic energy and the looming threat it posed to civilization.

Prophetic Warnings and Humanity's Future

The potential for nuclear devastation has lingered as a constant reminder of humanity's capacity for self-destruction. Many religious leaders warned that the misuse of atomic power could lead to divine judgment, echoing apocalyptic prophecies about fire, smoke, and the end of the world. For those who saw the development of atomic energy as a fulfillment of prophecy, the power of the atom symbolized humanity's final test; a choice between wisdom and destruction, between restraint and apocalypse.

In a world that has witnessed the horrors of Hiroshima and Nagasaki, the looming threat of nuclear annihilation remains one of the most potent symbols of the apocalyptic age. To this day, nuclear weapons continue to be a sobering reminder of humanity's potential to bring about its own end, serving as both a warning and a call for humility in the face of powers that could easily spiral beyond human control.

The Cold War and the Stakes of Nuclear Armageddon (1945-1991)

East vs. West: ideological conflict seen as forces of good and evil

The ideological divide between East and West during the Cold War created a powerful narrative of two forces locked in an existential battle. On one side stood the United States and its allies in the West, who championed democracy, individual freedom, and capitalism. On the other side was the Soviet Union, along with its allies in Eastern Europe and beyond, advocating for communism, state control, and a society founded on class equality. This stark dichotomy wasn't just a political conflict; it was a worldview, a sense that these opposing systems embodied moral values that went beyond borders, influencing millions of people across the world. Each side saw itself as representing the true path forward, while the other was perceived as dangerous, deceptive, or morally wrong.

A World Divided: The Good vs. Evil Narrative

The Cold War's ideological clash framed the East as oppressive and godless in the minds of many Western citizens, while the West, particularly the United States, was seen as a beacon of freedom and moral righteousness. Politicians and cultural influencers on both sides fanned this narrative, crafting a moral and religious undertone that depicted the West's resistance to communism as part of a larger battle between "good" and "evil." This narrative pervaded everything from government speeches and propaganda to school curricula and religious sermons.

The United States saw itself as the leader of the "Free World," rallying other nations to join the fight against the "Red Menace." In contrast, the Soviet Union presented itself as a liberator of oppressed people, positioning its ideology as a global movement that would free humanity from the shackles of capitalist exploitation. This sense of moral superiority justified military actions, interventions, and alliances on both sides. From Korea and Vietnam to Afghanistan and Latin America, the superpowers competed for influence and control in countries across the globe, each seeking to tip the ideological scales in their favor.

Religious Overtones and the "Godless East"

In the West, particularly in the United States, the Cold War was often framed as a religious conflict as well as an ideological one. The Soviet Union's official atheism reinforced Western fears that communism was not only anti-capitalist but anti-God. This fear led to heightened religiosity in the U.S. and an alignment between national identity and religious belief. American leaders painted the Soviet Union as a godless nation, where churches were suppressed, religious beliefs were stifled, and citizens were indoctrinated with atheistic teachings. Religious leaders, especially evangelicals, spoke of the Soviet Union as a threat not only to political freedom but to Christianity itself.

This perception was so strong that phrases like "In God We Trust" became central to American identity during this period. In 1956, the U.S. adopted this phrase as the national motto, and "under God" was added to the Pledge of Allegiance in 1954, further cementing the idea that the U.S. stood on the moral high ground. The "God-fearing" West was seen as holding the moral compass, standing against an atheistic regime that disregarded spiritual values. For many, this wasn't just a political struggle; it was a holy war, a defense of faith and religious freedom against the oppressive forces of secularism.

Mutual Demonization: The Red Scare and Propaganda

Both sides engaged in extensive propaganda campaigns to demonize the other. In the United States, the "Red Scare" led to an intense fear of communism infiltrating American society. Political leaders like Senator Joseph McCarthy famously conducted anti-communist "witch hunts," accusing government officials, Hollywood figures, and ordinary citizens of harbouring communist sympathies. People lived in fear of being accused of disloyalty to their country. This era left a lasting impact, with the label of "communist" becoming synonymous with disloyalty and even treason.

In the Soviet Union, similar efforts were underway to paint the West, particularly America, as the embodiment of capitalist corruption and moral decay. Soviet leaders and media depicted the U.S. as a society driven by greed, inequality, and injustice. Propaganda emphasized stories of poverty, racial discrimination, and crime in Western countries, presenting communism as a force of justice that could remedy these societal ills. Citizens were taught to see the West as a morally bankrupt adversary and to distrust Western ideas and media.

Influence on Pop Culture: Films, Literature, and Art

This clash of ideologies infiltrated pop culture on both sides of the Iron Curtain. In the U.S., movies and literature often portrayed communists as villains, with spies, defectors, and heroes fighting against the "Red Menace." Films like *Red Dawn*, *Rocky IV*, and *Dr. Strangelove* showcased themes of Cold War rivalry, playing up the East vs. West tension and reinforcing the notion of communism as an ever-present threat. Books like George Orwell's *1984* highlighted the dangers of totalitarianism, a veiled critique of communist regimes, and warned of a future where individual freedom could be crushed by state control.

In the Soviet Union, similar efforts were made to create a narrative that glorified communist values and depicted Western societies as places of suffering, exploitation, and moral degradation. Literature, music, and films promoted Soviet ideals and showcased heroic workers and soldiers who embodied the values of the communist state. Art was censored and controlled, aligning cultural output with state-approved messaging. This intense ideological shaping of culture kept citizens aligned with their respective nations' views and goals.

Proxy Wars and the Global Battlefield

The ideological divide between East and West often led to direct confrontations in the form of proxy wars, where the superpowers supported opposing sides in conflicts across the globe. These wars were waged in countries like Korea, Vietnam, and Afghanistan, with devastating consequences for the people caught in the middle. For each side, these battles were a microcosm of the broader Cold War conflict. The U.S. aimed to prevent the "domino effect," fearing that if one nation fell to communism, neighbouring countries would follow. In Vietnam, for instance, the U.S. committed immense resources to combat communist forces backed by the Soviet Union and China, leading to one of the most controversial wars in American history.

For the Soviet Union, supporting leftist movements around the world was seen as a way to counter Western influence and spread communist ideals. They provided military, financial, and logistical support to regimes and rebel groups aligned with socialist and anti-capitalist ideologies. The result was a fractured world, with countries in Africa, Asia, and Latin America becoming battlegrounds for the ideological struggle between East and West. Each side viewed these conflicts as morally justified, fighting not just for territory or influence but for the hearts and minds of people worldwide.

The Nuclear Threat as a Moral Battleground

Nuclear weapons added an apocalyptic dimension to this ideological battle. Both superpowers raced to develop and stockpile nuclear weapons, each with the power to wipe out entire cities. The doctrine of "Mutually Assured Destruction" (MAD) meant that neither side could strike without risking its own annihilation, creating a precarious balance that held the world in suspense. Leaders on both sides justified their nuclear arsenals as necessary to protect their values and ideologies. It was a twisted morality where the threat of mass destruction was seen as a safeguard of peace and a protector of ideological purity.

The ideological battle between East and West became a justification for policies and decisions that would otherwise have been seen as extreme or even immoral. The Cold War's narrative of "good" versus "evil" made it easier for each side to rally support, maintain control, and push forward with actions that had far-reaching consequences. It was a psychological, cultural, and spiritual war, with each superpower determined to shape the world in its own image. This high-stakes standoff had a profound impact on global society, setting the stage for the political and cultural landscape of the modern era, and leaving a legacy that would shape international relations long after the Cold War ended.

Doomsday Clock, nuclear proliferation, and the prospect of total annihilation

The concept of the Doomsday Clock emerged in 1947, symbolizing humanity's proximity to global catastrophe; originally due to nuclear weapons but later encompassing other existential threats as well. Created by the Bulletin of the Atomic Scientists, the clock uses the metaphor of "minutes to midnight" to represent how close humanity is to self-destruction. Midnight signifies a hypothetical point of no return; essentially, an irreversible disaster on a global scale. Since its inception, the clock has been adjusted numerous times, depending on global events, shifts in international relations, and technological developments. The Doomsday Clock has become a haunting reminder of the dangers posed by nuclear weapons and other threats to humanity's survival.

Nuclear Proliferation: The Spread of Destruction

The end of World War II marked the dawn of the nuclear age, as the U.S. dropped atomic bombs on Hiroshima and Nagasaki in 1945. These bombings demonstrated the unparalleled destructive power of nuclear weapons and initiated an arms race between the U.S. and the Soviet Union. Other nations; such as the United Kingdom, France, and China; soon developed their own nuclear capabilities, creating a global stockpile of warheads capable of obliterating civilization. This spread of nuclear weapons, known as nuclear proliferation, was fuelled by fear and a desire for strategic advantage.

Proliferation became especially concerning as more countries sought to acquire nuclear weapons, potentially destabilizing international relations. Nations like Israel, India, and Pakistan eventually joined the nuclear club, heightening global tensions. The United Nations attempted to counteract this trend through various non-proliferation efforts, including the Treaty on the Non-Proliferation of Nuclear Weapons (NPT) in 1968. However, despite these efforts, the number of nuclear weapons continued to rise, as did the fear of their use.

The competition for nuclear dominance led to a vast array of weapons, from hydrogen bombs to intercontinental ballistic missiles (ICBMs). The superpowers invested in "second-strike" capabilities, meaning that if one side were attacked, it could retaliate with devastating force. This doctrine, known as Mutually Assured Destruction (MAD), was meant to deter either side from launching a first strike. Yet, the sheer volume of nuclear arms created a volatile situation, where even an accident or miscalculation could trigger catastrophic consequences.

The Doomsday Clock and Public Fear of Total Annihilation

The Doomsday Clock became an influential symbol of the global threat, particularly during periods of heightened tensions. Every time it inched closer to midnight, it sent a shockwave through the public consciousness, reminding the world that nuclear war could break out at any time. During the Cuban Missile Crisis in 1962, for instance, the clock seemed to tick ever closer, as the U.S. and Soviet Union came perilously close to nuclear conflict. The Bulletin of the Atomic Scientists responded by adjusting the clock's hands, signalling how dangerous the situation had become.

Throughout the Cold War, the clock moved back and forth in response to diplomatic developments, arms control agreements, and technological advancements. Treaties like the Strategic Arms Limitation Talks (SALT) and the Intermediate-Range Nuclear Forces Treaty (INF) managed to slow down the arms race, prompting the clock's hands to move back from midnight temporarily.

But these intervals of hope were often short-lived, as new conflicts and technologies reignited the threat of annihilation.

For ordinary citizens, the Doomsday Clock became a powerful symbol of anxiety. Media reports about the clock's adjustments created widespread public fear and uncertainty. Civilians were taught to "duck and cover" in schools, and fallout shelters became commonplace in American homes. The sense of a looming doomsday deeply impacted the psychology of entire generations, influencing everything from popular culture to politics.

The Possibility of Nuclear Annihilation and Doomsday Scenarios

With the massive expansion of nuclear arsenals, theorists began to explore doomsday scenarios that could result from a full-scale nuclear exchange. One of the most terrifying was nuclear winter; a concept proposed by scientists who suggested that the detonation of a large number of nuclear weapons could send massive amounts of smoke and debris into the atmosphere, blocking sunlight for months or even years. This would lead to a dramatic cooling of the Earth's surface, causing widespread crop failure and famine. Such a scenario implied that even if some parts of the world survived the initial blasts, they would face a prolonged, catastrophic aftermath.

The idea of nuclear winter underscored the fact that nuclear war wouldn't just affect warring nations; it could potentially wipe out civilization as a whole. Entire ecosystems, water supplies, and climates would be altered, making human survival nearly impossible. This sense of finality reinforced the existential dread surrounding nuclear weapons, pushing activists, scientists, and even political leaders to seek ways to mitigate the risk.

As a result, various disarmament and anti-nuclear movements gained traction. Organizations like the Campaign for Nuclear Disarmament (CND) and global peace marches pressured governments to consider the moral and humanitarian costs of nuclear weapons. Public figures and scientists joined the call, arguing that humanity couldn't rely on the fragile balance of Mutually Assured Destruction to prevent catastrophe. Even with safeguards in place, there was an undeniable risk that nuclear annihilation could occur by accident, miscalculation, or the actions of rogue actors.

The Doomsday Clock Today: A Continuing Symbol of Caution

The Doomsday Clock endures as a symbol of the delicate state of global security, still adjusted annually by the Bulletin of the Atomic Scientists based on threats that include nuclear proliferation, climate change, and artificial intelligence. The clock's relevance extends beyond the Cold War, reflecting a broader spectrum of existential threats that endanger humanity. Each adjustment serves as a reminder of the fine line we walk and the high stakes involved.

With nuclear arsenals still in place and modern challenges adding to global instability, the clock remains a constant reminder of the potential for total annihilation. It emphasizes the need for vigilance, international cooperation, and a renewed commitment to peaceful resolution of conflicts. Although the Cold War has ended, the Doomsday Clock continues to signify the ever-present danger that humanity faces, urging us to consider the long-term consequences of our actions in the pursuit of power and technological progress.

Rise of William Branham's prophecies, interpreting contemporary events as signs of the end times

William Branham, a prominent American preacher in the 20th century, became widely known for his prophecies and for interpreting contemporary events as signs of the impending end times. Branham's teachings and prophetic visions resonated with a generation grappling with rapid changes in society and the looming existential threats posed by nuclear warfare, political upheaval, and moral shifts. His followers viewed him as a prophetic voice, a man chosen by God to reveal divine mysteries and prepare humanity for what he described as the imminent Second Coming of Christ. His teachings emphasized moral purity, a return to foundational Christian beliefs, and an awareness of the "signs of the times."

Branham's Prophetic Visions and End-Times Predictions

One of the most defining aspects of Branham's ministry was his series of visions, which he claimed were revealed to him by God. These visions, he asserted, showed him critical events that would unfold in the world, serving as harbingers of the last days. Among the most notable of his predictions was his vision of America's downfall, a prophecy that would become a focal point for his teachings on the decline of Western society.

Branham often referenced his "Seven Visions" prophecy, a series of seven distinct visions he claimed to have received in 1933, which he believed foretold the future. In these visions, Branham saw significant geopolitical events, technological advancements, and social changes that would escalate until the world reached a state of moral corruption. He interpreted these developments as indicative of the beginning of the end times.

In the first vision, Branham saw that the rise of Fascism in Italy and Nazism in Germany would ultimately lead to a devastating war. His second vision predicted that America would enter the conflict, which aligned with the U.S. joining World War II. The following visions pointed to cultural and technological developments, but the seventh and final vision was the most apocalyptic. In it, he saw America burning in flames, symbolizing its eventual destruction, which he interpreted as a divine punishment for moral corruption and the abandonment of God.

Interpretation of Contemporary Events as Fulfillments of Prophecy

Branham viewed various events of his era as evidence of a moral and spiritual decay. The Cold War, with its ideological conflicts, nuclear arms race, and potential for global annihilation, was seen as a direct fulfillment of his apocalyptic predictions. The burgeoning tensions between the U.S. and the Soviet Union, he preached, were manifestations of a deeper spiritual battle between good and evil. These contemporary events became touchstones in his sermons, used to illustrate the coming wrath that, he warned, would befall humanity if it did not repent and turn back to God.

Branham also saw the advancement of technology and the embrace of secularism as warning signs. The rapid progress in science and technology, he argued, was not merely a mark of human achievement but a step closer to the fulfillment of his visions. For example, he expressed concerns over innovations in atomic weaponry and materialism, viewing these as symbols of humanity's growing alienation from God. In his eyes, the obsession with worldly knowledge and power represented the same sin that led to the fall of civilizations in the past.

Moral Decline and the Apocalyptic Sign of Modesty

Branham strongly emphasized the theme of modesty and moral conduct, particularly in relation to women's roles and attire. In his teachings, he expressed concern over what he perceived as a decay in traditional values, especially around femininity and family roles. He viewed the shift towards modern fashion and societal changes in women's roles as signs of the end times, claiming that such changes symbolized a loss of innocence and an embrace of ungodly behaviour.

His teachings on modesty extended to his views on the broader moral climate of society. Branham interpreted the rising acceptance of behaviours that he considered sinful; such as increased promiscuity, secularism, and a rejection of Christian principles; as evidence of an impending judgment. This perceived moral decline, he preached, was a sign that humanity was drifting further from God, fulfilling prophecies that pointed to the moral corruption that would characterize the last days.

The True Bride of Christ and the Church's Role in the End Times

In Branham's theology, he described the concept of the "True Bride of Christ"; a remnant of faithful believers who would uphold Christian values amidst a world that had turned its back on God. He distinguished between the true Bride and what he called the "false church," which, in his view, had become corrupted by political and cultural influences. Branham's vision of the True Bride emphasized a return to the teachings and practices of the early Christian church, unadulterated by what he saw as modern compromise.

According to Branham, only those who adhered strictly to God's word would be saved in the end times. This group, he claimed, would not be swayed by popular trends, secular ideologies, or the cultural shifts that he believed marked the moral decay of society. The Bride of Christ, as he described it, was meant to be a beacon of purity and obedience, a community that would resist the world's temptations and await the Second Coming.

The Modern World's Misunderstanding of Life and the Approach of the Apocalypse

Branham often spoke against what he viewed as the modern world's misguided priorities and misunderstanding of life's true purpose. He argued that humanity's focus on material success, intellectual achievements, and physical pleasures had led people away from God. In his eyes, this misunderstanding reflected a fundamental failure to grasp the importance of spiritual salvation.

Branham urged his followers to reject the values of a society that, he believed, idolized wealth, pleasure, and power, warning that these pursuits would ultimately lead to destruction.

His teachings suggested that the modern world was on a collision course with divine wrath. He interpreted events such as the rise of secularism, the erosion of family structures, and the global spread of ideologies that he saw as anti-Christian as signals of the approaching apocalypse. The fascination with new philosophies, social movements, and scientific discoveries, he warned, represented humanity's dangerous detachment from God's truth.

Branham's Teachings on the End of Days: The Final Judgment

For Branham, the end of days was not merely a distant theological concept but a real, imminent event. He believed that the world was rapidly approaching a final judgment, in which those who had rejected God's teachings would face divine retribution. Branham warned of a time when God would judge nations and individuals for their sins, particularly the sin of turning away from divine principles. This judgment, he preached, would not only punish sinners but also usher in a new era of divine justice, restoring God's order.

Branham's apocalyptic teachings included vivid depictions of catastrophic events that he believed would mark the end times; natural disasters, wars, moral decay, and the decline of traditional values. His warnings often evoked fear but also served as a call to repentance. He emphasized that there was still time for people to turn back to God and escape the coming judgment, but he cautioned that the window of opportunity was closing rapidly.

Present Day and the Rise of Modern Prophecies

The Digital Age and Decline of Morality (Late 20th Century - Early 21st Century)

Moral decay in modern times, internet and media's role in spreading immorality

In the digital age, the rapid advancement of technology and the unprecedented spread of information have profoundly influenced society, reshaping nearly every aspect of human life. While the internet and media have opened pathways for innovation, connection, and knowledge, they have also introduced new and complex challenges to moral and ethical standards. For many, this period represents a marked decline in societal values, as immorality seems to proliferate unchecked through the very tools once envisioned as gateways to progress and enlightenment.

The Internet's Influence on Modern Morality

The internet, a monumental creation of the late 20th century, brought the promise of boundless information and the ability to connect people across the globe instantly. However, with this openness came a flood of content that has both shaped and, in many cases, degraded moral standards. In particular, the anonymity and accessibility of the internet have allowed for behaviours, discussions, and content that would previously have been relegated to the fringes of society to become mainstream.

The spread of pornography, for instance, has reached levels unimaginable in previous eras. What once might have been hidden or limited to specific communities is now accessible with just a few clicks. This ease of access has normalized explicit content, leading to growing concerns about its effects on individuals' perception of relationships, self-worth, and the sanctity of intimacy. Studies have shown that continuous exposure to such content can shape attitudes toward relationships and sexuality, encouraging a more transactional view of human connection and fostering unhealthy expectations.

Social media has also played a pivotal role in this moral transformation. Platforms like Facebook, Instagram, Twitter, and TikTok have not only revolutionized the way people communicate but also significantly influenced social standards and values. These platforms often incentivize behaviours that prioritize self-image, popularity, and material wealth over virtues like humility, kindness, and self-restraint. Many young people today navigate a world where "likes" and "followers" serve as primary indicators of worth, leading to increased anxiety, competition, and often a sense of inadequacy.

Moreover, social media's algorithm-driven models have fuelled a culture of comparison and superficial judgment. Influencers and celebrities; figures often idealized by youth; showcase lifestyles that are far from attainable for most, promoting materialism and reinforcing the idea that happiness can be achieved through wealth and physical perfection. As a result, a culture of vanity and self-centeredness has flourished, overshadowing traditional values that once promoted community and genuine connection.

The Media's Role in Shaping Morality

Beyond social media, mainstream media has also contributed to the shifting landscape of moral values. With television, movies, and music reaching nearly every corner of the globe, the content people consume heavily influences their beliefs, behaviours, and worldviews. While media can serve as a powerful tool for positive storytelling and education, it also has a darker side, as it often sensationalizes violence, glamorizes materialism, and promotes increasingly explicit content. Traditional family values, moral responsibility, and virtues of patience and integrity are often cast aside in favor of instant gratification, individualism, and excess.

Television shows and movies frequently depict characters engaging in morally ambiguous behaviour, often without consequences. Infidelity, greed, dishonesty, and violence are portrayed in ways that normalize such behaviours, making them appear acceptable, or even glamorous. This shift not only affects individual viewers but also shapes cultural standards. What was once frowned upon now becomes tolerated or celebrated in popular media, reinforcing the idea that ethical boundaries are malleable and open to personal interpretation.

Impact on Family Structures and Relationships

With these cultural shifts, traditional family structures have also faced significant changes. The digital age has introduced pressures and distractions that previous generations did not encounter. Family dinners and face-to-face conversations have often been replaced by screens, and interactions once central to building bonds are now diluted by the constant presence of digital devices. Parents struggle to instill values in a world where children have access to a vast array of content beyond their control. As a result, many families experience strain as they try to bridge the gap between traditional values and the influences of modern culture.

Relationships, too, have been affected. Dating apps and social media have altered the way people meet, interact, and understand love. The value of commitment has diminished as these platforms encourage a consumer-like approach to relationships, where individuals are "swiped" and assessed based on superficial traits. This shift has raised concerns about the erosion of deep, meaningful connections, as people may increasingly view each other as commodities rather than as individuals deserving of respect and care.

The Rise of Relativism and Moral Ambiguity

Another key aspect of the digital age is the rise of moral relativism; the belief that moral principles are not universal but instead vary based on personal or cultural perspectives. This shift has led to an erosion of common moral standards, replaced by a "live and let live" philosophy that rejects objective morality. With information at everyone's fingertips, people are empowered to find beliefs that align with their desires, and this customization of morality has led to a fragmented and often contradictory set of values within society.

Moral relativism has permeated much of popular culture and political discourse, creating an environment where there is little consensus on right and wrong. Actions once condemned across cultures are now subject to debate, and individuals are encouraged to "find their truth" rather than adhere to a common moral framework. While this openness has allowed for greater tolerance and acceptance of diverse perspectives, it has also led to confusion and conflict as societies grapple with differing definitions of morality.

Growing Concerns Among Religious and Ethical Thinkers

The moral changes in the digital age have not gone unnoticed, particularly among religious leaders, ethicists, and community organizers who warn of the long-term consequences of this shift. Many religious groups interpret these changes as signs of an impending spiritual crisis, viewing the erosion of traditional values as a fulfillment of warnings found in ancient texts about a time of widespread immorality before a period of divine judgment.

Some religious thinkers interpret the decline of moral standards as a modern-day parallel to biblical narratives of moral corruption. They point to the rampant materialism, hyper-sexualization, and the glorification of violence in popular media as evidence that society is turning away from core spiritual principles. According to these perspectives, the widespread acceptance of behaviours and lifestyles once considered immoral signals the beginning of a collective moral descent, marking a pivotal moment that could lead to divine consequences.

Consequences of Moral Decline in Society

The consequences of this moral shift extend beyond individual behaviour, impacting society at large. Rising rates of depression, anxiety, and loneliness, particularly among younger generations, suggest that the very tools designed to connect people may, in fact, be contributing to a greater sense of isolation and discontent. Additionally, the erosion of trust, the loss of shared values, and the emphasis on individualism over community have led to societal fragmentation and increased polarization.

In response, some communities have begun advocating for a return to foundational moral values, urging individuals to seek meaning beyond the superficial allure of the digital world. These movements often promote practices such as mindfulness, meditation, and family bonding activities that emphasize presence, community, and introspection over the digital distractions that have come to dominate daily life.

The digital age has undoubtedly brought remarkable advancements and opportunities, but it has also introduced new moral challenges that reflect a deeper cultural shift. The widespread accessibility of information and the influence of media have reshaped societal values, often leading individuals away from traditional principles and into a realm of moral ambiguity and relativism. As religious and ethical thinkers continue to interpret these trends, many see the changes of the digital age as not just a societal evolution but as a sign of the times; a possible precursor to greater spiritual consequences. This perspective serves as a call for introspection, reminding people of the enduring importance of foundational moral values, even amidst the rapidly changing landscape of the modern world.

New idols: technology, celebrity, wealth; rejection of traditional values

As the digital age progresses, society has seen a rise in new idols; technology, celebrity, and wealth; that increasingly shape cultural values and personal aspirations. These idols often overshadow traditional virtues, leading to a rejection of principles that once grounded communities and promoted ethical cohesion. In this context, technology, fame, and material success become not just ambitions but central symbols of value and identity.

Technology as a Modern Idol

In contemporary society, technology is no longer just a tool; it has become a defining force in people's lives, reshaping communication, work, and even relationships. Technology is now a primary driver of identity, influencing how people perceive themselves and each other. With the rise of smartphones, artificial intelligence, and constant digital connection, individuals have become heavily dependent on devices and platforms that allow them to communicate, entertain, and define their existence. For many, the constant connectivity has shifted from a means of productivity to an all-consuming priority, creating a reliance that borders on worship.

Social media platforms, for instance, are designed to captivate attention and elicit emotional responses. Algorithms reward frequent engagement, encouraging users to check their phones continuously, reinforcing the importance of virtual validation. People often measure their self-worth through "likes," comments, and shares, creating a value system where online presence equates to personal success. The "idolization" of technology is particularly evident in the way it has redefined social interactions; people frequently prioritize virtual relationships over real-life connections, choosing digital approval over meaningful face-to-face exchanges.

The Celebrity Phenomenon

Celebrity culture has a similar, if not even stronger, grip on modern society. With the advent of the internet and social media, the concept of celebrity has expanded to include not only actors, musicians, and athletes but also influencers, content creators, and social media personalities. The modern celebrity is not just famous for achievements or talents but often gains attention through carefully curated online personas. Social media platforms have given rise to "everyday celebrities"; individuals who achieve fame by showcasing an attractive lifestyle, wealth, or perceived charisma, shaping their followers' ideas of success.

For many people, these celebrities become idols, representing a lifestyle and social status they aspire to emulate. Fans develop emotional attachments to their favourite personalities, following every update and often adopting similar habits, fashion, or even worldview. Celebrities influence everything from fashion to political opinions, wielding an influence that would have been unimaginable in earlier eras. They are often looked to as modern-day "prophets" of culture, promoting trends and ideologies that shape societal values. This focus on celebrity reflects a societal shift where admiration for virtuous character is often displaced by adoration for fame and image.

The danger lies in how this fixation on celebrities fosters a culture of superficiality and comparison. Young people, in particular, measure their own lives against these curated snapshots, leading to feelings of inadequacy, envy, and discontent. This has contributed to a growing epidemic of self-esteem issues, as many struggle to reconcile their reality with the idealized, filtered world presented by celebrities and influencers.

The Pursuit of Wealth and Material Success

In addition to technology and celebrity, wealth has become another dominant idol of modern society. Financial success is often viewed as the ultimate goal, with material wealth symbolizing personal worth and achievement. While the pursuit of economic stability has always been important, the digital age has amplified the allure of wealth, with constant exposure to lifestyles that flaunt luxury, convenience, and exclusivity. Wealth is portrayed as the pathway to freedom, power, and happiness, leading many to equate financial success with the pinnacle of human achievement.

This idolization of wealth manifests in several ways. Many people prioritize career success, often sacrificing relationships, personal well-being, and even ethical standards in their quest for financial gain. In this environment, money becomes a measurement of self-worth, driving behaviours that prioritize profit over community or integrity. Economic success becomes the primary measure of an individual's "value" to society, while virtues like compassion, humility, and generosity are often sidelined.

Businesses and corporations also play into this idolization of wealth, emphasizing profit and consumerism. Advertising bombards individuals with messages that link happiness to material possessions, implying that life is incomplete without the latest products. This has created a consumer culture where people are encouraged to constantly upgrade, acquire, and consume, leading to cycles of debt and an ever-growing ecological footprint. This focus on consumption fuels the belief that fulfillment is attainable only through the accumulation of wealth and material goods, perpetuating a sense of inadequacy and unending desire.

Rejection of Traditional Values

As these modern idols; technology, celebrity, and wealth; have gained prominence, traditional values have increasingly been sidelined. Values such as humility, simplicity, self-restraint, and community-oriented living are often viewed as outdated in an age that prizes self-promotion, instant gratification, and individual achievement. Where past generations may have placed greater emphasis on integrity, faith, family, and community, the new idols suggest a more individualistic worldview where personal success and external validation take precedence.

This shift has weakened communal bonds, as people increasingly prioritize their own ambitions over collective well-being. Traditional institutions like family and faith communities, which once provided a moral foundation and support network, face challenges as their influence wanes in modern culture. As family units spend more time isolated on individual devices and less time engaged in meaningful conversations, the bonds that previously sustained families weaken. Community organizations and churches, once centres of shared moral values and support, are often perceived as less relevant, as people shift their allegiance to online communities or self-focused activities.

This rejection of traditional values reflects a deeper philosophical change: a shift from intrinsic values (focused on who a person is) to extrinsic values (focused on what a person has or portrays). The intrinsic values that traditionally defined personal character and virtue are being overshadowed by values that emphasize outward appearance and acquisition. This philosophical shift has contributed to a cultural narrative that often undervalues integrity, kindness, and empathy, favouring instead a focus on image, success, and consumption.

Spiritual Implications and Concerns

For religious and philosophical thinkers, the rise of these modern idols is often seen as a significant spiritual crisis. Many interpret this societal shift as a fulfillment of ancient prophecies that warned against idolatry and the pursuit of false gods. Scriptural texts across various religions caution that a focus on wealth, power, and worldly pursuits can lead to moral decay and separation from spiritual truth. These thinkers argue that the modern age has redefined idol worship in the form of technology, celebrity, and wealth, drawing people away from the values that foster inner peace and moral clarity.

Religious leaders, in particular, warn that idolizing these aspects of modern life risks creating a generation disconnected from spiritual principles. Technology, in particular, is seen as both a powerful tool and a potential trap; one that can enrich lives but also distract from deeper, more meaningful pursuits. The intense focus on celebrity and wealth, meanwhile, is seen as evidence of a society increasingly obsessed with image and status, rather than character and humility.

The spiritual concern is that, by placing hope and purpose in transient, material pursuits, people risk losing touch with the eternal principles that offer lasting fulfillment and guidance. The rejection of traditional values in favor of these modern idols is seen as a path that could lead to moral and spiritual desolation; a departure from the foundational virtues that have grounded and guided humanity across generations.

Consequences for the Individual and Society

The elevation of technology, celebrity, and wealth to the status of idols has deep and lasting consequences. At an individual level, this shift fosters discontent, as people often chase after external validation without finding genuine fulfillment. The constant need for approval through digital means, the relentless pursuit of wealth, and the desire for fame often leave individuals feeling hollow and disconnected from themselves. Anxiety, depression, and loneliness have surged as people grapple with the pressures of maintaining an idealized image and constantly comparing themselves to unattainable standards.

On a societal level, this fixation on external achievements and appearances has contributed to a sense of division and isolation. Community bonds weaken, and people become increasingly focused on personal success, often at the expense of collective well-being. The sense of solidarity, once cultivated through shared values and mutual support, is diminished as individuals pursue self-interest. The growing environmental crises and social inequalities are direct consequences of a culture that prioritizes consumption, wealth, and status over responsibility, empathy, and stewardship.

The rise of technology, celebrity, and wealth as modern idols reflects a profound shift in societal values. This transformation challenges traditional notions of morality, community, and spirituality, placing external validation and material success above character, virtue, and collective well-being. As society continues down this path, there are growing concerns about the long-term impacts on both individual fulfillment and societal health. The pursuit of these modern idols often leads to a cycle of unfulfilled desires, as people realize that genuine happiness cannot be found in transient things. This era calls for a return to foundational principles and the recognition that lasting peace and purpose come not from what we possess or portray but from who we are and how we treat one another.

William Branham's interpretations of this age as the rise of "false prophets"

William Branham, a significant figure in the 20th-century Pentecostal movement, interpreted the modern age through the lens of what he termed the "rise of false prophets." He believed that this phenomenon marked a dangerous era of spiritual deception, where many individuals and institutions would distort religious truth for personal gain, leading believers away from genuine faith. According to Branham, this wave of falsehood, disguised as religious guidance, would contribute to the moral and spiritual decay that he saw as evidence of humanity's slide toward the end times.

Understanding "False Prophets" in Branham's Teachings

To Branham, a "false prophet" was not only a specific individual leading others astray but also represented any force that promoted deceptive ideologies under the guise of righteousness. In Branham's view, these false prophets would appear charismatic, knowledgeable, and influential, gaining large followings and spreading beliefs that seemed virtuous on the surface but, in reality, would weaken and corrupt genuine spirituality.

He saw this deception occurring not only in religious circles but also in the broader cultural and intellectual landscape, where modern ideologies and philosophies increasingly questioned or outright rejected traditional beliefs. For Branham, these influencers worked as false prophets in a new way; through culture, education, and even entertainment; to erode society's moral foundations and promote lifestyles that departed from scriptural teachings.

Branham's Warnings Against Religious Deception

Branham believed that false prophets would often appear within organized religion itself, disguised as leaders claiming to speak for God while ultimately prioritizing their interests. He warned that churches and religious leaders would increasingly compromise on doctrine and accommodate worldly values, attempting to stay relevant or attract larger congregations. In his view, this compromised form of religion would mislead people by diluting or misrepresenting biblical truth, leading to a form of "lukewarm Christianity" that lacked spiritual depth and power.

He argued that many religious leaders in his day embraced the secular values of fame, wealth, and social influence, turning away from the core teachings of humility, simplicity, and devotion. He saw this shift as a symptom of false prophecy, warning that these leaders' messages would resonate with worldly desires rather than spiritual truth. Instead of guiding people toward salvation and genuine spiritual growth, Branham saw them drawing believers into superficial, material-focused lifestyles.

False Prophets in the Context of Modern Technology and Media

With the rise of technology, particularly radio, television, and later digital media, Branham believed that false prophets gained an unprecedented platform to reach and influence the masses. He predicted that media would amplify the voices of deceptive leaders, allowing their messages to spread rapidly and globally. In his view, this would further corrupt society, as individuals became bombarded with contradictory teachings and diluted truths. He warned that people would find it increasingly difficult to discern genuine faith from falsehood amid so much noise and confusion.

Branham saw media-driven culture as a powerful tool that false prophets would wield to normalize practices and beliefs contrary to Christian teachings. He believed that these voices would advocate for moral relativism, secularism, and other ideologies that drew people away from traditional faith, offering a watered-down version of Christianity that catered to popular opinion rather than divine truth.

Social and Cultural Icons as "Prophets" of Modern Belief Systems

Branham argued that secular culture had created its own prophets, individuals who promoted ideologies and lifestyles that contradicted the Bible. He saw these figures not only as entertainers, influencers, and intellectuals but as agents of a spiritual deception that lured people away from faith. To Branham, the widespread admiration for cultural icons was a modern form of idolatry, as these figures became the "prophets" of society's new values; values that often conflicted with or openly mocked religious principles.

He believed these modern prophets preached the "gospel" of self-empowerment, relativism, and hedonism, which, in his view, undermined humility, obedience to God, and moral discipline. This shift, he warned, would have disastrous consequences for both individuals and society as a whole. As people idolized and emulated these figures, Branham felt they would lose their spiritual grounding, succumbing to values that centered on personal pleasure and fulfillment rather than a life guided by faith and service.

Branham's Prophecies on End-Time Deception

One of Branham's most profound concerns was that this rise of false prophets was a key sign of the end times, echoing biblical prophecies about mass deception preceding judgment. He frequently referenced scriptures, particularly from the books of Matthew and Revelation, which warned about a time when "many false prophets shall rise, and shall deceive many" (Matthew 24:11). He viewed this prophecy as especially relevant in his time, seeing the world's turn toward secularism, immorality, and materialism as a precursor to the final judgment.

Branham saw himself as a prophet called to warn believers against the seduction of these false doctrines and to prepare them for the coming trials. He urged his followers to remain vigilant and steadfast, adhering strictly to biblical teachings and rejecting the diluted doctrines promoted by false prophets. For him, these deceptive influences were not merely an intellectual threat but an existential one, with souls at stake.

The True Bride of Christ Amid Deception

Central to Branham's teaching was the concept of the "true Bride of Christ," a select group of believers who would remain faithful and pure in a time of great deception. He described this group as those who would reject the lure of false prophets and uphold genuine, undiluted Christian faith. According to Branham, the true Bride would be set apart, standing firm against the pressures of a world that had fallen into moral chaos. This faithful remnant, he believed, would be rewarded in the end, remaining spiritually "alive" in the face of a world turning spiritually "dead."

Branham taught that the Bride would recognize the truth and separate themselves from the compromised church, which he often referred to as the "harlot church"; a metaphor for religious institutions that had betrayed their original faith. He saw this division as a fulfillment of biblical prophecy, where the true followers of Christ would be tested and ultimately separated from those who had been led astray by false teachings.

September 11 and the War on Terror (2001 - Present)

9/11 attacks, a moment of global shock and end-of-world fears

The September 11 attacks in 2001 marked a pivotal moment in global history, profoundly impacting not only international relations but also the psyche of societies around the world. As two planes crashed into the Twin Towers of the World Trade Centre in New York City and another struck the Pentagon, the immediate aftermath created an atmosphere of shock, fear, and a burgeoning sense of impending doom.

The Immediate Impact of 9/11

In the wake of the attacks, the world witnessed a dramatic transformation in how nations viewed security and terrorism. The shocking nature of the attacks; targeting iconic symbols of American power and economic might; left many questioning the stability of their own countries. The images of destruction and chaos broadcasted worldwide fuelled an environment rife with anxiety, leading to a belief that the world had entered a new, more dangerous era.

For many, the catastrophic loss of life; nearly 3,000 souls; coupled with the devastating imagery of collapsing buildings and people fleeing for their lives, evoked a sense of apocalyptic foreboding. The attacks were not only an assault on the United States but also an attack on global ideals of freedom, democracy, and security. The horror of that day became synonymous with notions of an impending apocalypse in the minds of many, who began to wonder if this was a signal of worse things to come.

Religious and Cultural Interpretations of the Attacks

The September 11 attacks prompted various religious interpretations, particularly among Christian communities. Many turned to biblical prophecies, interpreting the events through a lens of eschatology; the study of end times. Pastors and theologians began preaching about the signs of the times, warning congregations that the attacks could herald a series of judgments leading to the end of days.

These interpretations often referenced scriptures that spoke of tribulation, wars, and the rise of a global system that could be seen as aligning with end-times prophecies. In some circles, the idea that the attacks were a form of divine judgment for perceived moral failings in the United States gained traction. This notion suggested that the increasing secularization, materialism, and moral decay of society had drawn the ire of God, thus manifesting in catastrophic events like 9/11.

Political and Social Fallout

Politically, the attacks prompted the United States to launch the War on Terror, which included military operations in Afghanistan aimed at dismantling al-Qaeda and removing the Taliban from power. This unprecedented military response furthered feelings of insecurity and global instability.

The idea that terrorism could strike anywhere at any time added to the sense of dread, leading to a pervasive belief that the world was becoming increasingly hostile and unpredictable.

Socially, the fallout from the attacks resulted in a rise in xenophobia and Islamophobia, as many in the United States and around the world viewed Muslims and those from Middle Eastern backgrounds with suspicion. The narrative surrounding 9/11 often conflated terrorism with Islam, leading to a generalized fear that further exacerbated tensions between cultures and religions.

Fear and the Rise of Conspiracy Theories

In the years following 9/11, fear of further attacks fuelled conspiracy theories that circulated widely, including claims that the government had prior knowledge of the attacks or that they were orchestrated to justify wars in the Middle East. These theories often intertwined with apocalyptic fears, suggesting that the attacks were part of a larger, sinister plan to bring about a new world order or to pave the way for the Antichrist.

The notion that the attacks signalled the beginning of a series of catastrophic events aligned with biblical prophecies gained traction in certain evangelical circles. Many began interpreting global political shifts, natural disasters, and ongoing conflicts as signs of the impending apocalypse, each event viewed through the lens of a world on the brink of chaos.

The Role of Prophetic Voices

In the wake of 9/11, prophetic figures like William Branham (whose teachings have been revisited by some in the light of contemporary events) were invoked to frame the attacks within the context of end-time prophecies. His warnings about moral decay, the rise of false prophets, and the impending judgment were echoed by modern preachers who saw parallels between his teachings and the current global landscape.

These voices called believers to recognize the signs of the times, urging them to remain vigilant and prepared for what they perceived as a spiritual battle manifesting through political and social turmoil. This narrative emphasized the need for spiritual awakening, a return to biblical truths, and a rejection of worldly distractions in preparation for the final events prophesied in scripture.

The September 11 attacks left an indelible mark on global consciousness, fundamentally altering how people perceive safety, security, and the future. In many ways, it catalyzed a cultural shift toward an apocalyptic mindset, as individuals and communities began to interpret events through a prophetic lens, questioning the implications of a world filled with violence and uncertainty.

As the War on Terror continues to unfold and global tensions persist, the fear instilled by 9/11 remains a powerful undercurrent in contemporary society. The events of that day serve as a reminder of the fragility of peace and the complexities of faith in a world increasingly marked by conflict, prompting ongoing reflection on the moral and spiritual state of humanity as it grapples with the realities of a post-9/11 world.

Escalation of terrorism, religious extremism, and an increase in prophetic warnings

The early 21st century has been marked by an alarming escalation of terrorism and religious extremism, which has profoundly shaped global dynamics and sparked a renewed wave of prophetic warnings from various religious communities. This era not only highlights the complexities of ideological conflict but also underscores the ways in which fear and uncertainty have mobilized prophetic narratives across faith traditions.

The Surge of Terrorism and Extremist Ideologies

In the aftermath of the September 11 attacks, the world saw a significant rise in terrorist activity, often rooted in radical interpretations of religious beliefs. Groups like al-Qaeda and later ISIS (Islamic State of Iraq and Syria) gained notoriety for their brutal tactics and expansive propaganda campaigns. They exploited political instability, social discontent, and grievances in the Muslim world, positioning themselves as defenders of their faith against Western imperialism and oppression.

1. Global Impact of Extremism: Terrorism became a global phenomenon, as extremist groups carried out attacks not only in the Middle East but also in Europe, Africa, and Asia. Major incidents, such as the bombings in London (2005), the Paris attacks (2015), and the Manchester Arena bombing (2017), exemplified the transnational reach of these groups. These attacks were often accompanied by chilling messages aimed at instilling fear and showcasing the supposed strength of the terrorist movements.

2. Ideological Justification: Extremist groups framed their violent actions as part of a divine struggle, often citing religious texts to justify their brutality. They presented a binary worldview that painted their enemies as forces of evil, and themselves as champions of a pure faith. This ideological framing not only attracted followers but also intensified polarization within societies, leading to a climate of fear and mistrust.

The Role of Religious Extremism

As terrorist activities escalated, so too did the prominence of religious extremism, which increasingly became associated with mainstream religious identities. This association has often led to a backlash against entire communities, with Muslims in particular facing heightened scrutiny and discrimination.

1. Misinterpretation of Faith: The actions of extremist factions have often been mischaracterized as reflective of the broader Islamic faith, leading to widespread misconceptions about Islam as a whole. Many Muslims have sought to combat these narratives by emphasizing their faith's teachings on peace, compassion, and community, but the damage to public perception has been profound.

2. Rise of Anti-Muslim Sentiment: In many Western countries, the fear of terrorism fuelled anti-Muslim sentiments and policies. This climate of fear often led to calls for increased surveillance, profiling, and even outright discrimination against Muslim communities. The negative impact on societal cohesion and the rise of hate crimes against Muslims became alarming trends that reflected the complexities of religious extremism in contemporary society.

Prophetic Warnings and Apocalyptic Narratives

In the context of increasing terrorism and extremism, many religious communities began to issue prophetic warnings, interpreting these events through an apocalyptic lens. This surge in prophetic voices sought to make sense of the chaos and provide guidance in a world that seemed increasingly perilous.

1. Emergence of Prophetic Voices: Religious leaders, particularly within evangelical and charismatic Christian circles, began to frame contemporary events; ranging from terrorist attacks to natural disasters; as signs of the end times. This trend was characterized by an urgency to awaken the faithful to the moral and spiritual decay that they believed was indicative of approaching judgment.

2. Interpretative Framework: Many of these prophetic warnings drew upon biblical texts and historical precedents, suggesting that the current state of the world mirrored scenarios described in scripture. Interpretations of passages from the Book of Revelation, the Book of Daniel, and other prophetic texts were frequently cited, reinforcing the belief that humanity was on a trajectory toward catastrophic conflict and divine intervention.

3. Calls for Spiritual Renewal: Prophetic messages often called for spiritual renewal, repentance, and a return to traditional values. These warnings sought to mobilize believers to confront moral decay within society, emphasizing the importance of faith in the face of mounting fear. The rhetoric used by these leaders sometimes echoed apocalyptic themes, framing the current challenges as critical moments that could lead to redemption or destruction.

Cultural Reflections and Responses

The intersection of terrorism, religious extremism, and prophetic warnings has had far-reaching cultural implications. Media narratives often fueled apocalyptic fears, shaping public perception and discourse surrounding terrorism and its consequences.

1. Media Representation: News outlets frequently sensationalized terrorist incidents, reinforcing narratives of fear and insecurity. The portrayal of terrorists as embodiments of evil contributed to a societal narrative that emphasized a clash of civilizations, fostering an environment of distrust and polarization.

2. Increased Interest in Prophetic Literature: In response to the fears and uncertainties of the times, there has been a resurgence in interest in prophetic literature and teachings. Books, sermons, and online platforms dedicated to eschatology proliferated, providing a space for believers to engage with the idea of an impending apocalypse.

3. Interfaith Responses: Amidst the chaos, interfaith dialogue initiatives emerged, aiming to combat extremism and promote understanding among different faith communities. Religious leaders from various traditions came together to emphasize shared values and common humanity, striving to counter the narrative that equated faith with violence.

The escalation of terrorism and religious extremism in the early 21st century has reshaped global dynamics and sparked a profound wave of prophetic warnings. As societies grapple with the implications of violence and fear, the need for understanding, compassion, and spiritual renewal becomes increasingly urgent.

In this turbulent landscape, the intertwining of faith, ideology, and prophetic discourse continues to shape public consciousness. As prophetic voices rise amidst the chaos, humanity stands at a crossroads, confronted with the choice between fear and hope, violence and understanding, destruction and redemption. The outcomes of this struggle will not only determine the future of nations but also define the moral and spiritual trajectory of humanity as it navigates the challenges of a world in crisis.

Growing sense that the final battle is brewing, as East and West tensions rise

As the early 21st century unfolded, a growing sense emerged among many that the world was on the brink of a monumental confrontation; a final battle that some believe could be the culmination of centuries of ideological and spiritual conflict. This perception was fuelled by rising tensions between East and West, political upheavals, and a series of global crises that seemed to echo apocalyptic prophecies across various cultures and faiths.

The Historical Context of East vs. West Tensions

The tensions between Eastern and Western civilizations have deep historical roots, often characterized by political, religious, and cultural conflicts. The Cold War had already established a narrative of a polarized world, but the post-9/11 era reignited these sentiments with a new intensity.

1. Resurgence of Nationalism: In recent decades, nationalist movements have gained momentum across both the Eastern and Western blocs. In the West, there has been a rise in populism, often fuelled by fears of immigration, economic instability, and a perceived loss of cultural identity. In the East, countries like Russia and China have sought to assert their power on the global stage, often challenging Western hegemony. This resurgence of nationalism has exacerbated tensions, with both sides viewing the other as a threat to their way of life.

2. Ideological Clashes: The ideological divide remains significant, with the West often promoting democratic values and human rights, while some Eastern regimes emphasize state sovereignty and collectivism. This dichotomy has been evident in international conflicts, trade disputes, and diplomatic relations, often leading to a sense of inevitability regarding a larger confrontation.

The Role of Religious Narratives

Amid these geopolitical tensions, religious narratives have played a crucial role in shaping perceptions of an impending final battle. Many believers across various faith traditions have interpreted current events through the lens of prophecy, framing them as signs of a larger cosmic struggle.

1. Islamic Eschatology: In Islamic teachings, the concept of a final battle, known as the Battle of Armageddon or the Day of Judgment, is a significant theme. Some interpretations suggest that the conflict between the West and the Muslim world could be a precursor to this ultimate confrontation. Radical groups have exploited these beliefs to recruit followers, framing their struggles as part of a divine mission against perceived Western oppression.

2. Christian Apocalyptic Views: Similarly, many Christians have interpreted contemporary events, including conflicts in the Middle East, as fulfillments of biblical prophecy. The imagery of battles in the Book of Revelation, particularly those involving forces of good and evil, has been invoked to suggest that the final confrontation is drawing near. Some believe that the re-establishment of Israel and tensions surrounding Jerusalem could trigger the events leading to the Second Coming of Christ.

3. Interfaith Tensions: The growing animosity between various religious groups has further intensified these apocalyptic beliefs. Attacks on places of worship, hate crimes, and sectarian violence have contributed to a narrative of a world divided along religious lines, heightening fears of a final clash between faiths. This division not only fuels extremism but also undermines interfaith dialogue and cooperation.

Global Crises and Their Impact

Various global crises, including environmental disasters, economic instability, and health pandemics, have also been perceived as signs of an approaching reckoning. These crises often exacerbate existing tensions and lead to competition for resources, further intensifying East-West conflicts.

1. Environmental Degradation: The ongoing climate crisis has raised alarms globally, with many interpreting natural disasters as divine judgment or warnings of an impending apocalypse. The struggle for resources; such as water, arable land, and energy; has increasingly pitted nations against each other, creating a fertile ground for conflict. As climate change exacerbates existing inequalities, fears of resource wars loom large on the horizon.

2. Economic Inequality: Global economic disparities have widened, leading to increased dissatisfaction among populations. In the West, economic uncertainty has bred populism and anti-globalization sentiments, while in the East, rapid industrialization has created its own set of challenges, including labour exploitation and environmental degradation. This growing sense of injustice has the potential to ignite conflicts that could escalate into larger confrontations.

3. Health Crises: The COVID-19 pandemic further highlighted the fragility of global systems and the interconnectedness of humanity. The varying responses of Eastern and Western nations to the crisis have deepened mistrust, with accusations of blame and mismanagement fostering an environment of fear and paranoia. As nations grapple with the pandemic's aftermath, the potential for rising tensions remains high.

Cultural Reflections and Public Sentiment

The increasing belief that a final battle is brewing has permeated popular culture, political discourse, and everyday life. Many people, feeling the weight of uncertainty, have turned to prophetic interpretations of current events as a means of making sense of the chaos.

1. Popular Media and Literature: Movies, television shows, and literature have often explored themes of apocalyptic conflict, reflecting societal anxieties about the future. The rise of dystopian narratives, in which East and West are pitted against each other in catastrophic wars, resonates with audiences who perceive the world as increasingly precarious.

2. Political Rhetoric: Political leaders have sometimes invoked apocalyptic language to galvanize support or justify military interventions. The rhetoric of "us vs. them" has gained traction, further entrenching divisions and feeding into the narrative of an impending clash.

3. Public Perception: Surveys indicate a growing belief among people that the world is heading toward a catastrophic event. This sentiment is often coupled with a sense of helplessness, as individuals struggle to comprehend the complexities of global affairs. Many feel a deep yearning for spiritual guidance and clarity amid the chaos.

The combination of geopolitical tensions, ideological divides, and religious narratives has created a growing sense that the final battle is brewing as East and West tensions rise. As individuals grapple with the uncertainties of the present, the fear of an apocalyptic confrontation looms large in the collective consciousness.

Navigating this complex landscape requires not only an understanding of the historical and cultural contexts but also a commitment to fostering dialogue and cooperation across divides. As humanity stands at the precipice of potential conflict, the choices made in this critical moment will determine whether the world moves toward destruction or reconciliation. The narratives we embrace, the actions we take, and the values we uphold will ultimately shape the future of humanity as it faces the challenges of a world in crisis.

The Antichrist and the Rise of False Prophets

Exploration of "Antichrist" Figures in Modern History, Secularism as a False Religion

Throughout history, the term "Antichrist" has been used to describe figures that embody evil or opposition to Christ, representing a challenge to the moral and spiritual order established by Christianity. In modern times, the concept has evolved, expanding beyond individual leaders to encompass broader social, political, and ideological movements that some perceive as antithetical to Christian teachings.

1. The Evolution of the Antichrist Concept

In biblical prophecy, particularly in the New Testament, the Antichrist is often portrayed as a singular, malevolent figure who will emerge during the end times to deceive the masses and lead them away from the truth of Christ. This figure is commonly associated with tribulation, persecution, and moral decay. However, interpretations of who or what the Antichrist might be have varied significantly over the centuries.

a. Historical Figures: Various historical figures have been labelled as Antichrists by different groups, often in response to perceived threats to their faith or society. For example, leaders like Julius Caesar, Napoleon Bonaparte, and Adolf Hitler have been cited as embodiments of the Antichrist due to their tyrannical regimes, promotion of secular ideologies, or persecution of Christians and Jews. These interpretations often reflect the anxieties and moral struggles of the times, projecting fears of absolute power and moral corruption onto specific individuals.

b. Modern Antichrist Interpretations: In contemporary discussions, the notion of the Antichrist has broadened to encompass systemic issues rather than solely individual figures. This perspective aligns with the belief that societal and cultural movements; particularly those promoting secularism, materialism, and relativism; can act as forces that undermine spiritual values and lead people astray.

2. Secularism as a False Religion

One of the most prominent concepts within modern interpretations of the Antichrist is the rise of secularism, which some view as a false religion that undermines traditional faith and moral values. Secularism advocates for a separation of religion from civic affairs and public education, often promoting a worldview based on reason and empirical evidence rather than divine revelation.

a. The Secularization Process: Over the past few centuries, particularly since the Enlightenment, there has been a marked shift toward secularism in Western societies. This transformation has manifested in various ways, including the diminishing influence of religious institutions, the rise of scientific rationalism, and the increasing acceptance of diverse belief systems.

While these developments have fostered greater freedom of thought and expression, they have also led to a perceived erosion of moral foundations.

b. Implications of Secular Ideals: Many religious individuals argue that secularism promotes a moral relativism that undermines the objective truths and values found in religious teachings. In this view, the prioritization of personal autonomy and self-interest can lead to a culture where ethical standards are fluid and subjective, fostering a sense of chaos and confusion regarding right and wrong.

c. The Rise of New Idols: Secularism often brings with it a new set of idols, including the veneration of technology, wealth, and celebrity. These idols can distract individuals from spiritual pursuits and foster a culture of superficiality, where material success and status are valued above spiritual integrity. Critics argue that this cultural shift not only reflects a rejection of traditional values but also creates a vacuum that can be filled by false prophets; charismatic figures who offer empty promises of fulfillment without the grounding of genuine spiritual wisdom.

3. The False Prophets of Our Time

The rise of false prophets is often associated with the idea that charismatic leaders or ideologies can mislead people, leading them away from the truth. In the context of secularism, false prophets may emerge as figures who advocate for ideologies that seem appealing but ultimately lack the depth and truth found in genuine spiritual teachings.

a. Charismatic Leaders: In modern society, charismatic leaders often arise within political, social, and even religious movements, presenting themselves as visionaries or saviours. Some of these figures may espouse secular ideologies that promise utopian outcomes, appealing to the desires for progress, equality, or security. However, their teachings may lack a foundation in ethical or spiritual truth, leading followers down a path of disillusionment or conflict.

b. The Role of Media and Technology: The advent of mass media and the internet has amplified the influence of these false prophets, enabling them to reach broader audiences. Social media platforms, in particular, have allowed for the rapid dissemination of ideologies and charismatic messages, often blurring the lines between truth and deception. This phenomenon raises concerns about the vulnerability of individuals to manipulation and the potential for misinformation to flourish.

4. The Call for Discernment

In light of the rise of modern Antichrist figures and the influence of secularism as a false religion, there is a growing call for discernment among believers and spiritual seekers. Many argue that it is crucial to remain vigilant against the allure of false teachings and to seek a deeper understanding of faith that can withstand the challenges posed by contemporary society.

a. Grounding in Spiritual Truth: Believers are encouraged to deepen their understanding of their faith and to seek wisdom through prayer, study, and community engagement. By grounding themselves in the teachings of their religious traditions, individuals can cultivate the discernment necessary to navigate a world filled with competing ideologies and charismatic leaders.

b. Emphasizing Spiritual Values: There is a renewed emphasis on the importance of spiritual values such as compassion, humility, and integrity, as a counter to the materialism and individualism often promoted by secular ideologies. This call encourages individuals to prioritize relationships, community, and the pursuit of a higher purpose over the fleeting satisfaction of worldly desires.

As the world navigates the complexities of modern life, the exploration of Antichrist figures and the rise of secularism as a false religion serve as poignant reminders of the ongoing battle for truth and moral clarity. The call to discernment and the commitment to spiritual integrity are more relevant than ever as individuals confront the challenges of a rapidly changing world.

By understanding the historical context of these concepts and remaining grounded in faith, individuals can resist the allure of false prophets and ideologies that seek to undermine the foundations of their beliefs. In doing so, they can contribute to a more compassionate, just, and spiritually enriched world, ultimately standing against the forces that threaten to lead humanity astray.

Examination of Branham's Views on World Leaders, Politics, and Power as Apocalyptic Signs

Branham's views on world leaders, politics, and power are significant as they reflect his apocalyptic perspective, which frames contemporary events as manifestations of prophetic significance. He believed that various political figures and movements were indicative of the approaching end times, aligning with a broader narrative of moral decline and spiritual warfare.

1. Branham's Prophetic Framework

Branham's teachings often integrated his interpretation of scripture with his observations of global events. He positioned himself as a prophet, asserting that he received divine revelations that illuminated the spiritual significance of historical and political developments. His framework suggested that understanding the actions of world leaders and the state of global politics could provide insights into God's plan for humanity and the unfolding of prophetic events.

2. World Leaders as Indicators of Spiritual Conditions

a. Moral and Spiritual Corruption: Branham frequently spoke about the moral decay prevalent in political leadership, emphasizing that corrupt leaders were signs of an impending apocalypse. He believed that the rise of immorality among those in power reflected a broader spiritual decline in society. Branham's critiques extended to the political systems themselves, which he viewed as increasingly disconnected from divine principles.

b. Specific Leaders as Antichrist Figures: Branham identified certain political figures as potential embodiments of the Antichrist. For instance, he often referred to leaders like Adolf Hitler, whom he viewed as manifestations of evil due to their oppressive regimes and persecution of

144

vulnerable populations. Branham's rhetoric framed these leaders as harbingers of judgment, suggesting that their actions were part of a larger spiritual conflict between good and evil.

3. Political Events as Prophetic Fulfillments

a. Global Conflicts and Tensions: Branham interpreted major global conflicts; such as World War II and the Cold War; as significant events in the prophetic timeline. He believed that these conflicts were not merely historical occurrences but were intricately tied to biblical prophecies regarding the end times. Branham posited that the chaos and destruction resulting from such wars were precursors to the ultimate confrontation between good and evil, symbolizing the final battle foretold in scripture.

b. Political Alliances and Movements: Branham paid particular attention to international alliances and geopolitical shifts. He viewed these movements as manifestations of divine judgment, interpreting the realignment of nations as signs of the approaching end. For example, he spoke about the establishment of Israel as a nation in 1948 as a pivotal event, believing it fulfilled biblical prophecy and indicated the nearing of the end times.

4. The Role of Spiritual Authority in Politics

Branham emphasized the importance of spiritual authority over political power, asserting that true leadership must align with divine principles. He warned against the dangers of secularism and the erosion of faith in political spheres. In his teachings, he often contrasted spiritual authority with worldly power, suggesting that leaders who deviated from biblical truths would ultimately lead their nations to ruin.

a. The Church's Responsibility: Branham believed that the church had a critical role in guiding political leaders and influencing society. He encouraged believers to remain vigilant and prayerful, advocating for a return to spiritual values as a means of countering the moral decay he perceived in governance. This perspective positioned the church as a necessary counterbalance to the secularization of political systems.

5. Branham's Legacy and Influence on Contemporary Prophetic Movements

Branham's views on world leaders and politics have had a lasting impact on various prophetic movements within Christianity. His emphasis on the spiritual significance of political events resonates with many contemporary believers who view current global issues through a prophetic lens.

a. Apocalyptic Interpretations Today: Modern prophetic voices often echo Branham's teachings, drawing parallels between current political leaders and apocalyptic narratives. The lens through which they interpret global events remains rooted in a belief that the signs of the times indicate the imminent return of Christ and the unfolding of final judgment.

b. The Continued Relevance of Branham's Teachings: Branham's teachings continue to be relevant in discussions around morality, leadership, and the intersection of faith and politics. His prophetic insights serve as a foundation for believers navigating an increasingly complex world, encouraging them to seek understanding through a spiritual framework.

The Gog and Magog Prophecy and the Looming World War III

Biblical Prophecy of Gog and Magog: Interpretations and Potential Nations Involved

The prophecy of Gog and Magog is one of the most compelling and mysterious passages in the Bible, capturing the attention of theologians, historians, and modern prophecy enthusiasts alike. This prophecy is found primarily in the Old Testament, specifically in the Book of Ezekiel, chapters 38 and 39, and later in the Book of Revelation, where it takes on an apocalyptic tone. Both accounts describe a climactic and cataclysmic battle involving powerful forces that will descend upon Israel, an event that many believers interpret as part of the end times narrative.

1. The Origin of the Gog and Magog Prophecy

a. Ezekiel's Vision: The prophet Ezekiel first describes Gog and Magog in vivid terms, foreseeing a massive coalition of nations that will come against Israel in a battle of devastating proportions. In Ezekiel 38:2-3, God speaks to Ezekiel, saying, "Set your face against Gog, of the land of Magog, the chief prince of Meshech and Tubal." Here, Gog is presented as a ruler, while Magog represents a land or people group.

The prophecy continues to describe Gog's armies gathering from the "far north" to attack Israel, bringing with them an overwhelming force comprising multiple nations. Despite the power and ferocity of this alliance, God reassures that He will intervene directly, bringing about a miraculous victory for Israel.

b. Revelation and the End Times: The Book of Revelation, written centuries after Ezekiel, picks up the theme of Gog and Magog in a new context. In Revelation 20:8, Gog and Magog appear once more, symbolizing the forces of evil that Satan will rally at the end of the Millennium to battle against the faithful. This final showdown signifies the ultimate battle between good and evil before the establishment of God's eternal kingdom.

2. Historical Interpretations of Gog and Magog

Throughout history, the identity of Gog and Magog has been widely debated. The names "Gog" and "Magog" have been associated with various historical and mythical figures, regions, and nations over the centuries.

a. Early Jewish and Christian Thought: In early Jewish and Christian writings, Gog and Magog were often connected to distant lands and peoples who lay beyond the known world. Some interpreted them as representing barbarian tribes on the fringes of the Roman Empire, such as the Scythians or Huns. Early interpretations saw them as symbolizing foreign threats; peoples who might one day invade and wreak havoc on more "civilized" lands, fulfilling the prophecies of Ezekiel.

b. Medieval and Renaissance Views: During the Middle Ages and Renaissance, various rulers and theologians saw Gog and Magog as representing invaders from the East, including Mongol and Tatar forces who threatened Europe from Asia. These Eastern powers were often depicted as apocalyptic enemies in Christian thought, resonating with the sense of dread surrounding the fulfillment of Ezekiel's vision.

3. Modern Interpretations and the Cold War Era

In more recent times, particularly during the Cold War, the prophecy of Gog and Magog took on new geopolitical associations. Many prophecy interpreters began to speculate that Gog and Magog represented powerful nations that could lead an attack on Israel, setting the stage for World War III.

a. Russia as "Gog": A popular interpretation, especially among American evangelicals, associates Gog and Magog with Russia. This view stems from Ezekiel's description of the armies of Gog coming from the "far north," which, when plotted on a map, points toward Russia. The prophecy's language of a vast, overpowering military force also seems to align with Russia's historical role as a global superpower.

This interpretation became particularly popular during the Cold War, as the United States and the Soviet Union engaged in a tense standoff that many saw as apocalyptic in nature. Some viewed the Soviet Union's atheistic policies and aggressive stance toward the West as fitting with Gog's characteristics, envisioning Russia as the primary antagonist in a final conflict against Israel.

b. Allies of Gog; A Coalition of Nations: Ezekiel's prophecy also mentions other nations that will join forces with Gog, including Persia (modern-day Iran), Cush (commonly identified with Ethiopia or Sudan), and Put (Libya). Many prophecy scholars interpret this coalition as a group of Middle Eastern and African nations that could align against Israel in the end times.

Iran, in particular, has been seen as significant in this interpretation due to its historical and modern-day tensions with Israel, as well as its influence in the broader Middle East. Other nations in North Africa and the Middle East, such as Libya, have also been speculated as part of this alliance, contributing to the broader anticipation of an apocalyptic conflict centered on the Holy Land.

4. Interpretations of Gog and Magog in Contemporary Geopolitics

As modern conflicts and alliances shift, interpretations of Gog and Magog continue to evolve. With the resurgence of Russia's presence on the world stage, some prophecy scholars have reignited the notion that Russia may play a role in the ultimate fulfillment of Ezekiel's vision. Meanwhile, rising tensions in the Middle East, particularly around Israel and Iran, have also fueled discussions about the prophecy's relevance today.

a. Russia and Iran's Modern Alliance: Recent alliances between Russia and Iran have only added to the speculation, as both nations have significant military influence in Syria, which borders Israel. For those who interpret these alliances through the lens of prophecy, such developments may seem like modern echoes of the ancient coalition described in Ezekiel, sparking renewed interest in how current events may be unfolding according to biblical prophecy.

b. Broader Global Tensions and "End of Days" Warnings: In today's global climate of political and military tension, with shifting allegiances and escalating conflicts, the prophecy of Gog and Magog resonates with many who believe the world is on the brink of unprecedented upheaval. With the ongoing development of nuclear weapons and the spectre of large-scale warfare, the concept of a final showdown; an "Armageddon"; remains a potent topic in apocalyptic discourse.

5. Theological Implications of the Gog and Magog Prophecy

a. Divine Intervention and the Power of God: Ezekiel's prophecy not only highlights the threat posed by Gog and Magog but also emphasizes God's promise of protection over Israel. The prophecy reassures that, in the face of overwhelming opposition, God Himself will intervene, ensuring Israel's survival and demonstrating His power to all nations. This promise of divine intervention serves as a cornerstone of hope for believers who anticipate the fulfillment of the prophecy.

b. Prophetic Reassurance of Ultimate Justice: The final confrontation between good and evil, as foreshadowed by Gog and Magog, assures believers that justice will ultimately prevail. For Christians who view the Gog and Magog prophecy as a key component of the end times narrative, it represents God's ultimate triumph over the forces of darkness, offering a vision of justice and restoration in the wake of apocalyptic chaos.

Conclusion: The Ongoing Relevance of Gog and Magog

The prophecy of Gog and Magog continues to fascinate and intrigue, with interpretations adapting to each new historical and political era. Whether seen as a literal prediction of future nations clashing over Israel or as a symbolic representation of the ongoing spiritual battle between good and evil, the prophecy resonates with a timeless message of vigilance, faith, and the ultimate hope of divine justice. As global tensions persist, many who study biblical prophecy remain watchful, interpreting current events through the lens of ancient scripture, seeking signs of Gog and Magog in the unfolding story of our world.

Escalation of Conflicts in Eastern Europe, Asia, and the Middle East as Signs of Imminent War

As global tensions continue to rise, many prophecy scholars and commentators have looked to the escalation of conflicts in regions like Eastern Europe, Asia, and the Middle East as potential indicators of an impending, large-scale conflict. For those who interpret these developments through a biblical or prophetic lens, these regions represent more than just geopolitical hotspots; they are seen as key locations in the unfolding of end-time events, contributing to a sense of impending war on a global scale.

1. Eastern Europe: The Resurgence of Hostilities and Echoes of Old Tensions

a. Russian Aggression and the Specter of World Conflict: The ongoing hostilities in Eastern Europe, particularly the conflict involving Russia and Ukraine, have drawn significant attention as a potential catalyst for a broader, global confrontation. Russia's military actions and its expansionist aspirations have renewed fears reminiscent of the Cold War era, and many interpret these actions as signalling the revival of age-old conflicts between East and West.

For those who see biblical prophecy in these events, the resurgence of Russian aggression evokes Ezekiel's prophecy of a powerful force from the "far north" potentially mobilizing for a significant conflict. As Russia's influence extends across Europe, concerns of an all-out war are heightened, especially as countries in the region increase military spending, form alliances, and prepare for possible escalations. Some believers interpret this as a "Gog and Magog" style gathering, marking Russia as a potential antagonist in an approaching world war.

b. NATO and the Tensions of a Divided World: As tensions build in Eastern Europe, NATO's involvement has become a point of focus for many prophecy scholars. Some believe that NATO's strengthening role and its commitment to countering Russia's influence reflect an alignment of nations that could fulfill prophecies about global alliances in the final days. The potential for a world-shaking conflict between NATO-aligned countries and Russia raises concerns about a broader war involving multiple nations, reminiscent of the Armageddon narrative.

2. Asia: Rising Powers and the Gathering Storm

a. China's Global Influence and Military Expansion: In Asia, China's rapid military buildup and assertive stance in regions like the South China Sea are seen as part of a broader alignment of forces that could contribute to a world-shaping conflict. China's increasing role in the global economy, combined with its military expansion and assertive policies, has positioned it as a major power that could play a critical role in the future of global affairs. China's close alliance with Russia and its adversarial stance toward Western powers have led some to believe that it may play a significant part in an eventual end-time conflict.

Prophecy interpreters often draw connections between China's rise and biblical references to vast armies from the East. In Revelation 16:12, for instance, it describes the drying up of the Euphrates River to prepare the way for the "kings of the east," potentially referencing massive Eastern armies advancing toward the final battleground. China's position as a formidable power, with millions of soldiers and vast resources, leads some to see it as a possible fulfillment of this prophecy.

b. Tensions in Taiwan and the Risk of Regional Escalation: The situation in Taiwan also has significant implications for regional and global stability. China's claim over Taiwan and the United States' support of the island nation raise the stakes, as a conflict over Taiwan could easily draw multiple countries into a larger confrontation. For prophecy scholars, a war involving Taiwan could serve as a flashpoint that brings East and West into direct military engagement, igniting a conflict with far-reaching implications.

3. The Middle East: An Ongoing Centre of Conflict and Prophecy

a. Iran, Israel, and the Longstanding Struggle: The Middle East has long been viewed as a focal point of biblical prophecy, and current events continue to affirm its significance in the eyes of prophecy interpreters. The conflict between Israel and neighbouring nations, particularly Iran, has intensified in recent years. Iran's nuclear ambitions and its hostility toward Israel are seen as key elements in the potential buildup to an end-time conflict.

Prophecy scholars often point to scriptures that speak of conflicts involving Israel in the last days. Ezekiel's prophecy of Gog and Magog describes a coalition of nations coming against Israel, which many believe could include Iran and its allies. Iran's influence in Syria and Lebanon, along with its alliances with Russia and other anti-Western powers, raises concerns about a broader coalition that could fulfill these prophecies.

b. The Influence of Terrorist Organizations and Militant Groups: Militant groups such as Hezbollah, Hamas, and other factions throughout the Middle East add another layer of complexity to the region's conflicts. Supported by various nations hostile to Israel, these groups continue to engage in conflicts that destabilize the region and heighten the risk of large-scale warfare. These groups' ongoing threats against Israel and their connection to powerful allies amplify concerns that the Middle East is a powder keg on the verge of igniting a larger war, possibly drawing in nations from around the world.

c. Prophetic Views of Jerusalem and the Final Conflict: Jerusalem holds a special significance in end-time prophecy, as many believe it to be the location of key events leading to the return of Christ. The contested status of Jerusalem and its centrality in Israeli-Palestinian tensions are seen as symbolic of a larger spiritual battle. Various prophecies, particularly in Zechariah and Revelation, indicate that Jerusalem will be a focal point in the final struggle between good and evil. For believers, any escalation involving Jerusalem and surrounding nations resonates with prophetic warnings of the end times.

4. The Role of Prophetic Warnings and Global Awareness

As conflicts escalate across Eastern Europe, Asia, and the Middle East, many modern-day prophets and religious leaders interpret these events as clear warnings of imminent war and ultimate destruction. For example, William Branham and others spoke of a world filled with wars and conflicts in which East and West would face off in devastating battles. In Branham's visions, he forewarned of apocalyptic scenes of warfare and the looming shadow of nuclear destruction, emphasizing that humanity would ultimately face judgment for its rejection of spiritual truth and embrace of materialism and immorality.

5. The Global Perspective: A World at the Brink of Unprecedented Conflict

Today, the spread of information through media and the internet has made global tensions far more immediate and accessible to everyone. News of conflicts in one part of the world can now reach the rest of the globe in seconds, creating an atmosphere of heightened awareness and anxiety. This accessibility has amplified the sense that humanity is on the brink of a major, apocalyptic confrontation, and religious communities are increasingly vigilant, interpreting world events as markers in a divine timeline leading to the end.

For many believers, the convergence of crises in these critical regions signifies a warning that humanity may be approaching its final, catastrophic chapter. Modern prophecy scholars argue that we are living in a time when the conditions described in the Bible are being fulfilled, and that these escalating conflicts may indeed be leading up to the final conflict described as Armageddon.

The Stakes of Humanity's Survival: Nuclear Threats and the Approach of Armageddon

As tensions build among nations and powerful arsenals of nuclear weapons continue to grow, humanity faces an unprecedented threat to its very survival. Since the revelation of nuclear power during World War II, the stakes of global conflict have changed forever. Today, the potential for total annihilation looms larger than ever, leading many to question if we are on the brink of the prophesied end-time battle; Armageddon.

1. Nuclear Weapons: The Ultimate Tool of Destruction

a. The Nuclear Arms Race and Global Vulnerability: The Cold War introduced the concept of "Mutually Assured Destruction" (MAD), where the use of nuclear weapons by one superpower would lead to a devastating counterattack by the other, effectively ending life on earth. Although the Cold War ended, the nuclear threat remains as powerful and immediate as ever, with an estimated 13,000 nuclear warheads still in existence. As technology has advanced, so too has the destructive potential of these weapons, making the reality of a nuclear Armageddon more terrifying and real than ever before.

Modern nuclear capabilities mean that, in minutes, entire cities or even nations could be wiped off the map. With this kind of power in the hands of humans, any misstep, miscommunication, or intentional escalation could lead to catastrophic consequences. A single nuclear strike could trigger a chain reaction of retaliations, plunging the world into a nuclear winter with devastating consequences for human life, the environment, and global stability.

b. Proliferation of Nuclear Weapons and Rogue States: The expansion of nuclear capabilities to countries outside of the traditional nuclear powers has intensified the global threat. Nations such as North Korea, which actively seeks to increase its nuclear arsenal, pose unpredictable risks, as do ongoing tensions surrounding Iran's nuclear ambitions. These countries may view nuclear weapons as essential for self-defence, deterrence, or even as tools for asserting their influence on the world stage.

The presence of nuclear weapons in unstable or autocratic hands raises the stakes exponentially, heightening the possibility that a nuclear conflict could erupt in response to political or ideological motivations. Many religious and prophecy-focused groups see this unchecked proliferation as a sign that humanity is moving toward a point of no return, where the drive for power outweighs concerns for collective survival.

2. Prophetic Connections: Nuclear Weapons as Signs of the End Times

For those who interpret current events through the lens of prophecy, the existence of nuclear weapons fulfils some of the most ominous predictions of the end times.

a. Fire and Destruction Imagery in Biblical Prophecies: In the Bible, apocalyptic prophecies frequently refer to fire, brimstone, and destruction on a global scale. Passages from Revelation speak of burning cities, falling stars, and a cataclysm that scorches the earth; all imagery that resonates with the potential effects of nuclear warfare. For many believers, the capacity for nuclear destruction is not merely a scientific achievement but the realization of prophecies warning of mankind's ability to bring about its own end.

One of the most famous prophecies comes from Revelation 8:10-11, which describes a star called "Wormwood" falling from the heavens, turning waters bitter and bringing suffering to humankind. While interpretations vary, some see in this description a metaphor for the radioactive fallout and contamination that nuclear war could bring, polluting water sources and rendering land uninhabitable.

b. William Branham's Visions of Global Catastrophe: The prophetic preacher William Branham spoke extensively about the end times, warning that human civilization would face unparalleled destruction. He described vivid visions of cities engulfed in flames, clouds of smoke, and utter devastation. For Branham, these visions were not simply abstract symbols; he believed they were real, foreseen events that would mark humanity's final moments before the ultimate divine judgment.

Branham warned that America, in particular, was in danger of facing judgment for its moral and spiritual failings, and that a fiery destruction awaited if it continued down its current path. Many who follow his teachings view the current nuclear threat as the fulfillment of his warnings, with the potential for nuclear war seen as the culmination of human rebellion and a literal bringing of fire down from heaven.

3. The Concept of Armageddon: Humanity's Final Battle

a. Understanding Armageddon in the Context of Modern Conflict: The term "Armageddon" originates from the Book of Revelation, where it is depicted as the site of the ultimate battle between good and evil, waged at the end of days. Armageddon represents both a physical place; identified as Mount Megiddo in Israel; and a metaphor for the final showdown between the forces of darkness and light. Many view it as the moment where humanity faces its greatest test, with a decisive outcome for the soul of mankind.

In today's world, Armageddon is often associated with global warfare that threatens to eradicate human civilization. Nuclear conflict, with its unparalleled destructive capacity, is seen by many as the fulfillment of this apocalyptic vision. The possibility of a world-ending war involving nuclear weapons resonates deeply with the biblical narrative of Armageddon as a moment of ultimate destruction and reckoning.

b. Modern Interpretations: The East vs. West Confrontation: Many prophecy scholars believe that the escalating tensions between East and West, particularly between the United States and Russia or China, could signify the buildup to Armageddon. The rivalry between these superpowers, each with the capability to destroy the other many times over, echoes the biblical vision of opposing forces gathering for a final, devastating confrontation.

Eastern and Western ideological divides, combined with nuclear arsenals and geopolitical alliances, make the concept of Armageddon feel more immediate and plausible. This has led many to see current conflicts and the fragile balance of power as precursors to the ultimate battle described in prophecy.

4. The Growing Sense of Urgency Among Religious Communities

a. Calls for Repentance and Return to Faith: Faced with the looming threat of nuclear Armageddon, many religious leaders and communities are calling for repentance, emphasizing a return to moral and spiritual values as the only way to avert disaster. They urge individuals and nations to seek divine forgiveness, believing that a collective return to faith can stay God's hand and prevent total destruction.

Many churches and religious organizations interpret the nuclear threat as a wake-up call to humankind to turn back to God. Some encourage fasting, prayer, and other forms of spiritual discipline, believing that these actions can help avert the ultimate catastrophe. For them, the nuclear threat serves as both a warning and a reminder that the fate of the world may be tied to humanity's collective moral and spiritual choices.

b. Prophecies and Visions of Hope Amidst Despair: While the threat of nuclear annihilation looms, some prophecy interpreters hold on to the hope of divine intervention. They believe that God will ultimately protect the faithful, ensuring the survival of a remnant that will endure beyond Armageddon. Some visions and interpretations suggest that while humanity may face immense suffering, a period of renewal and restoration will follow, offering hope for those who remain steadfast in their faith.

5. Humanity's Role in Shaping the Future

The modern nuclear threat, while deeply terrifying, also emphasizes human agency and responsibility. It serves as a stark reminder that humanity holds in its hands both the power of creation and the power of destruction. Many believe that God has given humanity the freedom to choose its destiny, and the decisions made in these critical times could determine whether the world plunges into catastrophe or finds a way to peace.

For prophecy scholars, the choice before humanity is not merely a question of survival but a test of spiritual integrity, moral commitment, and reverence for divine law. Whether humanity chooses peace over conflict, compassion over hatred, and faith over secularism may ultimately determine if Armageddon remains a vision of the future or a tragic reality of the present.

The stakes of humanity's survival are higher than ever, as nuclear threats converge with prophetic warnings to create an atmosphere of urgency and reflection. With nuclear arsenals at the ready and ideological tensions escalating, humanity stands on the edge, contemplating both its past choices and the possibility of a cataclysmic end. The concept of Armageddon, once an abstract prophecy, now resonates as a very real, imminent danger; leaving the world to ponder its fate and what can be done to avoid the ultimate destruction.

Global Pandemics and Natural Disasters

Analysis of COVID-19 and Other Recent Pandemics as Apocalyptic Harbingers

In recent years, global pandemics like COVID-19, SARS, and Ebola have shaken humanity to its core, reminding people of the frailty of human life and society's vulnerability to unseen forces. For many, these pandemics seem to echo age-old warnings about the end times, stirring fears of an approaching apocalypse and encouraging closer examination of the events foretold in prophecy.

Pandemics have long been associated with apocalyptic imagery, dating back to ancient religious texts, which often describe pestilences as part of divine judgment or natural upheavals that signal the end of days. The impact of COVID-19 and other recent pandemics has rekindled these ideas, leading some to believe that these global health crises are more than biological phenomena; they could be signs of a world nearing its final chapter.

1. Pandemics in Biblical and Prophetic Texts: A Symbol of Judgment

a. Pestilence as a Warning of the End Times: Pandemics, often referred to as pestilences in the Bible, are mentioned repeatedly in apocalyptic literature. The Book of Revelation, for instance, speaks of the "Four Horsemen of the Apocalypse," where one of the riders brings pestilence, disease, and widespread suffering upon humanity (Revelation 6:8). This horseman symbolizes divine judgment upon a world gone astray, and many believe pandemics are manifestations of these ancient prophecies. Such references create a perception that modern-day pandemics like COVID-19 fulfill or echo these ancient warnings, showing humanity a glimpse of the impending end times.

In addition to Revelation, passages in the Old Testament mention plagues and pestilence as divine responses to widespread sin or societal corruption. When humanity becomes consumed by immorality, neglect of spiritual principles, or hubris, these texts suggest that plagues may serve as reminders of human frailty and the need for humility and repentance.

b. Prophecies of Modern-Day Prophets: Some modern prophetic figures, including William Branham, have made references to widespread disease as an indicator of moral decay and divine dissatisfaction. Branham, for example, warned that unchecked moral and spiritual decline would invite God's judgment, often manifesting through natural disasters, plagues, or global chaos. His warnings, among others, align with the idea that pandemics are more than coincidental; they serve as spiritual reminders, pointing to humanity's urgent need for redemption and a return to faith.

2. COVID-19: A Global Catastrophe and its Profound Impact

a. Unprecedented Scale and Global Response: COVID-19 rapidly emerged as one of the most severe global crises of the 21st century, spreading across every continent and disrupting daily life for billions. Governments instituted unprecedented lockdowns, health systems became overwhelmed, and economies experienced a dramatic downturn. For many, the sudden, all-encompassing nature of COVID-19 seemed to defy the typical experience of modern society's ability to contain crises, leading people to question if it was something greater; a warning, perhaps, of more profound challenges ahead.

The psychological impact of COVID-19 is profound. The isolation, loss, and constant anxiety have led to a global mental health crisis, with people experiencing increased depression, loneliness, and existential fear. These emotions, coupled with the overwhelming mortality rate and the rapid spread of the virus, have caused many to contemplate whether the pandemic was a harbinger of the end times. COVID-19's sweeping devastation echoes biblical descriptions of pestilences that precede divine judgment, suggesting that humanity is facing a moment of reckoning.

b. Pandemics and the Fragility of Modern Society: The COVID-19 pandemic has exposed vulnerabilities in even the most advanced societies. Medical supplies, healthcare infrastructure, and emergency preparedness proved inadequate, revealing how unprepared humanity is for global-scale crises. This realization has instilled fear and anxiety in many, underscoring the notion that no amount of technological progress can shield humanity from nature's unpredictable wrath.

COVID-19 has also highlighted divisions within society, with misinformation, political polarization, and social unrest rising amid the crisis. These fractures may symbolize deeper issues within humanity; moral and spiritual fractures that pandemics only amplify. For those looking at these events from a prophetic perspective, COVID-19 has unveiled humanity's collective fragility, signalling that the end could be closer than imagined.

3. Lessons and Spiritual Reflections During the Pandemic

a. Calls for Repentance and Spiritual Awakening: Throughout history, pandemics have often been accompanied by calls for repentance and spiritual reevaluation. With COVID-19, religious leaders worldwide have urged people to reflect on their lives, values, and priorities. The pandemic's disruption of daily routines has given people an opportunity to reconsider what is truly important, encouraging many to turn back to faith and spirituality.

Some religious communities have interpreted COVID-19 as an opportunity to seek forgiveness, make amends, and realign with divine principles. For those with prophetic inclinations, the pandemic is seen as God's way of shaking humanity, pushing it to confront its moral failings and renew its spiritual commitments. This interpretation aligns with Branham's and other prophets' teachings, who have warned that humanity must return to faith and moral integrity to avoid divine wrath.

b. Pandemic as a Test of Humanity's Compassion and Unity: The COVID-19 pandemic also serves as a test of humanity's ability to come together in times of crisis. While pandemics bring widespread suffering, they also present opportunities for collective compassion, unity, and resilience. Many religious perspectives hold that pandemics reveal humanity's potential to rise above individual interests and to prioritize communal well-being. This pandemic, however, has exposed both the strengths and weaknesses of this potential.

For believers, the pandemic's challenges serve as a reminder that humanity must overcome its divisions to survive the coming trials. Prophetic interpretations see the pandemic as a preview of the moral and spiritual tests humanity will face in the end times. If humanity can learn compassion, selflessness, and humility now, it may stand a chance against even greater apocalyptic trials to come.

4. Other Recent Pandemics: A Pattern of Warning Signs

a. Ebola, SARS, and MERS as Warning Events: Before COVID-19, other pandemics like Ebola, SARS, and MERS served as early indicators of a global health crisis. While they did not reach the scale of COVID-19, these pandemics demonstrated how easily diseases could spread in our interconnected world. For some, these events were early warnings; a series of "birth pains," as some prophecies describe; leading up to a larger crisis.

Religious scholars and prophecy interpreters point to these earlier pandemics as pieces of a broader pattern, suggesting that each outbreak is part of a buildup toward a more catastrophic event. As each pandemic unfolds with greater global reach, it appears to fulfill the concept of an escalating series of plagues that would mark the end times.

b. Prophetic Patterns and the Urgency of the Times: From a prophetic viewpoint, the succession of pandemics in recent decades aligns with biblical teachings that the end times will be marked by a steady increase in natural and human-made disasters. This "intensifying pattern" is seen by many as evidence that humanity is progressing toward a decisive climax, with pandemics serving as clear indicators that time is running out.

Religious communities, aware of these patterns, often stress the urgency of returning to faith and preparing spiritually for what is to come. The rise in pandemics is interpreted as a message for humanity to heed the warnings, turn back from moral decay, and prepare for a time of divine intervention.

5. Pandemics and the Fulfillment of End-Time Prophecies

The rise of pandemics like COVID-19, coupled with environmental disasters and moral decay, seems to echo key elements of biblical prophecy. The convergence of these events has led many to view the present age as a fulfillment of ancient predictions regarding the last days. With humanity facing both a biological and spiritual crisis, the urgency for repentance, compassion, and moral reform is more pressing than ever.

As pandemics continue to emerge and impact humanity on an unprecedented scale, people are left to wonder whether these events are simply random or part of a larger, prophetic sequence leading toward the end of days. For those who interpret these events through a spiritual lens, pandemics like COVID-19 are not just biological challenges; they are divine wake-up calls, urging humanity to heed the signs, reflect on its moral direction, and prepare for a future that may be as uncertain as it is inevitable.

Rise of Natural Disasters: Fires, Earthquakes, Floods Seen as Divine Judgments

In recent decades, the frequency and intensity of natural disasters have increased dramatically, prompting concern and speculation about their origins and implications. For many, this surge in catastrophic events; raging wildfires, devastating earthquakes, floods, and extreme weather; aligns with the warnings in prophetic texts, which describe such phenomena as divine judgments and signs of an impending apocalypse. These disasters are not merely environmental; they are viewed as spiritual harbingers, suggesting that humanity is being called to confront its moral failures and return to faith.

1. Biblical Prophecies and Natural Disasters: Signs of Divine Displeasure

a. Fire as a Tool of Judgment: In the Bible and other religious texts, fire frequently appears as an instrument of divine judgment. The destruction of Sodom and Gomorrah, where fire rained down to punish the cities' immoral behaviour, serves as one of the most striking examples of fire's symbolic role in executing God's wrath. For those who interpret modern natural disasters as acts of judgment, widespread wildfires are seen as a contemporary echo of this ancient event. In recent years, places like California, Australia, and the Amazon rainforest have experienced massive wildfires, with intense flames consuming vast landscapes and displacing countless people. Many interpret these fires as signs that humanity's actions; its greed, environmental abuse, and moral decay; are angering divine forces.

b. Earthquakes and Their Apocalyptic Significance: Earthquakes, too, have biblical significance. In the New Testament, Jesus mentions earthquakes as one of the indicators of the end times, warning that they will increase in frequency and intensity as humanity approaches the final days. Earthquakes are unique in their sudden, ground-shaking impact, symbolizing the idea of the earth itself rebelling against human misdeeds. In recent years, earthquakes have caused devastation across regions like Haiti, Nepal, Japan, and Indonesia, resulting in massive loss of life and prompting many to view them as warnings of divine displeasure.

c. Floods as Signs of Renewal and Wrath: Flooding holds a complex role in religious texts, often symbolizing both destruction and the possibility of renewal. The story of Noah's Ark recounts how God used a flood to cleanse the earth of sin, sparing only those who lived righteously. Today's devastating floods; such as those in Pakistan, China, and various coastal regions; are seen as a reminder of humanity's vulnerability before divine forces. For some, floods represent another call to repentance, reminding humanity that if it does not change its ways, it may face further calamity.

2. The Increase in Frequency and Severity of Disasters

a. Climate Change and the Prophetic Connection: While science attributes the increase in natural disasters to climate change, many believe this explanation does not negate their spiritual significance. Instead, they view human-caused climate change as a symptom of humanity's moral decay; greed, selfishness, and disregard for the earth. In this sense, the climate crisis aligns with prophecy, indicating that humanity's disregard for divine principles has manifested in environmental catastrophe. From this perspective, fires, earthquakes, and floods are not random or solely natural events; they are interconnected, resulting from human negligence of both environmental and spiritual responsibilities.

b. Patterns of Intensification: The pattern of intensifying natural disasters fits well with prophetic teachings that describe the end times as marked by increasing turmoil and destruction. Just as the Bible describes the last days as filled with "birth pains" that escalate over time, modern disasters are seen as growing warnings that humanity is running out of time. As each new disaster exceeds the last in intensity and destruction, the world appears to be following the exact path foretold in prophecy.

3. Divine Judgment and the Call to Repentance

a. A Call to Moral Reform: For those who interpret these events spiritually, natural disasters are more than tragic occurrences; they are calls for humanity to reform its ways. The increase in disasters is viewed as a series of divine wake-up calls, urging people to abandon sinful behaviour and return to a life centered around faith, compassion, and humility. This view sees God using these events to encourage humanity to reject materialism, selfishness, and corruption, reminding people of their duty to care for the earth and each other.

Religious leaders often interpret disasters as warnings, suggesting that these events are intended to lead humanity toward introspection and repentance. They emphasize that only by addressing the root causes of greed, moral decay, and environmental disregard can humanity avoid further judgment and potentially stave off the ultimate disaster; the final apocalypse.

b. Fulfillment of Prophecies about Environmental Chaos: Prophecies from figures like William Branham emphasize that the end times will be marked by chaos on a global scale, with nature itself appearing to turn against humanity. Branham's teachings specifically warned of increased natural disasters, which he saw as signs that humanity's moral decline had reached a tipping point. His followers view today's events as fulfillment of these predictions, interpreting every catastrophe as confirmation that the end times are approaching.

4. The Interconnected Nature of Disaster and Morality

a. Humanity's Responsibility and the Need for Spiritual Awakening: From a spiritual perspective, the rise in natural disasters is a reflection of humanity's broken relationship with both the earth and divine principles. The Bible frequently discusses humanity's role as steward of creation, a role that has been largely neglected in favor of exploitation and consumption. As humanity's disrespect for the environment and each other intensifies, so do the consequences. Fires, floods, and earthquakes thus serve as reminders of the responsibilities humanity has failed to uphold, urging a return to spiritual values and environmental responsibility.

b. Apocalyptic Views on Restoration and Renewal: Some view these natural disasters as a necessary part of the process leading to an eventual restoration of the world. Just as a fire clears a forest to allow for new growth, these disasters are seen as part of a divine cleansing process. However, this interpretation is not without its sombre undertone: it suggests that humanity's refusal to repent and realign with divine principles could result in an overwhelming catastrophe from which only the righteous will emerge. In this view, disasters are both judgment and preparation for a final renewal; a painful but essential step toward a new spiritual era.

5. Public Fear and Spiritual Awakening in Response to Disasters

a. Growing Public Concern and Awareness: As people witness more frequent and intense natural disasters, there is a growing sense of unease and introspection about the future. Public fear and curiosity about prophetic interpretations have surged, with many seeking answers about the spiritual significance of these events. This renewed interest in prophecy and spiritual guidance has brought apocalyptic teachings back into popular discourse, encouraging people to consider the deeper, moral implications of environmental disasters.

b. Shift Toward Faith and Spiritual Communities: Many people affected by natural disasters find themselves turning to faith as a means of comfort and understanding. Disasters prompt people to reconsider what truly matters, pushing them toward community, compassion, and spirituality. Religious communities often step in to provide support, interpreting these events through a prophetic lens and offering hope and guidance. This shift toward faith in response to natural disasters reflects an underlying desire for meaning and a return to foundational principles amid chaos.

6. Looking Ahead: What Do These Signs Mean for the Future?

The rise of natural disasters, coupled with moral decline and technological advances, presents a complex and unsettling picture for humanity's future. Many believe that these events are signalling the imminent fulfillment of prophecy and a final warning for humanity to change its ways. Fires, floods, earthquakes, and other catastrophes appear to be building toward a climactic event, leading many to prepare spiritually and morally for what lies ahead.

For those who interpret natural disasters as divine judgments, these events are not random but carefully orchestrated signs intended to awaken humanity. In this perspective, the only path forward is through repentance, spiritual renewal, and a genuine commitment to change. Whether these disasters are viewed scientifically or spiritually, they present a profound challenge that asks humanity to reconsider its actions and priorities in an age of unprecedented upheaval.

Growing Human Impact on Nature and Climate Change as an End-Times Event

The profound impact humans have had on the natural world has dramatically altered the environment, leading to significant ecological shifts and contributing to what many see as signs of the "end times." From large-scale industrialization to deforestation, pollution, and the relentless extraction of natural resources, human activities have reshaped landscapes, disrupted ecosystems, and pushed the planet toward a state of ecological crisis. Climate change, seen by many as the ultimate consequence of humanity's disregard for nature, embodies what some view as a sign of divine judgment or an apocalyptic event in the making.

1. Humanity's Role in Shaping the Earth's Future

a. Industrialization and Pollution: The Industrial Revolution marked a turning point where technology and machinery began to drive human progress, transforming economies and societies worldwide. However, this progress came at a cost. Factories and transportation systems fuelled by coal and oil released massive amounts of carbon dioxide, sulfur dioxide, and other pollutants into the air, leading to smog, acid rain, and contamination of natural resources. Industrial waste discharged into rivers and oceans disrupted aquatic ecosystems, poisoning water supplies, killing marine life, and harming communities dependent on these resources.

b. Deforestation and Habitat Destruction: Deforestation, driven by agriculture, logging, and urban expansion, has decimated forests worldwide. Forests act as the planet's lungs, absorbing CO_2 and producing oxygen. As they disappear, CO_2 levels in the atmosphere rise, intensifying the greenhouse effect and warming the earth. Beyond climate implications, deforestation has destroyed countless animal habitats, leading to the extinction of species and the collapse of ecosystems. This destruction of natural habitats highlights humanity's prioritization of economic gains over environmental stewardship, a trend that many see as a moral and spiritual failing.

c. Overexploitation of Resources: Human society has increasingly exploited the earth's resources, including fossil fuels, minerals, and precious metals. As populations grow and economies expand, this consumption has only accelerated, leading to the depletion of resources and the disruption of ecological balance. Overfishing, mining, and unsustainable agriculture have depleted soils and oceans, risking future food and water security. Many see this reckless consumption as a form of idolatry, with humanity worshiping wealth and progress at the expense of nature's integrity; a direct violation of the divine mandate to steward the earth responsibly.

2. Climate Change as a Catalyst for the "End of Days"

a. Rising Temperatures and Extreme Weather Events: One of the most concerning effects of climate change is the rapid rise in global temperatures, which has resulted in increasingly erratic and extreme weather patterns. Heatwaves, hurricanes, droughts, and floods have become more frequent and severe, devastating communities and ecosystems alike. Prophetic teachings often warn of chaos in nature as a precursor to the end times, and many view these unprecedented weather patterns as a fulfillment of those warnings. The deadly combination of rising temperatures, water scarcity, and extreme weather events points to a world in distress, unable to support its inhabitants as it once did.

b. Melting Ice Caps and Rising Sea Levels: The warming climate has caused polar ice caps and glaciers to melt at an alarming rate, contributing to rising sea levels. This rise threatens coastal cities and island nations with flooding, displacement, and economic ruin. Entire communities are at risk of disappearing as oceans encroach upon once-secure lands. In the Bible and other religious texts, the idea of rising waters often symbolizes judgment and cleansing; a return of a flood-like event, reminiscent of Noah's Ark. For many, this modern-day flood is not only a scientific consequence of climate change but also a metaphorical reflection of humanity's failures, a sign of divine displeasure with the state of the world.

c. Loss of Biodiversity: Climate change, coupled with habitat destruction, has led to a dramatic loss of biodiversity. Species extinction rates have accelerated, with many scientists warning that we are on the brink of the "sixth mass extinction." In religious prophecy, the destruction of animal life and the natural world is often seen as a harbinger of the end times. Some interpret this mass die-off as a sign that the balance of life on earth has been disrupted beyond repair, a warning that humanity's continued disregard for nature may bring about catastrophic consequences for all forms of life.

3. Prophetic Interpretations of Climate Change as Divine Judgment

a. Climate Catastrophe as Punishment for Human Pride: Prophetic figures and religious leaders have often spoken about the dangers of pride and hubris, cautioning that humanity's belief in its dominion over nature could lead to ruin. William Branham, among others, warned that humanity's technological and scientific achievements, while impressive, might ultimately bring judgment upon the world if not used responsibly. Branham's followers interpret climate change as a direct consequence of humanity's excessive pride; believing that the earth's resources were endless and could be consumed without restraint. This hubris, they argue, is part of a broader moral and spiritual decay that prophecy has long warned would invite divine punishment.

b. Disregard for Creation as a Sin: Many religious teachings emphasize the importance of respecting creation as a divine gift. According to this view, the earth and its resources were given to humanity under the condition of responsible stewardship. By polluting the earth, destroying ecosystems, and causing widespread suffering among God's creatures, humanity has violated its covenant with the divine. Climate change, in this context, is not merely a result of greenhouse gases or industrial activity; it's a divine reckoning, a call for humanity to account for its sins against creation. This perspective sees natural disasters and climate crises as part of God's efforts to reclaim the earth from those who would defile it.

4. Spiritual and Ethical Responses to Climate Change

a. A Call to Repentance and Change: For those who interpret climate change as an apocalyptic sign, the crisis is not just a physical challenge but a moral one. Religious and spiritual communities often advocate for repentance, urging individuals to adopt more sustainable, compassionate, and humble lifestyles. They view acts of conservation, environmentalism, and humility before nature as forms of repentance. The goal is not just to reduce emissions or clean up pollution but to realign humanity's relationship with the divine, recognizing that the earth's resources are gifts that must be respected, preserved, and shared equitably.

b. Return to Simplicity and Spiritual Values: Many spiritual leaders suggest that the solution to the climate crisis lies in a return to simplicity and traditional values. Materialism, consumerism, and the desire for constant technological progress are seen as forms of modern idolatry, which have distracted humanity from its core spiritual mission. By living more simply, embracing humility, and prioritizing community over consumption, individuals and societies can work toward restoring balance and, perhaps, averting further judgment.

c. Unity Across Faiths and Cultures: The global nature of the climate crisis has led many religious communities to advocate for unity and collaboration across faiths and cultures. Despite differences in doctrine, a common theme emerges: the need to protect and preserve the earth. Some interpret this unity as an opportunity for humanity to fulfill a divine purpose, putting aside divisions and working collectively to save creation. This unity is seen as both a moral imperative and a hopeful sign that humanity, even at the brink of disaster, can turn toward righteousness.

5. The Urgency of Action in Light of Prophetic Warnings

a. Last Chance for Humanity to Change: Prophecies about the end times often speak of a period of warning and opportunity; a window during which humanity can repent and change its ways before it is too late. Many believe that this period is now, that the increase in climate-related disasters is a final wake-up call. This urgency is reinforced by scientific warnings that time is running out to reverse environmental damage and prevent catastrophic outcomes. Spiritual leaders urge humanity to act swiftly, not only to save the planet but also to restore its relationship with the divine.

b. Consequences of Inaction and Final Judgment: For those who view climate change as part of apocalyptic prophecy, the stakes are high. Failure to heed these warnings could lead to a final judgment, a cataclysmic end to the world as we know it. Religious texts frequently describe scenes of fire, drought, famine, and other disasters as part of the end-times narrative, painting a picture of a world pushed to its limits by the consequences of human action. Many believe that without genuine repentance and significant changes, humanity may face divine retribution on a scale unprecedented in history.

The climate crisis, from this perspective, is not merely an environmental issue but a spiritual journey. Humanity is at a crossroads, and its future hinges on whether it can learn to respect creation, act with humility, and prioritize spiritual values over material gains. The natural disasters and crises brought on by climate change serve as both a mirror, reflecting humanity's sins, and a guide, pointing toward a path of renewal. For those who see climate change as an end-times event, the journey ahead is one of repentance, transformation, and ultimately, redemption; an opportunity to avert disaster and fulfill humanity's divine purpose.

The Final Chapters of Prophecy

Armageddon and the Gathering of Nations

Revelation's Vision of Armageddon: The Gathering of World Powers in a Final Conflict

The concept of Armageddon is one of the most widely recognized, dramatic symbols of the end times in biblical prophecy. Described in the Book of Revelation, it represents the ultimate confrontation between the forces of good and evil; a monumental clash in which the fate of humanity will be decided. Armageddon has been a topic of religious debate, theological interpretation, and even modern speculation as believers and scholars attempt to decode the message embedded in this ancient prophecy. As our current age faces unprecedented global challenges, many perceive these prophecies as more relevant than ever.

1. The Prophetic Origin of Armageddon: Revelation's Apocalyptic Vision

a. The Setting of Armageddon: The word "Armageddon" itself comes from the Hebrew phrase "Har-Megiddo," meaning the "Mountain of Megiddo." Historically, Megiddo was an ancient site of numerous battles and strategic significance in the northern part of Israel. While no mountain by that name exists, Megiddo's prominence in ancient warfare likely symbolized a place of immense conflict. In Revelation, the term is more symbolic, suggesting not a literal location but rather a climactic confrontation.

b. Imagery of Conflict in Revelation: Revelation paints a vivid picture of Armageddon as a chaotic scene in which nations and armies, influenced by demonic forces, gather to wage war against God and His followers. This battle serves as the culmination of a series of judgments poured upon the earth. It is a scene of cosmic upheaval: the sun darkens, the earth trembles, and supernatural signs appear. The setting indicates a final standoff, a moment of reckoning where God's justice and mercy intersect.

c. Forces of Good and Evil: In this vision, the forces of good are represented by Christ, often depicted on a white horse, symbolizing purity, victory, and divine authority. He leads the heavenly armies into battle, representing the final stand of righteousness. In contrast, the forces of evil consist of a coalition of earthly powers led by the Beast (often interpreted as the Antichrist), the False Prophet, and Satan himself, embodying deception, rebellion, and corruption. The gathering of these forces represents humanity's struggle with spiritual darkness, where deception blinds people to divine truth, leading them to oppose God's plan.

2. Modern Interpretations: Nations Aligning in Global Conflict

a. The Idea of Armageddon in Current Events: For many, the current state of global affairs appears to echo the apocalyptic vision of Armageddon. Geopolitical alliances are increasingly polarized, and tensions between superpowers continue to escalate. From the rise of nuclear threats to ideological clashes, the sense of an impending global conflict feels closer than ever. The alignment of nations on various fronts; economic, military, and ideological; has led some to believe that this is a prelude to the ultimate gathering predicted in Revelation.

   b. The Influence of Political and Religious Leaders: Political and religious leaders worldwide often find themselves on opposite sides of intense ideological divides. With the increasing spread of authoritarianism, nationalism, and religious extremism, some leaders appear to embody the traits associated with the Antichrist and the False Prophet, figures who deceive the masses and lead them into rebellion. For many, the potential rise of such figures is seen as a sign of the end times; a signal that the forces of darkness are preparing for their final act.

   c. Technology's Role in Gathering the Nations: Modern technology has enabled a level of global interconnection unprecedented in human history. Social media, news outlets, and digital platforms have amplified ideological divides and made it possible for people around the world to rally around causes or leaders instantaneously. Some interpret this global reach and interconnectivity as a means by which the "gathering of nations" could take place, facilitated by technology and driven by increasingly shared (or divisive) ideologies. The digital age, thus, becomes a tool in fulfilling the prophecy, enabling nations to align and mobilize in ways that were previously unimaginable.

   3. The Spiritual Battle Beneath the Surface

   a. Deception as a Key Element: One of the central themes of Armageddon is deception; the ability of evil to convince people to turn against what is right. According to Revelation, the False Prophet and the Beast work to deceive the nations, leading them into rebellion against God. This deception manifests in various forms: moral confusion, the allure of power, and the promise of false peace. Today, many perceive the moral ambiguity and moral relativism prevalent in society as part of this deception, where traditional values are often discarded in favor of more subjective moral codes.

   b. Apostasy and Spiritual Decline: As the world drifts further from religious or spiritual values, many see a spiritual decline as contributing to the end times scenario. Armageddon, in this context, is not just a physical battle but a representation of humanity's spiritual state. Apostasy, or the abandonment of faith, is viewed as a precursor to the final battle, where the moral and spiritual foundation of society is shaken. Some interpret the widespread decline in religious observance, combined with the rise of secularism, as indicative of the world moving closer to this ultimate confrontation.

   c. False Prophets and Misleading Doctrines: Revelation speaks of false prophets who mislead people, drawing them into false religions and corrupt ideologies. In our age, false doctrines and misleading teachings have proliferated, both within religious circles and in secular ideologies. Many believe that the rise of alternative belief systems and the commercialization of spirituality reflect the work of these false prophets, whose mission is to dilute the truth and sway people from faith. The increased popularity of ideologies that prioritize self-interest, materialism, and relativism is seen as part of this trend.

4. Divine Intervention and the End of Human Rule

a. The Arrival of Christ as Judge: In Revelation, the final battle concludes with the intervention of Christ, who descends to bring justice and righteousness. This marks the end of human rule and the beginning of a new era under divine authority. The imagery of Christ leading the armies of heaven is symbolic of ultimate justice, representing the final victory of good over evil. For believers, this aspect of the prophecy provides hope and assurance, indicating that despite the horrors of the end times, God's ultimate plan will prevail.

b. The Defeat of Evil Powers: At Armageddon, the forces of evil are said to be defeated in a decisive and conclusive manner. Satan, the Beast, and the False Prophet are all cast into the lake of fire, symbolizing the total eradication of evil from the earth. This defeat signals the end of human suffering, corruption, and deception, and the beginning of a new era where God reigns supreme. It suggests a world restored to its original state of purity and peace, free from the influence of evil.

c. Renewal of Creation and the Promise of a New World: The conclusion of Armageddon is not just the end of the world but the start of a new beginning. Revelation speaks of a new heaven and a new earth, a restored creation where pain, suffering, and death are no more. This promise of renewal is central to the prophecy, signifying that the trials and tribulations of the end times are a necessary precursor to a world reborn. This vision of a renewed creation serves as a source of comfort and encouragement for believers, offering a glimpse of the future that awaits after the final battle.

5. Contemporary Reflections on the Timing and Nature of Armageddon

a. Current Global Tensions as Precursors: The world today faces numerous tensions that seem to parallel the events leading up to Armageddon. From escalating conflicts to economic instability and environmental crises, the signs appear ominous to those familiar with biblical prophecy. These tensions make the vision of Armageddon feel imminent and tangible, not just as a religious prophecy but as a plausible outcome of current global trajectories.

b. Urgency for Spiritual Preparation: Many religious communities interpret the signs of the end times as a call for spiritual readiness. Believers are encouraged to strengthen their faith, resist deception, and uphold moral principles in the face of growing corruption. Spiritual leaders urge their communities to remain vigilant, interpreting these times as an opportunity for repentance and transformation. For them, the purpose of prophecy is not to instill fear but to guide humanity toward redemption and readiness.

c. The Hope of Redemption Beyond Armageddon: Although Armageddon is portrayed as a time of great suffering, it is also a time of great hope. The promise of Christ's return and the establishment of God's kingdom on earth is a source of profound inspiration for believers. The prophecy of Armageddon ultimately leads to a restored world, free from sin and suffering. For many, this hope fuels their resilience and determination to persevere, trusting that, even in times of darkness, the story of humanity ends not in destruction but in divine restoration.

Examination of Geopolitical Alliances, Prophetic Interpretations, and Signs in Current Events

As the concept of Armageddon looms large in end-times prophecy, the focus has increasingly shifted toward understanding modern geopolitical alliances and their potential alignment with ancient prophetic texts. To believers, the realignment of nations and emergence of new alliances are not random but are significant indicators that these prophecies are approaching their fulfillment. Through this lens, contemporary global events become signs, pieces of a larger puzzle pointing to a prophesied gathering of nations and a final confrontation.

1. The Relevance of Geopolitical Alliances in Prophecy

a. Nations in Prophecy: Various biblical passages, especially in Ezekiel, Daniel, and Revelation, have been interpreted as references to specific nations involved in the end-times scenario. Many scholars and religious leaders have speculated on the identities of these nations, often associating certain modern powers with the "kings of the north and south" (interpreted as powers from Europe and the Middle East), "Gog and Magog" (interpreted as a possible alliance involving Russia or other northern powers), and other significant alliances.

These ancient descriptions are thought to refer symbolically to regions rather than specific nations, implying that, in the end times, these regions would be dominated by particular powers or coalitions. For instance, many Christians view the United States, Europe, Russia, China, and certain Middle Eastern countries as primary players in these prophecies due to their influence and ideological power.

b. The Rise of Strategic Alliances: The global political landscape has changed dramatically, especially in recent decades, with alliances shifting and new tensions emerging. NATO, the European Union, and economic alliances across Asia and the Middle East illustrate how the world's powers are increasingly intertwined. This integration of economic, military, and political interests echoes the prophecies of a time when powerful alliances would shape the world's destiny, potentially leading to a final confrontation.

c. East vs. West Tensions as Fulfillment of Prophecy: Many believers interpret the enduring conflict between Eastern and Western ideologies as a modern representation of the biblical battle between forces of good and evil. The polarization between democratic and authoritarian regimes, as well as the ideological battle between secularism and religious belief, heightens the significance of these alliances. For example, China's close ties with Russia and ongoing tensions with Western countries are seen by some as aligning with prophecies that predict Eastern alliances becoming significant players in the end-times conflict.

2. Prophetic Interpretations of Today's Geopolitical Landscape

a. The Revival of Nationalism and Populism: The resurgence of nationalism and populist movements worldwide is seen as a prophetic sign, symbolizing a retreat from the ideals of global cooperation and unity that have defined recent decades. Many interpret this rise in nationalist sentiment as evidence of division; a necessary prelude to the final, prophesied gathering of nations. Biblical texts indicate that in the last days, "nations shall rise against nation, and kingdom against kingdom" (Matthew 24:7), a description that resonates with today's frequent national disputes.

b. Jerusalem as a Focal Point of Conflict: In prophetic literature, Jerusalem is often described as the centre of end-times conflict. Today, Jerusalem and Israel remain focal points of geopolitical tension, particularly in relation to Palestinian issues and regional hostilities in the Middle East. Prophecies state that all nations will be drawn to the area in the end times, with Jerusalem becoming a "burdensome stone" (Zechariah 12:3) for the world. Current events like peace negotiations, hostilities, and international alliances involving Israel are therefore seen as fulfilling these ancient predictions.

c. Religious Tensions and "False Prophets": Religious extremism and the proliferation of radical ideologies are significant themes in prophecy, particularly concerning the rise of "false prophets" who lead people away from the truth. In recent years, ideological and religious tensions have intensified globally, with numerous factions claiming divine backing for their agendas. Some see these events as evidence of the prophetic warning that, in the end times, false prophets and leaders will deceive many, drawing them into a false sense of security or righteousness before the final judgment.

3. Signs in Current Events: Global Upheavals as Warnings

a. The COVID-19 Pandemic and Its Aftermath: For many, the COVID-19 pandemic symbolized a major sign of the end times, representing a global crisis that brought humanity to a collective pause. The pandemic disrupted economies, strained healthcare systems, and revealed vulnerabilities in even the most powerful nations. This unprecedented event has led some believers to view it as a precursor to even greater calamities prophesied to come, a warning for humanity to prepare for the times ahead.

b. Economic Instability and Inflation: Prophecies often mention global economic turmoil as a marker of the end times. In recent years, inflation, recession fears, and financial inequality have become pressing concerns, echoing biblical descriptions of financial collapse and scarcity, such as in Revelation's description of a time when basic commodities become inaccessible for the common person (Revelation 6:6). Many view these economic struggles as precursors to the prophesied financial collapse of the world's system.

c. Environmental Disasters as Judgments: Natural disasters; hurricanes, floods, wildfires, and droughts; have become more frequent and severe, a fact that many see as part of God's judgment. Environmental crises, such as the Amazon fires and melting polar ice, contribute to the narrative of a world "groaning" under the weight of sin, as described in Romans 8:22. These natural events are seen as divine warnings, pushing humanity to consider their spiritual state and the environmental impact of their actions.

d. The Digital Revolution and the "Mark of the Beast" Interpretations: The rapid advancement of technology has also sparked prophetic concerns, particularly around digital tracking, surveillance, and data collection. The concept of a "Mark of the Beast" (Revelation 13:16-18) has been widely interpreted to mean a system of control or economic restriction imposed on individuals who refuse to comply with a dominant world order. Modern technologies like microchips, digital IDs, and surveillance systems are perceived as paving the way for this prophecy's fulfillment, enabling authorities to monitor and control individuals on an unprecedented level.

4. The Warning of Imminent Judgment and Divine Intervention

a. The Urgency of Prophetic Signs: With the increasing convergence of global events and prophetic signs, many feel an urgency to heed these warnings, interpreting them as clear markers of an imminent divine intervention. The sense of urgency permeates religious communities who interpret the chaotic state of world affairs; wars, natural disasters, pandemics, and technological control; as evidence that the time is near. The message, therefore, is one of preparation, prompting individuals to realign their values, reflect on their faith, and prepare spiritually for what is to come.

b. Hope and Redemption Beyond Armageddon: Although these signs forewarn of intense trials, prophecy ultimately points to a message of hope. For believers, the fulfillment of these prophecies signifies not just the end of an age of suffering but the beginning of divine restoration. The Bible promises a future where justice prevails, suffering is eradicated, and peace reigns; a new creation that follows the final judgment. In this vision, Armageddon is not the end but the doorway to a renewed world in God's presence, encouraging believers to remain steadfast, even as the signs intensify.

As we look at these geopolitical shifts and global events through the lens of prophecy, the call is clear: a spiritual readiness to face an uncertain future with faith and resilience. Prophecies of the end times serve as a reminder that, while humanity may face unparalleled trials, divine purpose remains at the heart of these events. This chapter ultimately invites reflection on our place in history, prompting each person to consider their role and relationship with faith as these prophetic signs unfold.

Potential Scenarios for World War III and Global Collapse

In the shadow of Armageddon, the specter of World War III has gripped the minds of many as a potential final chapter in humanity's history. From rising international tensions to the proliferation of nuclear weapons, modern events present a chilling scenario where global collapse might unfold in ways that could fulfill ancient prophecies. While it's impossible to predict the future precisely, several key factors and potential scenarios stand out as pathways to this feared global conflict.

1. East vs. West: The Ideological Battle Resurfaces

The ideological divide between the East and the West; often seen as a struggle between authoritarianism and democracy; remains a fundamental aspect of global conflict. This divide can be traced back to the Cold War, but today, it has intensified with new rivalries and alliances.

a. U.S. and NATO vs. Russia and China: One scenario envisions a full-scale confrontation between the United States and NATO allies on one side and Russia and China on the other. Tensions have escalated due to territorial disputes, economic competition, and differing political ideologies. In recent years, clashes over Ukraine, Taiwan, and the South China Sea have hinted at potential flashpoints where a regional skirmish could escalate into a larger war. If diplomatic channels fail, even a single miscalculation or aggression could trigger a rapid escalation.

b. Proxy Conflicts in the Middle East and Asia: Another scenario involves prolonged proxy conflicts, where smaller nations become battlegrounds for global superpowers. Syria, Yemen, and other volatile regions could see new waves of conflict, as global powers intervene to support opposing factions. These proxy wars might ignite a larger conflict, with the superpowers unable to withdraw or de-escalate as commitments deepen and stakes rise.

c. Cyber Warfare and Technological Competition: The digital realm adds a new dimension to the potential for conflict. Cyberattacks on critical infrastructure, financial systems, and government institutions could serve as a prelude to World War III. With global dependence on technology, a significant cyberattack could cripple economies, disrupt supply chains, and destabilize nations, driving them toward open conflict. Both the U.S. and China have invested heavily in cyber capabilities, and an unchecked escalation in this domain could act as a trigger for military retaliation.

2. Resource Scarcity and Environmental Strain

As natural resources become more limited, competition over essential commodities could lead to global conflict. Prophetic interpretations of the end times often highlight war over scarcity as a sign of humanity's final descent into chaos.

a. Water Wars and Energy Conflicts: Regions like the Middle East, Northern Africa, and parts of Asia are increasingly facing water shortages due to climate change, overpopulation, and pollution. Countries might go to war to secure access to freshwater, particularly as populations grow and supplies dwindle. Similar conflicts could arise over oil, natural gas, and rare earth minerals essential for technology and weaponry. A scramble for these resources would intensify existing hostilities, drawing other nations into the fray.

b. Climate Refugees and Border Tensions: As climate change displaces people, the strain on nations already struggling with economic or social challenges will increase. Mass migrations could lead to a crisis of unprecedented scale, with millions seeking refuge across borders. Nations might respond by militarizing their borders, leading to clashes with neighbouring states and contributing to a global refugee crisis that spirals into conflict.

3. Nuclear Standoff and Mutually Assured Destruction

The existence of nuclear arsenals presents one of the most immediate and devastating paths to World War III. While major powers generally avoid direct conflict to prevent nuclear annihilation, the risks of escalation remain.

a. Accidental Launch or Escalation: An unintentional nuclear launch, due to a technical error or miscommunication, could quickly escalate. The "Doomsday Clock" has highlighted how close the world is to a potential nuclear event, emphasizing the fragility of global security. In such a scenario, even a single launch could trigger a rapid retaliation, setting off a chain reaction that would result in widespread destruction.

b. Limited Nuclear Engagement and Fallout: Some analysts propose a scenario involving "limited nuclear strikes" where smaller, tactical nuclear weapons are used in specific regions. While these are intended to be localized, any use of nuclear weapons risks global escalation. The radioactive fallout from even limited strikes could contaminate food and water supplies, worsen climate change, and push humanity toward collapse. A "limited" nuclear war might spiral into a larger conflict as other nuclear-armed states react to the precedent set.

c. North Korea, Iran, and the Risk of Rogue States: Countries like North Korea and Iran, with nuclear or near-nuclear capabilities, add a further layer of unpredictability. With fragile alliances and often-unpredictable leadership, these nations could trigger a major conflict either by using nuclear weapons or by provoking reactions from other global powers. If North Korea were to launch an attack on South Korea, for example, the U.S. and its allies would be compelled to respond, risking a larger engagement with China.

4. Economic Collapse as a Catalyst for Global Conflict

Economic crises have historically led to war, as nations seek to regain stability or distract from domestic issues through military action. In the modern world, the interconnectedness of global economies means that a collapse in one region can rapidly spread, creating the perfect storm for conflict.

a. Inflation, Debt, and Financial Instability: Recent years have seen rising inflation, widening economic disparities, and high national debts, all of which strain national economies. If a major economy were to collapse, the impact on trade and global markets would be profound. Unemployment and poverty would rise, and governments might resort to military intervention to stabilize or redirect unrest. Economic collapse could drive nations into competition over resources and land, leading to international conflicts that risk escalating.

b. Currency Wars and Economic Sanctions: The weaponization of economic tools, such as sanctions and trade embargoes, has intensified tensions. Nations have increasingly used these tools as an alternative to direct military action, but they also serve as a spark for conflict. Sanctions on countries like Russia and Iran have led to retaliatory actions, with nations exploring alternative economic alliances that challenge the existing global financial order. Economic wars, combined with political hostility, can create the conditions for a traditional war.

5. The Final Conflict and Prophetic Interpretations of World War III

For believers in prophecy, these scenarios don't just represent random geopolitical possibilities; they are seen as part of an inevitable climax. Prophetic interpretations often frame World War III as a battle that culminates in the return of Christ and the ultimate judgment of humanity.

a. Armageddon as the Culmination of World Conflict: According to Revelation, the battle of Armageddon will draw nations together in a final confrontation in the Middle East. The idea that the world's powers will eventually converge in one location, whether by coincidence or divine intervention, is a core element of many end-times narratives. This conflict, it is believed, will mark the end of human rule and the establishment of a divine kingdom, where Christ assumes authority over the earth.

b. Prophecies of "Wars and Rumours of Wars": In the Gospels, Jesus speaks of "wars and rumours of wars" as signs of the last days (Matthew 24:6). For those who see prophecy unfolding, the frequent mention of war and the near-constant state of global tension are seen as indicators that the world is on the brink of the final, prophesied conflict. This belief fuels the sense that a cataclysmic event is not only possible but imminent.

6. Humanity's Choice and the Hope for Redemption

Despite these ominous scenarios, there is also a belief that humanity can make choices that lead to redemption rather than destruction. This view sees World War III not as an inevitable reality, but as a warning of the dangers of unchecked ambition, greed, and hatred. Spiritual leaders and peacemakers emphasize the potential for global cooperation, urging individuals to pursue values of humility, charity, and faithfulness to prevent such a catastrophe.

a. A Call for Global Repentance: Many religious voices advocate for repentance and spiritual renewal as a way to avert the final judgment. The belief here is that through prayer, ethical reform, and a return to spiritual values, humanity can appeal for divine mercy. This view holds that although humanity may be on the brink, there remains a chance for intervention if individuals and nations turn back to higher principles.

b. A Future Beyond Destruction: For believers, even the potential destruction brought by World War III is not the end. Prophecies suggest that divine intervention will ultimately bring peace and restoration, with a new world emerging from the ashes of the old. This belief in an eventual divine kingdom motivates many to remain hopeful, even in the face of dire predictions, trusting that God's plan will ultimately restore justice, peace, and harmony.

As we stand at this crossroads, the looming threat of World War III serves both as a warning and a call to reflection. The decisions made by leaders and individuals today could either fulfill or avert the worst of these prophecies. Whether or not the world descends into the final, prophesied conflict, these scenarios remind humanity of the consequences of division, hostility, and the failure to uphold shared values. For now, the path remains open, with each person invited to reflect on their role in shaping the future; for better or for worse.

The End of the World and the New Beginning

Prophecies of the End: What Believers Expect Versus What the World Is Preparing For

As we approach the final chapter, the notion of "the end" remains as complex as it is varied, split between the interpretations of believers and the secular plans for survival. In ancient scriptures, apocalyptic teachings, and spiritual prophecies, the end of the world is portrayed as both a time of judgment and renewal. For believers, this end marks the ultimate fulfillment of divine promise, a definitive separation of good from evil and a new world of peace, led by a higher power. Yet, from a secular perspective, the end of the world is often framed as a catastrophe to prepare for; whether through technology, survival strategies, or scientific breakthroughs designed to protect humanity from extinction.

As these two perspectives converge, a chasm emerges between faith and human intervention, with each trying to answer the profound question of what comes next. The stakes are high, and in this closing chapter, we explore the unique ways these views diverge and, sometimes, intertwine, as the world braces itself for an unknown tomorrow.

1. Believers' Vision of the End: Prophecy and Fulfillment

a. Divine Judgment and the Return of Christ: For many believers, especially within Christian and prophetic traditions, the end of days is inseparable from divine judgment. This period will be marked by Christ's return, the resurrection of the dead, and the final judgment of all souls. According to Revelation and other apocalyptic texts, Jesus will return to confront evil, with Satan and his followers condemned for eternity, while the faithful are ushered into an era of divine peace. Believers hold that this event will be unmistakable; a supernatural event that no human power can prepare for or prevent, seen as the culmination of centuries of prophecy.

b. The Rise of the New Jerusalem: One of the most potent images of this future is the New Jerusalem, a divine city that will descend from heaven, according to Revelation. This city, with gates of pearl and streets of gold, symbolizes the fulfillment of God's promise, a new dwelling place where God will dwell with humanity. For many, this vision represents hope: the promise of a world free from suffering, where sin and sorrow have no place, and all things are made new. It is the ultimate reward for enduring faith and righteousness, a vision of utopia that no earthly planning or preparation can replicate.

c. Separation of the Righteous and the Wicked: Prophecies in the Bible, the Qur'an, and other sacred texts foretell that at the world's end, a final division will occur, marking the last separation between the righteous and the wicked. For believers, this judgment is based on one's faith, actions, and adherence to divine principles. This is not a battle for survival; it is the culmination of a moral and spiritual journey. Believers see this as a divine sorting process, where every soul's true nature is revealed, leaving no room for deception. In this way, the end of the world is not feared but anticipated, viewed as the ultimate justice and the fulfillment of a long-awaited promise.

2. The World's Approach: Technology, Preparedness, and Scientific Solutions

In contrast, the secular world often approaches the end as a survival problem, something to be managed, planned for, and, if possible, avoided altogether. With a growing recognition of threats such as climate change, nuclear war, pandemics, and the unpredictable advancements in artificial intelligence, modern society invests heavily in plans and technologies aimed at preventing or surviving a catastrophic event.

a. Scientific Preparedness: Scientists and policymakers have crafted strategies to counter scenarios like asteroid impacts, super-volcanic eruptions, or nuclear disasters. The construction of bunkers, underground cities, and global seed vaults, like the Svalbard Global Seed Vault, are all practical steps designed to ensure that humanity can endure through a crisis. For these thinkers, the "end" is not the divine judgment of believers but a hurdle in human history; an apocalyptic challenge to overcome through innovation and resilience.

b. Colonization of Other Planets: Visionaries like Elon Musk have championed the idea that humanity must become an interplanetary species. Mars, in particular, has been targeted as a potential new home for humanity. Colonizing other planets is seen by some as the ultimate insurance policy against earthly disasters, providing a "backup" for human civilization. This approach reflects a starkly different vision of the future from traditional religious prophecies. Instead of a New Jerusalem descending to earth, we see visions of humanity ascending into the stars, creating a kind of "New Earth" on distant worlds.

c. Artificial Intelligence and the Quest for Immortality: The rapid development of artificial intelligence and biotechnology is also shaping secular visions of the end. Technologies that extend human life, enable mind uploading, or create powerful artificial general intelligences (AGIs) are sometimes presented as ways to transcend death and achieve a kind of digital immortality. Transhumanists and futurists imagine a future where humanity can sidestep natural limits and even death itself. This vision stands in stark contrast to traditional beliefs in a spiritual afterlife, focusing instead on technological evolution as the path to transcendence.

3. Overlapping Signs and Prophetic Interpretations in the Modern World

Interestingly, while secular and religious views differ on the nature of the end, both recognize and respond to signs that echo across time.

a. Signs of Judgment in Natural Disasters and Global Crisis: Many believers see an increase in natural disasters, wars, pandemics, and societal unrest as signs of imminent judgment, fulfilling prophecies of tribulation and trials that precede the end. At the same time, the scientific community sees these issues as signs of environmental degradation, climate change, and the natural consequences of human action. This overlap creates a complex tapestry where both groups are aware of imminent crisis but view it through different lenses; one sees it as divine judgment, the other as an environmental reckoning.

b. Moral and Ethical Decay: From a religious perspective, the abandonment of traditional values, increasing violence, and the spread of immorality are signs of a morally decaying world, ripe for judgment. For secular thinkers, these issues are often linked to the impact of globalization, changes in societal norms, and new challenges in governance and social cohesion. Though they interpret the causes differently, both acknowledge that human society is reaching a moral tipping point, further feeding into end-of-days expectations.

c. Prophets, Visionaries, and Thought Leaders: Just as prophets in various religious traditions have spoken of an end, contemporary secular thinkers often act as modern prophets, issuing warnings about existential risks from technology, environmental collapse, and unchecked power. Figures like Stephen Hawking and Elon Musk have warned of AI and environmental collapse as potentially civilization-ending threats, echoing themes that resonate with religious prophecies about human hubris leading to downfall.

4. Convergence or Divergence? Humanity's Ultimate Path Forward

As we reach what many consider to be a pivotal moment in history, the question remains: Will humanity follow a path that aligns with prophecy, or will it forge a new way forward through technology and survivalism?

a. The Choice Between Faith and Control: For believers, the end of days is inevitable, ordained by divine will and beyond human control. This outlook suggests that no technology or preparation can prevent what is coming. However, for those aligned with the secular world, the goal is to control, delay, or avoid the end entirely. The tension between these two perspectives raises a profound question: Is the future something we can shape, or is it preordained?

b. Potential for a New Era of Cooperation: There is also the possibility that these differing perspectives could inspire cooperation. By combining spiritual wisdom with scientific knowledge, humanity might find a path that respects both the sacred and the practical. For some, this cooperation could be seen as the beginning of a new age; one where humanity collectively seeks a higher purpose, united by a shared goal of preservation and moral renewal.

c. Redemption or Transformation? Ultimately, humanity stands at a crossroads where it must choose between two destinies: one that leads to redemption and divine fulfillment, and one that aims to transform the human experience beyond previous limits. Whether this moment is the end or a new beginning is a choice yet to be made, influenced by faith, human will, and the mysteries that lie beyond.

From Prophecy to Reality: A Chronological Unfolding of End-Time Signs
1. The Ascension of Jesus and the Early Church (1st Century)

After Jesus ascended, His disciples carried forth His teachings, laying the foundation for what would become the global Christian faith. In His last words, Jesus prophesied that His followers would face persecution and suffering for His name's sake, and that there would be wars, famines, pestilences, and signs in the heavens. These signs were meant to indicate the beginnings of what many call the "last days" ; the era leading toward the final judgment.

Fulfillment:

Soon after, early Christians faced intense persecution under the Roman Empire, particularly under emperors like Nero. Many were martyred, fulfilling Jesus' prophecy of suffering and persecution. The destruction of Jerusalem in 70 A.D., a massive event that scattered the Jewish people, was also prophesied by Jesus, marking a significant moment seen by believers as a prophetic foreshadowing of a later scattering.

2. The Spread of Christianity and Conflict with Empires (2nd - 5th Century)

As Christianity spread through the Roman Empire, the faith clashed with Rome's pagan roots, eventually leading to the conversion of Emperor Constantine in the 4th century. But this period also saw the rise of many heresies and false teachings within Christianity, which prophecy watchers saw as fulfilling warnings about false prophets and misleading doctrines.

Fulfillment:

The internal conflicts within Christianity over heresies; Gnosticism, Arianism, and others; mirrored warnings found in New Testament prophecies. This was interpreted as the early church's struggle against deception and moral decay, foreshadowing greater spiritual conflicts ahead.

3. The Rise and Fall of Empires, the Crusades, and the Black Death (6th - 14th Century)

During the Middle Ages, many believed prophecies in Revelation spoke of great conflicts between powers, especially the Islamic caliphates and Christian empires. The Crusades were waged between these two faiths, and prophecies of war between nations seemed to unfold before people's eyes. In the 14th century, the Black Death struck Europe, killing millions, and many believed this pandemic was a sign of God's judgment.

Fulfillment:

The Crusades, seen as holy wars for control over Jerusalem and the Holy Land, were viewed by many Christians as a fulfillment of prophecies about conflict in the Holy Land. The Black Death, due to its massive death toll, was seen as a fulfillment of pestilences and famines prophesied as signs of the times, marking a grim period many thought was the beginning of the end.

4. The Protestant Reformation and Rise of Modern Nations (16th - 18th Century)

The Protestant Reformation was a period of religious upheaval. Martin Luther and others challenged the authority of the Catholic Church, accusing it of corruption. This period saw the fracturing of Christianity, which many viewed as the rise of the "false church," as described in

Revelation. Meanwhile, the Age of Exploration began, with European nations seeking to expand and dominate new territories.

Fulfillment:

The Protestant Reformation fulfilled what some believe were prophecies about a divided church, with conflicts between different interpretations of the faith. This era also led to new empires and colonial expansions, which fuelled conflicts and wars, seen as a fulfillment of prophecies predicting wars between kingdoms and nations.

5. The French Revolution and the Rise of Secularism (18th - 19th Century)

The Enlightenment brought a wave of secularism, challenging the religious status quo. The French Revolution, in particular, was seen by many as a rebellion against God's order, with secular ideologies replacing traditional faith and morality. The concept of human rights and democracy spread across the world, changing the political landscape and leading to further conflicts among nations.

Fulfillment:

Prophecies of lawlessness and a turning away from God are seen by believers as being fulfilled by the Enlightenment's impact. With faith increasingly challenged, the idea of a godless society, as prophesied, became more widespread. Revolutions worldwide fuelled new political ideologies that sought to push God out of governance, signalling to some an era of rising rebellion against divine order.

6. World War I and World War II: The Birth of Global Conflicts (20th Century)

World War I was the first true global conflict, unleashing destruction on a massive scale. Then came World War II, with unprecedented horrors, including the Holocaust, which many saw as a fulfillment of the suffering predicted for the Jewish people in biblical prophecy. In 1948, the State of Israel was established, a monumental event prophesied thousands of years earlier, seen as a fulfillment of the "gathering of the Jews" back to their homeland.

Fulfillment:

World War I and II were interpreted as the "wars and rumours of wars" that Jesus prophesied. The Holocaust, as well as the formation of Israel, was seen as a significant fulfillment of Old Testament prophecies, especially those foretelling the return of the Jewish people to Israel. These events cemented the belief among prophecy watchers that the end times were indeed approaching.

7. The Cold War, the Doomsday Clock, and Nuclear Threats (1945 - 1991)

The Cold War between the United States and the Soviet Union brought the world to the brink of nuclear annihilation. The "Doomsday Clock," a symbolic timepiece reflecting the likelihood of a man-made apocalypse, was introduced, serving as a constant reminder of the threat of total destruction.

Fulfillment:

The Cold War's nuclear tension was seen as an indicator of potential end-times conflict, aligning with prophecies of a final, destructive battle. The nuclear threats were perceived as the potential fulfillment of fire-based judgments prophesied in various religious texts, especially with the ability to destroy entire cities in an instant.

8. Rise of Technology, Digital Age, and Moral Decline (Late 20th Century - Present)

The internet and digital technologies changed the world but also gave rise to new forms of immorality, from the spread of violence to the erosion of traditional values. Social media, celebrity culture, and the worship of technology have led many to believe that idolatry in a modern form has returned.

Fulfillment:

The rise of idolatry, warned about in both Old and New Testaments, is seen as taking shape in the worship of technology, fame, and wealth. The moral decline facilitated by the internet and the new avenues for spreading immorality align with prophetic warnings about the depravity of humanity in the end times.

9. September 11 and the War on Terror (2001 - Present)

The 9/11 attacks and the subsequent War on Terror marked a new era of religious and ideological conflict. This was seen as the beginning of a great conflict between the East and the West, setting the stage for future global tensions.

Fulfillment:

For prophecy believers, 9/11 and the subsequent wars between ideologies echo the prophecies of worldwide conflicts that will precede the final battle. The rise in religious extremism is seen as a further sign of division, foretelling a world primed for an ultimate confrontation.

10. COVID-19, Pandemics, and Natural Disasters (2020 - Present)

The COVID-19 pandemic and increased natural disasters; wildfires, hurricanes, earthquakes, and floods; have only reinforced apocalyptic fears. Some see these as divine judgments and signs of the increasing frailty of humanity, while others see them as proof of human impact on the earth, fulfilling prophecies about "birth pains" as described in Matthew 24.

Fulfillment:

Pandemics and natural disasters were specifically prophesied as end-times events. The frequent and devastating nature of recent disasters leads many to believe that these are signs of judgment or at least that the earth is preparing for a dramatic change. Climate change and environmental degradation, seen as human-driven, also connect with prophecies of the earth groaning under human sin and corruption.

Current World State and Conclusion

In today's world, the convergence of these events has led many to believe that we are living in the end times. Believers see the rise in immorality, religious conflict, technological idolatry, and global instability as validations of ancient prophecies. Prophets and religious leaders have long warned that humanity's moral decline, combined with the desire for power and domination, would lead to an ultimate reckoning. The current state of the world, from political tensions to natural disasters, echoes the prophecies of a world on the brink of both destruction and, potentially, divine renewal.

To believers, each historical milestone serves as a layer, building up to an imminent climax, while skeptics see a challenging but natural series of events. Nonetheless, the unfolding of history continues to align with prophecies made millennia ago, leading many to prepare for a significant shift, an "end of days" that may finally bring humanity to account.

Closing Thoughts

To those who have journeyed through these pages, thank you for taking the time to explore the unfolding of history, prophecy, and the intricate weave between them. I hope this book has prompted you to reflect on the events, ideas, and connections presented and to consider their meaning in light of our current world.

As you close this book, ask yourself: Do you believe these events align with ancient prophecies? Is there more to uncover, or perhaps another chapter in history that you think might add depth to what has been shared?

If you feel there's something that deserves further exploration, or if a particular event stands out as a missing piece, I would love to hear your thoughts. Whether you believe, question, or simply want to share a new perspective, please feel free to reach out. You can contact me at **ezekybahii@gmail.com**; your insights are valuable and may very well contribute to an ever-expanding conversation.

Thank you once again for reading,

Eze Bahii

Milton Keynes UK
Ingram Content Group UK Ltd.
UKHW031434151124
451150UK00007B/36

9 798227 386625